Between the Ambo and the Altar

Between the Ambo and the Altar

Biblical Preaching and The Roman Missal,
Year C

Guerric DeBona, OSB

LITURGICAL PRESS
Collegeville, Minnesota

www.litpress.org

For Noreen, Mike, and Bill
Lauren, Ashley, Liam, and Chloë

"A joyful heart is life itself,
  and rejoicing lengthens one's life span."
                              —Sirach 30:22

Contents

Holy Week

Easter Time

Ordinary Time

Solemnities of the Lord during Ordinary Time

Introduction: Biblical Preaching and the New *Roman Missal*

The Geography of the Homily

It is no exaggeration to say that we live in a world choked with words. From texting with smartphones to blogging on the Internet, we face a glut of language day after day. Paradoxically, we strain to establish relationships with one another that really connect. Indeed, this age of global messaging has been far from communicative. Instead, we are a culture of individual selves, more often isolated than not by the very words we form, longing for true community and reconciliation. In the end, no multiplication of words or virtual encounters via the latest technology will satisfy the human yearning for connecting to the deepest center of our being and the lives of others. Only the Word made visible will satiate that terrible hunger.

That is the mission of Christian preaching when the community of faith gathers as the eucharistic assembly: to unearth a liberating Word to the weary, the downtrodden, and the alienated. As Christ tells those gathered to hear the words of Scripture broken open to them in the synagogue at Nazareth at the beginning of his ministry in Galilee, God has sent him "to proclaim liberty to captives / and recovery of sight to the blind, / to let the oppressed go free, / and to proclaim a year acceptable to the Lord" (Luke 4:18-19). The liturgical homily exists, then, for the purpose of deepening the faith of the baptized. In the often quoted words from *Sacrosanctum Concilium* of the Second Vatican Council, "By means of the homily, the mysteries of the faith and the guiding principles of the christian life are expounded from the sacred text during the course of the liturgical year" (52). Preaching is meant to guide the Christian community into a deeper celebration of the Eucharist and engage the faith

1

community in the "richer fare" of the Scriptures as they unfold in the Sunday Lectionary and in the experience of the faith community.

This banquet of God's saving word served at the eucharistic celebration emerges from the Scriptures and the church's liturgy itself. As the *General Instruction of the Roman Missal* says, the homily "is necessary for the nurturing of the Christian life. It should be an explanation of some aspect of the readings from Sacred Scripture or of another text from the Ordinary or the Proper of the Mass of the day and should take into account both the mystery being celebrated and the particular needs of the listeners" (65). The preacher, then, engages the assembly in its particular historical horizon with the language of faith and tradition in order to draw the congregation into the paschal mystery of Christ's sanctification for his church. Preaching is a grace-filled convergence among preacher, text, and God's people. As a constitutive component of the liturgy, the homily "points to the presence of God in people's lives and then leads a congregation into the Eucharist, providing, as it were, the motive for celebrating the Eucharist in this time and place."[1] As the USCCB document *Preaching the Mystery of Faith: The Sunday Homily* enjoins us, "Every homily, because it is an intrinsic part of the Sunday Eucharist, must therefore be about the dying and rising of Jesus Christ and his sacrificial passage through suffering to new and eternal life for us."[2] The preacher facilitates the congregation's discovery of the Word unfolding in the very midst of sacred space and, in so doing, discloses the mystery of God's faithful love, together with the thanks and praise that is at the heart of the Eucharist, the height and summit of our worship as the people of God. As Pope Benedict XVI writes in *Verbum Domini*, quoting *Sacrosanctum Concilium*,

> Here one sees the sage pedagogy of the Church, which proclaims and listens to sacred Scripture following the rhythm of the liturgical year. This expansion of God's word in time takes place above all in the Eucharistic celebration and in the Liturgy of the Hours. At the center of everything the paschal mystery shines forth, and around it radiate all the mysteries of Christ and the history of salvation, which become sacramentally present: "By recalling in this way the mysteries of redemption, the Church opens up to the faithful the riches of the saving actions and the merits of her Lord, and makes them present to all times, allowing the faithful to enter into contact with them and to be filled with the grace of salvation." For this reason I encourage the Church's Pastors and

all engaged in pastoral work to see that all the faithful learn to savor the deep meaning of the word of God which unfolds each year in the liturgy, revealing the fundamental mysteries of our faith. This is in turn the basis for a correct approach to sacred Scripture.[3]

I have titled this preaching commentary *Between the Ambo and the Altar* in order to locate the liturgical geography of the homily and call attention to the place of preaching as the site for the faithful "to savor the deep meaning of the word of God which unfolds each year in the liturgy, revealing the fundamental mysteries of our faith." As is well known, for many years the sermon functioned as a kind of misplaced little island at the Roman liturgy; it became a harbor for boatloads of parish announcements or themes that were loosely drifting out to sea. Most of these were well-intentioned sermons but something like castaways unmoored, poorly integrated into the liturgy itself. When the restoration of the ancient *homilia* was promulgated with the Second Vatican Council, the character of preaching the Word shifted from a lone island adrift in a vast ocean to a strategic bridge connecting two vast continents. The purpose of the homily in the age of the new evangelization is to preach the Good News of Christ's saving work as it is disclosed in the entire Bible, God's living Word among us, and this disclosure is to lead the baptized assembly to praise, thanksgiving, and mission. "The homily is a means of bringing the scriptural message to life in a way that helps the faithful to realize that God's word is present and at work in their everyday lives. It should lead to an understanding of the mystery being celebrated, serve as a summons to mission, and prepare the assembly for the profession of faith, the universal prayer and the eucharistic liturgy. Consequently, those who have been charged with preaching by virtue of a specific ministry ought to take this task to heart" (*Verbum Domini* 59). By accounting for God's activity in Christ throughout salvation history, the homily deepens the faith of the Christian assembly, instilling in the faithful a heartfelt desire to gather at the eucharistic sacrifice. So by definition, the homily exists for the sake of the hearer of the Good News, to transition this congregation from Word to sacrament, from the ambo to the altar. And from the altar to mission.

The present series, which ends with this volume, is meant to be an application of preaching in the context of the church's Lectionary inside the language of the Sunday liturgy. From the perspective of the Sunday homily and the interests of those who preach week after week, there remains a marvelous opportunity to discover a dialogue that exists between the liturgical texts—the presidential prayers and eucharistic prayers, the prefaces for Ordinary Time as well as feasts and solemnities—and the Scriptures themselves. I think we should view our dialogue with the Sunday liturgy as both culturally local and broadly universal. Just as the Scriptures have been passed down to us and are made applicable for our day by exegetical methods such as historical criticism and other ways of study, so too are we able to draw in the church's liturgical tradition for the homily as a constitutive dialogue partner. As of this writing, there have already been some fine introductions to the translation and implementation of the new *Roman Missal* (2011), such as Paul Turner's *Pastoral Companion to the Roman Missal* (WLP, 2010). Indeed, the probing of the vast resources of the liturgy and the Scriptures from which this celebration has emerged allows for what Louis-Marie Chauvet calls *"la Bible liturgique."*[4] Drawing from Chauvet and echoing the *GIRM*, Edward Foley and Jon Michael Joncas remind us that the preacher may explore further resources for the homily, among them the "liturgical bible," which "may refer to all liturgical texts apart from the lectionary." These include the major and minor euchologies such as the eucharistic prayers, prefaces, collects, the invariable (e.g., the "Holy, Holy"), and optional texts for the day (e.g., prayers for the blessing of an Advent wreath or newly restored Blessing over the People during Lent), "as well as the words of the hymns, songs and acclamations that are sung during worship."[5] I hasten to add that this liturgical language is not simply a resource for the preacher, but the living text of the faith community that has unfolded over the centuries. Yes, we are a historical, culturally specific faith community but always in dialogue with sacred history and how God has shaped us through the mediation of the church. The liturgy and the Scriptures that are the spine of the Body of Christ, as it were, form a marvelous dialectic for the preacher to witness the proclamation of the Good News of Jesus Christ.

The Homiletic Arc

In addition to providing a resource for the preacher by way of commentary, my hope is that the present text will contribute to an understanding of homiletic process as well. After teaching preaching to seminarians for over a dozen years, and giving workshops to priests, deacons, and other ministers, I can say that one of the most difficult concepts to grasp—but one of the most essential to learn—is the essential organic unity of the homily. The late Ken Untener and others have stressed the frustration present in hearers in the congregation who complain about the homily having too many ideas and failing to challenge the call to mission in the world on a practical level.[6] Every preacher should certainly have some kind of method that serves as a kind of armature for the text, moving the homily along and structured around the listeners. We cannot rely on our subjective, privatized voice to preach to a community of believers. All of us have been trained as solitary writers from an early age, but those who preach write for a congregation of ears, not a single pair of eyes. In this regard, homiletic strategy is very much in order so that the baptized assembly might listen to the word of God with faith and understanding, unencumbered by the personal eccentricities of the preacher. For those who are interested in developing a method of homiletics more fully, I would recommend the works of David Buttrick, Eugene Lowry, and Paul Scott Wilson, all of whom have written extensively on crafting the homily.[7]

With *Between the Ambo and the Altar*, I have in mind something less like a method and more like process, moving from Scripture to liturgical text to homily. Therefore, I have structured the book around three coordinates that seem to me to be the most productive way of engaging a preaching dialogue between the Sunday Lectionary readings and the liturgical texts that surround them. The first section is meant to be a prayerful reflection on the Lectionary for the day. I have avoided commentaries but used only some (minor) native ability in biblical languages, together with a good study Bible. Over the years, I have found that scholarly biblical commentaries are quite useful but usually only *after* a kind of naïve reading of the text, a precritical reflection, which Paul Ricoeur has called "the first naïveté" or "the spontaneous immediacy of reader to subject matter."[8] Such reading of the sacred text allows me to sink deeply into the word of God without a gloss. At the same time, a study Bible with adequate footnotes affords the opportunity to make very general historical and textual connections that aid in the life of prayer and contemplation. I am suggesting, then, that this first section of exploring the biblical text become the initial starting point for the homily, best accessed about a week before the homily is to be delivered and, ideally, integrated into Morning or Evening Prayer.

The second section is devoted precisely to establishing a substantial connection with the liturgical texts and making some links with the Scripture. "Connecting the Bible and the Liturgy" is rather subjective and personal, and it is my hope that the preacher will bring a wealth of associations to such a process of connections between Scripture and the liturgy, or between the ambo and the altar. These musings on the prayers in the liturgy are meant to be pastoral suggestions for homiletic building blocks rather than formal theoretical arguments. To this end, I have taken each of the Lectionary cycles (A, B, C) and evinced some connection with the liturgical texts for that particular Sunday. My goal here is certainly not exhaustive; in fact, it is far from that. As every seasoned preacher knows, homiletics relies on making associations and connections for an increasingly diverse congregation of listeners. My aim is that preachers, new and experienced alike, will begin to mine the wealth of material already present in the liturgy and the Scriptures for a multicultural and multigenerational assembly. Although there are numerous elements in the "liturgical bible" to consider, as well as many possible partners for establishing the homiletic text, I have confined myself mostly to the newly revised translation of the presidential prayers and prefaces of *The Roman Missal* in an effort to glean material for preaching. There is a wealth of potential present in these texts for reflection. I have avoided historical explanations of the prayers, but simply recommend what might be considered a point of departure for constructing the liturgical homily. In some instances, I diverted to the original Latin as a way of mining the depth of the church's liturgy. So saying, the wise homilist's attention to these prayers demonstrates an attention to what *Fulfilled in Your Hearing* (1982) refers to as the preacher's unique role as "mediator of meaning." The preacher stands in the midst of the Christian assembly as an interpreter of the Word within a particular culture articulating a powerful witness, nurtured by the faith of the church. As Daniel McCarthy has demonstrated with his commentaries on selected Collects originally published in *The Tablet*, the liturgy itself is a catalyst to such preaching.[9] Careful meditation on the liturgical prayers in the manner of *lectio divina*, while reflecting on a given Sunday, solemnity, or feast that celebrates these days, will undoubtedly assist the preacher not only in the homily itself but also with the entire eucharistic liturgy for the various needs of these particular hearers of the Gospel.

Finally, I have included a third section on "Strategy for Preaching" as a kind of point of homiletic integration for each Sunday. As with the previous two sections, I hardly expect that each reader will come to the same homiletic text as I did in the course of this process, but I simply recommend one that strikes me as a plausible outcome of my own engagement with the texts. The paradigm remains the same, though, for each of the Sundays, feasts, and solemnities presented in the liturgical year. If we follow the process for preaching in this book, we move from a meditation on Scripture as it is given in the Lectionary then on to a connection of these texts with the liturgical prayers for the given Sunday (or perhaps some other relevant liturgical text) to the emergence of the homily itself. In terms of a watershed moment in preaching preparation, I regard the primary task of this third stage of the homiletic process a narrowing down to a single declarative sentence, which I have called here the homiletic core idea, but which has also been termed by others a "focus sentence."[10] Discovering a homiletic core idea, a foundation for an uncluttered, pristine armature from which to hang eight to ten minutes of words each week, is not easy, but absolutely necessary. It is the sentence that should be in the mind of every congregant after the homily is over in answer to the question, "What did you hear?"

Having come to a core homiletic sentence, the preacher will then need to develop practical tactics as to how this idea will become a reality for the congregation. For most Sundays, feasts, and solemnities, the best guide to understanding tactics is posing the question, What are some concrete images, relevant stories, or illustrations that will make the core homiletic idea a reality in the heart of the hearer? Tactics are culturally specific and will have strong pastoral application. The preacher ought to instinctively know that the day-to-day activity of the parish and the world at large will, by and large, inform tactics. If one is preaching to a youth group, there is no sense using stories, vocabulary, or illustrations that are more appropriate to the retired members of the parish. Then again, parishioners will be directly affected by the economic and political happenings around them, which will inflect the meaning of the homiletic core. If there has been a tragic death in the parish family, the homiletic event for the next Sunday (let's say, it is the Fifth Sunday of Lent, Year C, but the text to be preached will be the alternative Gospel for that day, which is the raising of Lazarus) will carry a different freight than if such sadness were not part of the community. Again, these homiletic strategies are only meant to be suggestive and not prescriptive.

As every seasoned preacher knows very well, abstractions are the kiss of death when it comes to homilies, and so the tactics for achieving a core homiletic idea should be as concrete as possible and structured in a way that the congregation may follow it with ease, with a logic that is slow and available. Remember—tactics are practical actions with measured goals; in this case there is a single target: the core homiletic idea. What must be done to achieve that goal? As I have suggested earlier, homiletic methods are designed to organize a structure around the listener. We cannot presume that simply because I am speaking the fruits of my meditation and study that the congregation is unpacking the homily and getting to the depth of the core homiletic idea. The homiletic idea gives something precious to the baptized, enfleshing the word of God; it is a deepening of the reality of faith, a pondering of the mysteries of Christ, an exploration into God's creation. So in order to get to a theological understanding of the word of God, we ought to taste the aroma of fresh bread in that language.

In a word: the people of God don't want our stale crumbs in our preaching. "Homilies are inspirational when they touch the deepest levels of the human heart and address the real questions of human experience."[11] The worst possible response anyone can evince after preaching the word of God is for a faithful member of the congregation to respond, "So what?" Good tactics in homilies, like creative strategic planning, ensure that there is a measurable outcome. "So what?" Homilists should take care that this primary question is the subtext of every preaching event because no congregation should walk away from the Eucharist with that question lingering in their hearts. If we don't have a method or a structure of some kind to achieve the incarnation of our words, then we may have a great private meditation, but not much by way of evangelization. Jesus did not preach in parables for nothing: they are stories designed around the hearer to challenge, affirm, and unfold the kingdom of God.

It is a great privilege to stand in the midst of the baptized assembly and mediate meaning for those who have faithfully gathered at

Introduction: Biblical Preaching and the New Roman Missal 9

the Eucharist. Our preaching begins long before we come to the ambo and remains in the hearts of the congregation well after we leave the altar. Pray God that our own words become sown in the field of the Lord and reap a bountiful harvest.

Feast of St. Gregory the Great
Saint Meinrad School of Theology and Seminary, 2012

Notes

1. United States Conference of Catholic Bishops, *Fulfilled in Your Hearing: The Homily in the Sunday Assembly* (Washington, DC: USCCB, 1982), 23.

2. United States Conference of Catholic Bishops, *Preaching the Mystery of Faith: The Sunday Homily* (Washington, DC: USCCB, 2012), 15.

3. Benedict XVI, Post-Synodal Apostolic Exhortation, *The Word of the Lord* (Verbum Domini) (Boston: Pauline Books, 2010), 52.

4. Louis-Marie Chauvet, "*La Dimensions bibliques des texts liturgiques,*" *La Maison-Dieu* 189 (1992): 131–47. Chauvet demonstrates the foundational influence of the biblical text on the Christian liturgy, citing just some of the more obvious examples.

5. Edward Foley, Capuchin, "The Homily beyond Scripture: *Fulfilled in Your Hearing* Revisited," *Worship* 73, no. 4 (1999): 355.

6. See Kenneth Untener, *Preaching Better* (Mahwah, NJ: Paulist Press, 1999).

7. See David Buttrick, *Homiletic* (Philadelphia: Fortress Press, 1987); Eugene Lowry, *The Homiletic Plot* (Louisville: Westminster John Knox, 2001); Paul Scott Wilson, *The Four Pages of the Sermon* (Nashville: Abingdon, 1999 [1980]).

8. See Paul Ricoeur, *The Symbolism of Evil*, trans. Emerson Buchanan (Boston: Beacon Press, 1967), 347–53.

9. Daniel McCarthy, *Listen to the Word: Commentaries on Selected Opening Prayers of Sundays and Feasts with Sample Homilies* (London: Tablet Publishing, 2009).

10. See Thomas Long, *The Witness of Preaching*, 2nd ed. (Louisville: Westminster John Knox, 2005 [1990]), 99–116.

11. United States Conference of Catholic Bishops, *Preaching the Mystery of Faith*, 15.

 **ADVENT**

First Sunday of Advent

Jer 33:14-16; Ps 25:4-5, 8-9, 10, 14;
1 Thess 3:12–4:2; Luke 21:25-28, 34-36

The book of Jeremiah is not typically associated with God's comfort in a time of great sorrow, but in the middle of chapter 32 there is a significant shift from the language of devastation to the promise of hope and rebuilding. Although God's face was seemingly eclipsed during the Babylonian invasion and its aftermath, the Lord says that a healing time has come and that prosperity will reign.

The capstone of that restoration is the covenant that the Davidic monarchy will be made new. "I will raise up for David a just shoot; he shall do what is right and just in the land." This messianic kingship will guarantee justice for Jerusalem. The Lord's unconditional promise has been renewed and that pledge will include an increase in offspring—"a just shoot." The Christian community understands this text as the messianic kingship of Christ and so the **First Reading** for the First Sunday of Advent looks forward to the coming of God in the flesh as an invitation to hope, new life, and regeneration.

If Jeremiah discloses a utopic vision in which the Davidic dynasty will multiply countlessly, in the **Second Reading** Paul reminds the Thessalonians that it is the Lord who builds their community in love as well: "May the Lord make you increase and abound in love / for one another and for all, . . . at the coming of our Lord Jesus with all his holy ones." The hope for the Christian community then and now resides in being "blameless in holiness before our God and Father" until the Lord appears. Like those in exile, we will be brought into a new messianic age, which Christ will initiate at his coming.

Unlike the first two readings for this Sunday, the **Gospel** of Luke paints a more dramatic and even desperate coming of the Son of

Man. The background of the signs and portents in Luke are related to his attempts to set the stage for the contemporary setting of the temple in Jerusalem. Having been rejected by the Jewish authorities, Jesus foretells the destruction of the temple, which is linked to persecutions, the fall of Jerusalem itself, and the coming of the Son of Man. All of these omens suggest a need for preparation and a readiness for the coming of God. The religious symbols—even the most important center of worship—will pass away. So Jesus advises his followers not to be drowsy or caught up in anxiety over the meaningless issues of daily life, but rather to "[b]e vigilant at all times." In these words we hear the promise of hope in both Jeremiah and Paul for the faithful when that advent of God appears. Such preparation mingled with the theological virtue of hope sets the stage for the liturgy of the First Sunday of Advent, which will move the worshiping congregation into a collective posture of vigil and waiting for the coming of God.

Connecting the Bible and the Liturgy

The **Collect** for the First Sunday of Advent more than hints at the connection between the Scripture and the liturgy today. We ask for "the resolve to run forth to meet your Christ / with righteous deeds at his coming." Similarly, Paul insists that the Thessalonians "be blameless in holiness before our God and Father." Finally, Jesus tells his disciples to "[b]e vigilant at all times and pray that you have the strength to escape the tribulations that are imminent and to stand before the Son of Man." At the same time, the biblical readings contrast a bit with the opening prayer in at least one significant way. As Jesus predicts the end time and its linkage with signs and portents of destruction, including the temple and Jerusalem, his image focuses on those who remain standing. Likewise, Paul advises the church at Thessalonica to bear with one another in love "at the coming of our Lord Jesus with all his holy ones." In my reading, these are static, almost passive images of exhortation, encouraging those to remain steadfast and faithful until the coming of the Lord. By striking contrast, the church asks God to give us "the resolve to run forth to meet your Christ." How can we account for these differing portraits between the biblical and liturgical readings? One is static and waiting; the other is running eagerly to meet the Lord. The answer is simple enough: we must hold all the readings in tension. One asks us to keep vigil, while the second enkindles a longing to be with the Lord. In a sense, our very eagerness to meet Christ becomes generated by a spirit of longing and vigil. Both the biblical and liturgical readings share a common feature: they are confident in the coming of the Lord and the hope necessary to maintain faith and love.

There are other elements of the **Presidential Prayers** that also call our attention to the necessity to keep vigil, even while we anticipate the joy of meeting the Lord face-to-face. The **Prayer over the Offerings**, for instance, asks God to "grant us to celebrate devoutly here below / [so that it may] gain for us the prize of eternal redemption." The use of a spatial displacement—we are "here below"— reminds us of our temporal state, but we also know that we will run for the "prize of eternal redemption," which is above. Additionally, the **Prayer after Communion** recalls that "we walk amid passing things," but asks God to help us "to love the things of heaven / and hold fast to what endures."

The church, then, is caught up in wonder these Advent days, poised between keeping watch and vigil, on the one hand, and longing to be already in the presence of God, on the other hand. It is this desire that fuels the season of Advent as we move toward the Day of the Lord.

Strategy for Preaching

We may think that we are far from the world of Jesus and the rejection he faced by the religious leaders in Jerusalem. But the kind of ossified religious structures that crippled the institution in Jesus' day can happen anywhere and at any time, even our own. Passivity, arrogance, self-righteousness: these are the qualities of any religious institution that has gone terribly wrong and needs a wake-up call— like the coming of God. And what is true for institutions remains doubly important for individuals because our collective is only as good as our individual lives. If we are not people of faith, hope, and love, continually being converted to the newness of God, then how can we expect any religious institution to be more than status quo? In this regard, the Lord's promise that he "will raise up for David a just shoot" who will do "what is right and just" remains a testimony to God's breaking into our tiny narcissistic world, which is to say the unleashing of God in the flesh, the incarnation.

As preachers of the Word, we may consider orienting the homily for today along the lines of a cultural confrontation or awakening. Indeed, most of the congregation will find themselves caught up in the frenzy of the time before Christmas as Advent moves along, but the Scriptures speak of the coming of "a just shoot," of being blameless until the Lord comes "with all his holy ones" and being "vigilant" in order "to escape the tribulations that are imminent." The Scriptures themselves break into our lives like Christ himself into history with a vibrant proclamation. So the core homiletic idea for today might be to revitalize the listener into the apocalyptic itself: we may have become used to being shocked so that God's coming has lost its edge; but the Lord is in our faces even now. Indeed, it is the Eucharist that will pray us into the eternal now of Christ's coming, a window into the eternal.

An introduction would, then, speculate on our dulling, even the commodification, of the apocalypse, entertaining ourselves with shock, violence, and the next new thing. In the end, we may ask ourselves during this Advent: Is it possible for God to surprise us? The answer to this question is yes, because the Son of Man will come to break into our world as Jesus says, not with special effects and shocking transitory things, but with a new shoot of justice and righteousness. Yes, we will be shocked by divine goodness. (Here it would be important to tease this concept out into concrete terms. What does being shocked by goodness and God's justice look like? This is naming grace in very specific ways.)

Love is breaking into a loveless world. How is that for a surprise? We do it every time we gather for Eucharist and share one bread and one cup (Prayer over the Offerings; Prayer after Communion). We have had glimpses already of God's righteousness; fragments of the incarnation have spilled over in our own day. Shoots of Jesse have sprouted. (Cite examples of those who are "abounding in love" in the parish and elsewhere.) This is the love for which we will wait and to which we will run (Collect). Isn't love worth waiting for? This is the question that guides this Advent season and our journey to the Day of the Lord.

Second Sunday of Advent

Readings from the Ambo

Bar 5:1-9; Ps 126:1-2, 2-3, 4-5, 6; Phil 1:4-6, 8-11; Luke 3:1-6

The book of the prophet Baruch, a selection from which is taken for the **First Reading**, is a very interesting example of how the word of God becomes living, vital, and very active according to new historical and liturgical contexts. We know, for instance, that Baruch was a friend and "secretary" to the prophet Jeremiah. Both prophets became associated with a bleak period in Israel's history, the exile of 597 BCE. Yet Baruch's text is filled with the hope God promises for his people during this period, even in the midst of a despairing nation. But the story does not end there. Baruch's text was resurrected in fragments during another tragic moment in the history of Israel—the horrendous seizing and violation of the temple by the Syrians in 168 BCE. The new edition of Baruch's text, with some emendations, became a source of consolation for a new nation experiencing an exile all its own.

The matter we might consider, especially during Advent as hearers and preachers of the Word in Christian community in the twenty-first century, is that the church has found itself in a kind of exile; it is marginalized by secular society, which tends to raid the temple of God's goodness and prioritize wealth and success while ghettoizing the poor, the elderly, and the unborn. At the same time, though, the church has at times polarized itself from the world by being more reactive than proactive, or by refusing to enter the kind of dialogue with the world that is at the core of the new evangelization. Bringing a light to the world is a mandate not only from *Gaudium et Spes* of the Second Vatican Council, but by the Savior himself who told his disciples to "go forth and preach to all nations."

Paul's Letter to the Philippians is unusually applicable to our present cultural condition because he speaks of "partnership." The word Paul uses here in the **Second Reading** is *koinonia*, an important New Testament expression denoting a life in community, which is to say, mutual partnership and self-giving. "I pray always with joy in my every prayer for all of you, because of your partnership for the gospel from the first day until now." Speaking and hearing the word of God is a matter of collaboration and sharing and listening attentively; this process of radical openness to *koinonia* fosters growth, so that we might "increase ever more and more in knowledge and every kind of perception, to discern what is of value."

God wants everyone back from exile. As the **Responsorial Psalm** reminds us, "Although they go forth weeping, / carrying the seed to be sown, / they shall come back rejoicing, / carrying their sheaves." In a very real sense, Luke's **Gospel** brings home the historical reality of the Word's transforming presence: it is not some generalized place into which the word of God has come to renew, but in "the fifteenth year of the reign of Tiberius Caesar." These are the very characters and places that will be overturned by God's reign in Christ, even as John the Baptist announces an even greater power: God's transmuting power of forgiveness and love. Clearly, Luke understands that the Word is living, since John has breathed new life into the words of the prophet Isaiah, *"Every valley shall be filled / and every mountain and hill shall be made low."* Such is the saving Word among us, bringing us out of exile and into the light of God's grace.

Connecting the Bible and the Liturgy

To the extent that we believe that the Lord is living and active in our lives now will determine how we are to understand the import of God's coming. Do we have faith that the Lord can do a new thing? Baruch uses very elaborate imagery to speak about taking off the "robe of mourning and misery; / put on the splendor of glory from God forever." The preaching of John the Baptist opens up a possibility of newness through repentance "for the forgiveness of sins." It is no wonder, then, that the **Entrance Antiphon** for today further reminds us of the power of God to break into our personal and collective history, even as the Lord came to Israel: "O people of Sion, behold, / the Lord will come to save the nations, / and the Lord will make the glory of his voice heard / in the joy of your heart." The Antiphon, taken from Isaiah, remains God's promise of both salvation and joy. This joy is so close we wear it like a garment, to borrow an image from the First Reading.

The recognition of God's active presence presumes that we are at a loss to save ourselves. So the **Prayer over the Offerings** allows for a plea for help when it says, "come, we pray, to our rescue / with the protection of your mercy." In a way, such a petition at the altar of God positions the congregation precisely within sight of a restored Jerusalem, "rejoicing that they are remembered by God." Baruch's words are indeed charged with the force of the present, the memory of grace, as we contemplate what must be undoubtedly the most comforting refrains at any time of the year: God is among us, Emmanuel.

In the midst of Advent, then, the Scriptures and the liturgy act in concert to remind us of the now of God's presence. Take off the mourning garment and put on God's glory now; partner with the Gospel of love now; prepare for the way of the Lord now. Indeed our very celebration of Word and sacrament is the occasion of the "nowness" of the immediacy of God in the flesh whose presence is welcomed by a contrite heart. The coming Nativity of the Lord becomes all the more an occasion to celebrate when we know that we can go forth with joy, already experiencing God's consoling and reconciling presence. Therefore the **Blessing at the End of Mass** in the **Prayers over the People** used for Advent deploys this oration: "May the almighty and merciful God, / by whose grace you have placed your faith / in the First Coming of his Only Begotten Son / and yearn for his coming again, / sanctify you by the radiance of Christ's Advent / and enrich you with his blessing. . . . So that, rejoicing now with devotion / at the Redeemer's coming in the flesh, / you may be endowed with the rich reward of eternal life / when he comes again in majesty." In other words, "put on the splendor of glory from God forever . . . you will be named by God forever / the peace of justice, the glory of God's worship." Christ has come, Christ is here, Christ will come again.

Strategy for Preaching

The skillful and attentive preacher will note the complexity that accompanies today's biblical and liturgical texts. In a sense, the foundational pastoral impulse for the homilist is supplied by Paul when he writes to the church at Philippi: "And this is my prayer: that your love may increase ever more and more in knowledge and every kind of perception, to discern what is of value, so that you may be pure and blameless for the day of Christ, filled with the fruit of righteousness that comes through Jesus Christ for the glory and praise of God." As the preacher deepens the faith of the baptized—always the task of the liturgical homily—the mission becomes discovering ways to structure a text that will invite the hearer toward a love of God that will "increase ever more and more." As I have suggested in an earlier section, a window into this invitation to love is uncovering the now moment of God's consolation (wrapped in our own repentance) so that our desire for the Lord and his coming at the end of Advent may become tangible and real. So the core homiletic idea for this Sunday might be that the Lord is already in our midst; we await the fullness of his presence at his future coming when the days of Advent have drawn to a close.

One way into this homiletic text is to draw heavily from the Prayer over the Offerings and the **Collect**; these prayers suggest a guiding image that could be accessed at the introduction and continued throughout the text: rescue, protection, and running in haste. Consider, for instance, a desperate situation, such as a fire, almost consuming everything we have—including our lives. We stand at the edge of the building waiting to leap into the net of our merciful rescuers. God delivers us like that. The homily might then ask the congregation to remember a consoling moment when such a comfort took place. Similarly, the Blessing over the People urges the congregation to remember the advent of the first coming of Christ in order to prepare for the coming of God in glory. The deliverance from being trapped in our shame of sin reminds us—as it did the people of Israel—that God's love endures and renews us from age to age. What has been promised now holds for the future as well. How can we not hasten to meet that love, now catching us in his net of mercy, now making our rough ways smooth when *"all flesh shall see the salvation of God"*?

Third Sunday of Advent

Readings from the Ambo

Zeph 3:14-18a; Isa 12:2-3, 4, 5-6; Phil 4:4-7; Luke 3:10-18

The prophet Zephaniah was active during the days of King Josiah and this short book straddles two extremes. The beginning of Zephaniah's text immediately engages the listener in the voice of God, who says that he will annihilate everything from the earth, much reminiscent of the Yahweh who brought the waters of the great Flood. The proximate cause of the Lord's anger is the wickedness of Judah and its idolatrous priests. At the same time, however, the last portion of Zephaniah's book, from which the **First Reading** has been extracted, discloses a God just as active in the fate of his people, but now overflowing with mercy and compassion, rejoicing with Judah and vindicating Jerusalem. "[H]e will rejoice over you with gladness, / and renew you in his love, / he will sing joyfully because of you, / as one sings at festivals."

The common thread that unites these two seemingly polarized representations of God is the coming of the "day of the Lord." One way or the other, God is going to enter history. That day will bring, in a word, justice for the remnant of Israel. Indeed, it is the elite and the privileged over whom God will exercise his power. So the Day of the Lord will mean freedom from injustice, together with its slippery companion, idolatry. For good reason, many of the liberation theologians of the 1960s and '70s in Latin America eagerly embraced Zephaniah's text because of the prophet's steadfast vision of reestablishing divine justice for the poor: a new order will come from God, who does not dwell apart, but announces his presence among us as one who will overturn injustice: "The LORD, your God, is in your midst."

In a sense, Paul and Luke pick up Zephaniah's very invitation to see the Lord acting in the here and now, albeit in different ways. John the Baptist becomes the sounding board for the question of righteous living when asked, "What should we do?" Interestingly enough, the portrait of John in Luke is very much a contrast to the depiction of him in the other **Gospel** narratives, and sounds like Zephaniah from the early portions of that prophet's text: John has advice for the elite of his day, including tax collectors (stop collecting more than is pre-scribed) and soldiers (do not falsely accuse anyone). Luke's John the Baptist sees the Lord as imminently present in the midst of the faithful remnant—purifying the nation with fire—even as God promised Zephaniah that divine justice would be coming on the Day of the Lord.

From Paul's perspective in the **Second Reading**, the Christian community cannot but rejoice because "[t]he Lord is near." Once again, the question becomes one of right action and justice for the community: "Your kindness should be known to all." The tender compassion of God becomes known as well—in the midst of the assembly. So we live inside the Day of the Lord, having "no anxiety at all, but in everything, by prayer and petition, with thanksgiving," we make our "requests known to God." The nearness of God is a nonnegotiable when it comes to understanding all these biblical readings; they lead us to a God who is already present among us and whose coming we are about to celebrate. That day will be so great that even the Lord himself will rejoice: "he will rejoice over you with gladness, and renew you in his love, he will sing joyfully because of you, as one sings at festivals."

Connecting the Bible and the Liturgy

Today's liturgy celebrating Gaudete Sunday could barely hope for better spokesmen for the joy the day implies than Zephaniah, Paul, and John the Baptist. As we have seen, all of these servants of the Lord are trumpets of the new hope that awaits God's people by a new in-breaking of the Lord in our day.

The biblical readings find a strong echo in the liturgical language of the **Responsorial Psalm**: "*Exulta et lauda quia magnus in medio tui Sanctus Israel.*" The initial word is also a gasp of joy—*Exulta!* We will remember the cry of the deacon with the *Exsultet* at the great

Vigil of Easter, amid the flickering candles. There too the church bids the people of God to rejoice greatly—and all creation with us: "Be glad, let earth be glad, as glory floods her, / ablaze with light from her eternal King, / let all corners of the earth be glad, / knowing an end to gloom and darkness." This excitement is mirrored, of course, in Zephaniah's cry: "Be glad and exult with all your heart, / O daughter Jerusalem! / The LORD has removed the judgment against you / he has turned away your enemies." As the hope for the messianic king unfolds, his coming looks ahead to the joy of Easter when that promise will be completed and fulfilled.

Clearly, the emphasis in the scriptural text lands squarely on celebration—ours and, interestingly enough, God's. The liturgy asks the Lord to make us mindful of our call to communal exultation with praise and thanksgiving, a foundation of this divine festival, while we look ahead to the celebration of the Lord's Nativity. "O God, who see how your people / faithfully await the feast of the Lord's Nativity, / enable us, we pray, / to attain the joys of so great a salvation / and to celebrate them always / with solemn worship and glad rejoicing" (**Collect**). Furthermore, the **Prayer over the Offerings** begs that "the sacrifice of our worship, Lord, we pray, / be offered to you unceasingly, / to complete what was begun in sacred mystery / and powerfully accomplish for us your saving work." Our celebration allows for a furtherance of what God has begun in Christ through the mystery of grace, and the same Christ will himself bring his work to completion through the Eucharist we celebrate. The **Communion Antiphon** prays as a fitting rejoinder to these prayers when it says, "Behold, our God will come, / and he will save us." The very anticipation of the Lord's coming increases our celebratory faculties. Gaudete Sunday is a time in which waiting itself becomes a joy because of the grace we know that will be ours on the promised day. And the Eucharist itself becomes the divine agent to "prepare us for the coming feasts" (**Prayer after Communion**).

Strategy for Preaching

Gaudete Sunday, as is well-known, is a day that anticipates the joys of the Nativity and beyond—the day of our salvation, when God himself will celebrate our liberation from the bondage to decay through the work of Christ. As such, this Sunday's readings point us, inevitably, in the direction of the messianic presence of Christ the Liberator, who, in his very person, evokes the Christian community into the refrain of the prophet Isaiah: "Cry out with joy and gladness: for among you is the great and Holy One of Israel." Our joy comes because the Lord is that near—is already near at hand in our celebration of the Eucharist.

Getting traditionally religious churchgoers to celebrate is a little like the extravagant father in Luke 15 attempting, apparently without much success, to induce his dour elder son to go to a party for his wayward prodigal. Joy is not always our default position when it comes to religion, oddly enough. But today is a timely reminder of true *gaudium*: that the Savior is near, so near that God will be throwing the celebration and dance for joy.

Being rescued from the death of sin should be the cause of happiness, not gloom. Returning again to Luke 15, the shepherd rejoices because he has found something he lost that was precious. So the core homiletic idea for today might be a tactfully placed question that could resemble something like this: What does it take for us to really celebrate the nearness of God?

To get at this question at this time of year requires a little dismantling of our binary, black-and-white thinking. It is easy to set up secular society as a fall guy, with materialism or irreligious behavior as its wicked consort. But these secular celebrations (such as Christmas itself) often are our gateway into a more sublime religious occasion of profound joy, the consciousness of which might be raised for the congregation. If the introduction suggested an evocative time when we were surprised by a Christmas gift from a parent—a long anticipated train set that found itself circulating a sparkling spruce tree that winter morning of our youth, or a red bicycle we will never forget—these gifts approach our collective joy to come: the unwrapping of God's mystery of the incarnation. We can only ask God to increase our joy (Collect). That unwrapping begins in Bethlehem, but is anticipated today by Zephaniah and the prophets as a day of salvation and merrymaking.

The wonder continues as Christ unveils the mystery of God's salvation in the proclamation of the Gospel (might use specific citations here), which continue to underline that the Lord is near (Responsorial Psalm). Finally, the paschal mystery of the life, death, and resurrection of Jesus is God's greatest gift to the Christian people, disclosed in the midst of a mystery and great rejoicing. This salvation is reason enough to rejoice (*Exsultet*). This salvation becomes what we anticipate not only today, but every day (Second Reading). Gaudete Sunday is a way of life, not just a single day. Let us rejoice, let us exult, "for great in [our] midst / is the Holy One of Israel!"

Fourth Sunday of Advent

Readings from the Ambo

Mic 5:1-4a; Ps 80:2-3, 15-16, 18-19; Heb 10:5-10; Luke 1:39-45

The prophet Micah lived during the time of Jotham, Ahaz, and Hezekiah, which places him (together with Amos, Hosea, and Isaiah) at the center of the turmoil and annihilation of the northern kingdom. Micah's prophetic warnings involve oracles that regard Jerusalem as faithless to its heritage and covenantal relationship with the God of the chosen people. A strange text chosen for a Sunday within days of Christmas, isn't it?

The **First Reading** softens the edge of Micah's oracle by beginning with chapter 5 and avoiding the verse immediately preceding it, recording the invasion from the Assyrians (although some texts, such as the NRSV, actually make the last verse of chap. 4 the beginning of chap. 5): "Now fence yourself in, Bat-gader! [translated by the NAB as a "fenced-in maiden," another name for Jerusalem] / 'They have laid siege against us!' / With the rod they strike on the cheek / the ruler of Israel." This prophecy of doom, however, finds a remedy in the redeemed sequence to follow: Bethlehem-Ephrathah becomes a city of hope, despite its size and insignificance. The small town is the locus point for the messianic dynasty, a new David, small of stature against a Goliath; it is a city that "shall stand firm and shepherd his flock / by the strength of the LORD, / in the majestic name of the LORD, his God; / and they shall remain, for now his greatness / shall reach to the ends of the earth; / he shall be peace." The English translation here makes a point to personify peace; the promised one shall not only bring peace, but the messianic king will be peace. The usual translation in English (as in the NRSV) is "he shall be the one of peace." But we have a Messiah who is not only going to take the place of a long line of Israel's kings and bring a peaceful reign, but embody peace itself. Indeed, this messianic king becomes clearly identified with the Savior in the Christian community as one who is simply, according to the translation as we have it in the Lectionary, "peace." By the end of this chapter, we will see that it is not any secular ruler who can bring peace, but God who will dismantle power and war and bestow peace in the form of a person. The **Responsorial Psalm** specifically involves this "shepherd of Israel" to "give us new life, and we will call upon your name."

God will also purify worship, making it right-worship as well—the sacred poles and the sorcerers and the soothsayers—cleansed by the new Davidic dynasty because, as the Letter to the Hebrews reminds us in the **Second Reading**, "Sacrifice and offering you did not desire, but a body you prepared for me." Such preparation is underway in the bodies of Elizabeth and Mary. Both the forerunner and the Anointed of the Lord will find a shrine in the house of these women. "Blessed is the fruit of your womb" underlines the text from Hebrews; a body is being prepared that will find its origins as both God and man. In a sense, the visitation we see depicted in Luke's **Gospel** represents a kind of super-intersection of God's will and human agencies, pathways to peace that have converged at the climactic time in salvation history and made possible by God's action in the world and the faith that the Almighty would triumph amidst the lowly and overturn the powerful. "Blessed are you who believed that what was spoken to you by the Lord would be fulfilled." These words imply that it is the house of faith that makes a body in preparation for the Lord, a fitting prelude to the celebration of the Nativity of the Lord. The church will become the Body that welcomes the messianic presence into its midst on the Day of the Lord.

Connecting the Bible and the Liturgy

On this last Sunday of Advent, the church is brought closer and closer to the celebration of the birth of the one "whose origin is from of old, / from ancient times." This Fourth Sunday of Advent draws us deeper into the contemplative stance of Elizabeth, the woman of prophecy, who would herself bear a prophet. Indeed, Mary's kinswoman stands in humble awe that such divine fulfillment should come to her own house when she says, "how does this happen to me, that the mother of my Lord should come to me?" This state of wonder is the antechamber to the Nativity of the Lord, where the faithful stand poised not in anxiousness and worry, but humble wonder and confidence that God's will is unfolding before their very eyes.

The **Prayer over the Offerings** allows the baptized assembly to participate in this divine disclosure of the incarnational mystery when that prayer creates an alliance between the gifts we bring, their sanctification, and the blossoming of the fruit of the womb of the Virgin Mary. "May the Holy Spirit, O Lord, / sanctify these gifts laid upon your altar, / just as he filled with his power / the womb of the Blessed Virgin Mary." In a certain way, the church at this moment becomes the womb waiting to bear the Promised One. The Scriptures have reminded us that God will cleanse us of our idols; that is what we ask through the sanctification of the Holy Spirit who overshadowed the Virgin. The congregation offers its gifts—which is to say, their wills in faith—so "that what was spoken to [them] by the Lord / would be fulfilled."

The (optional) Solemn Blessing given at the end of Mass and **Prayers over the People** affirm what has been promised by God for all the church. As we have joined ourselves to Mary and Elizabeth in our expectation of God's Anointed One who will deliver us, we ask that we be blessed by "the almighty and merciful God, / by whose grace you have placed your faith / in the First Coming of his Only Begotten Son / and yearn for his coming again." The blessing of the Lord comes to our house and so the presider continues the petition to "sanctify you by the radiance of Christ's Advent." It is well to note that the church has emphasized Advent as precisely the time of sanctification and the faith that has been nurtured and cultivated in the womb of the church purified. It is indeed faith in God's promise that makes Christ's first coming a mystical continuance of his coming again and in our celebration of the Eucharist where he embodies our peace. He "shall reach to the ends of the earth," past, present, and yet to come.

Strategy for Preaching

When it comes to contemporary preaching, the importance of attending to the "signs of the times" cannot be emphasized enough—

in and out of Advent. In these days of pyrotechnics, seemingly running amok in the entertainment industry and elsewhere, our culture has ironically lost its sense of wonder, the very thing these special effects, loud noises, and booming soundtracks seek to evoke. Honest to goodness contemplative awe seems marginalized to biblical narratives like the visitation in Luke and, indeed, religious worship rightly sanctified by God in many different traditions around the globe. We glibly throw around the word "awesome" so that when it comes to a genuine moment of jaw-dropping awe—of the kind we see in today's Scripture readings in the Lectionary—we are the ones who should be struck speechless.

How can the preacher enkindle a sense of contemplative wonder in the baptized assembly as we near the celebration of the Lord's Nativity? We have Elizabeth as our model and the liturgy to recall the mystery itself. Certainly the preacher faces a challenge because the goal of the homily, optimally speaking, ought to sanctify and not instruct, to deepen faith rather than deliver a message. The preacher is preparing the womb of the church for the Lord's Nativity. So the core homiletic idea for today might be, How have we been blessed and sanctified by the presence of the Lord who has already come so near? As we might intuit from this provocative question, the focus in this regard is meant to push the listener into a deeper contemplative reality of awe and wonder in preparation for the Nativity.

An introduction may draw from Elizabeth's witness, as I have suggested, since she and her house have been blessed by the nearness of the living God in Mary's haste to greet her cousin. Interestingly enough, the Lord has already visited Elizabeth in her barrenness, even before Mary's arrival at her house. Therefore the elderly woman is able to anticipate the greatest gift of sanctification to her house precisely because of a blessing already received. Here again, we sense the importance of contemplative evocation for the congregation who has already blessed and come near in countless ways.

If we allude to the language of the Solemn Blessing for Advent, we might notice a lovely point of departure for the homiletic text. The blessing affirms the faith of the congregation, which is a fruit of the womb of the church. To preach through the lens of this blessing suggests an invitation for the assembly to reflect on the gift of faith as a kind of child waiting to be born. An illustration here can be taken from the joys (and pains!) of the expectant mother who cares and nurtures life from its beginning. The role of the spouse and the children as collaborators further accentuates this child of faith waiting to be born. That faith will be led in trust by the Shepherd's gentleness (First Reading). And it is this same faith and trust that we bring to the altar (Prayer over the Gifts) for sanctification. The celebration of the Nativity will take us to the origins of our faith, hope, and love, the foundation of the house we have opened to allow God to enter. The gifts we welcome our divine guest with are our wills, our very lives (Second Reading).

Mary is the congregation this day—blessed already and awestruck because we too are doubly grateful for the Lord's presence in our midst (Gospel). Like Elizabeth, however, our faith rejoices in the womb of the church because we know that which was spoken to the Mother of God would be—will be—fulfilled in our hearing, in the presence of the baptized. In the end, we are witnesses to the work God has done within us, the awesome transformation of the incarnation ready to bud forth.

CHRISTMAS TIME

The Nativity of the Lord

Vigil Mass

Readings from the Ambo

Isa 62:1-5; Ps 89:4-5, 16-17, 27, 29;
Acts 13:16-17, 22-25; Matt 1:1-25

As with all three of the Masses for the celebration of Christmas, the readings selected for the Vigil Mass (celebrated before or after First Vespers of the Nativity of the Lord) maintain a character appropriate to the time surrounding the solemnity itself. Preachers, in particular, should attend to the way in which the readings from sundown on Christmas Eve through midnight and the break of day, shape the way the Nativity is experienced by the listening congregation. To this end, the Vigil readings are the very first to break the silence and vigil of Advent, exploding with joy and anticipation of what is to come. In a sense, the character of the Vigil Mass is a telescoped version of Advent, a liturgy brimming with the readings on the edge of the Day of the Lord.

The **First Reading** exemplifies such a powerful breaking into silence when Isaiah says, "For Zion's sake I will not be silent, / for Jerusalem's sake I will not be quiet, / until her vindication shines forth like the dawn / and her victory like a burning torch." Piercing silence like the dawn and the fire of a burning torch sets the ambiance for this powerful First Reading, taken from Isaiah, chapter 62, which is one of three oracles promising God's triumph. Clearly, this is the promise of victory, which has crested at this moment from all of Advent, a poem about new beginnings. God promises Zion and its territory another name: "My Delight" and "Espoused." Indeed this new name discloses even more: a covenantal relationship, that the Builder will marry his own creation. So this vindication, in the end, is less about vanquishing the enemy than an apocalyptic vision of the Builder re-creating a civilization of love—a marriage that will bring forth a holy people, redeemed by the Lord, "Sought Out, / A City Not Forsaken" (NRSV).

That same city is being re-created and brought out of the silence of shame in the **Gospel** as well. The genealogy of Jesus Christ appears to be anything but what we might call a pedigree for the messianic King. On the contrary, of the five women included, all except Mary are Gentiles or in some way associated with non-Jewish history. Needless to say, these women do not figure prominently in patriarchal history but are marginalized or powerless. Additionally, the kings mentioned in the genealogy are not proof of a royal line, nor are they, by and large, examples of fidelity and trust in God. And so, even a cursory glance at this genealogy of Jesus Christ, Son of David, tells us that a new cycle of earth's people are being brought into being: outside of a patriarchal configuration, indeed outside the will of the flesh but born of the Spirit. With the coming of Christ, this new generation will break the cycle of evil and sin, where, as Mary says in the *Magnificat*, the powerless will be blessed and the mighty overthrown. And God will once again, according to the promise made to Isaiah, direct a holy people.

Paul's speech in Acts (**Second Reading**) is part of his first of three missionary journeys to the Gentiles in the Mediterranean basin. Paul's retelling of salvation history in the synagogue in Antioch in Pisidia occurs after the reading of the Law and the Prophets. Not unlike Luke 4:16-21, Paul reinterprets history so that the story of salvation gains a new hearing. Paul bears witness to God's promise and "has brought to Israel a savior, Jesus." The speech will go on to proclaim that there is further Good News: that this Jesus has come to set free all who believe in him so that those bound to the Law would now be liberated—a people espoused to the Lord not by letter but by a new relationship.

Connecting the Bible and the Liturgy

The **Entrance Antiphon**, taken from Exodus 16:6-7, expresses the unique quality of the Vigil by its mixing of present and future: *Hodie scietis quia veniet Dominus*: "Today you will know that the

Lord will come." All during Advent the biblical and liturgical readings have pointed to the future; that future celebrated at the Vigil Mass for the Lord's Nativity is now. "[A]nd in the morning you will see his glory." I would like to think that this anticipation of the Lord in the morning is something like a bride who waits on the day of her wedding. Engaged during a period of "advent," Zion, Jerusalem, the Espoused, the City not Forsaken awaits her Lord, her Builder.

The **Collect** imagines that the anticipation of the Lord now mirrors our hope of redemption, welcoming the Redeemer, the Son as judge. In this sense, there is something apocalyptic about the Vigil Mass of the Lord's Nativity, much like Advent itself, since we experience the collapse of the future into God's now, an eschatological time made present to those gathered for worship. "O God, who gladden us year by year / as we wait in hope for our redemption, / grant that, just as we joyfully welcome / your Only Begotten Son as our Redeemer, / we may also merit to face him confidently / when he comes again as our Judge." At this point, we might recall the Collect for the First Sunday of Advent, which also imagines the Christian community joyfully running in anticipation to meet the coming Lord. Here we have come full circle on the Day of the Lord.

The anticipation of the Parousia interfaces well with the God who is so clearly in charge of history, a feature we see exemplified in the Gospel and Matthew's account of the genealogy of Jesus Christ. One gets the sense that it is going to happen because God desires it and nothing can block the vindication God intends to bestow on the Holy Ones. The Eucharist, then, becomes the sign of this beginning and end, the Alpha and Omega of our faith in God's ability to eradicate the power of sin and death through Christ. As the **Prayer over the Offerings** says, "As we look forward, O Lord, / to the coming festivities, / may we serve you all the more eagerly / for knowing that in them / you make manifest the beginnings of our redemption." Indeed the Eucharist is both now and yet to come, a foretaste of the eternal now, the kingdom that is to come. Here, the church is reminded once again that it is the Bride espoused and loved by the King, now about to be made manifest this day. Along these lines, an appropriate hymn to consider as a liturgical and biblical link for the Vigil is *Wachet auf, ruft uns die Stimme* ("Wake, Awake, for Night is Flying"), a 1599 Lutheran hymn by Philipp Nicolai. The text is based on the parable of the Ten Virgins in Matthew's Gospel and a popular Advent hymn, and certainly sounds the wake-up trumpet for this Vigil of the Lord's Nativity.

Strategy for Preaching

There are some very mature themes that emerge in the context of the Vigil Mass, but, as many will be quick to realize, the Vigil Mass in many parishes is often a liturgy focused on children. These little ones are plentiful and predictably excited and waiting for the Christmas moment to come into being. And there, most obviously, the preacher has a most important resource: the natural symbols in the congregation anticipating a future, like a child's anticipation of the holiday, already present in our midst. The presence of the children is all for the better because they provide a focal point to what will almost certainly be a "multigenerational homily" for a congregation of mixed devotions. There will be some preachers who will simply give a homily for children and hope that their parents and grandparents get something out of the preaching moment. Perhaps this will work, perhaps not. I suggest a model that mirrors the wedding homily in which the preacher has something to say to the couple as well as those who have gathered to witness the marriage vows. In the case of a multigenerational assembly present at the Vigil Mass (remembering to exegete the congregation for preaching as always), the core homiletic idea could be that God has once again surprised us by love and we wait together with our children to unwrap the gift of grace this very night.

I would suggest an introduction that addresses the children, perhaps pointing out what it might have been like to be loved into birth by their mothers. We know that children need concrete images and examples and do not relate at all to abstractions. For example, can you imagine how excited your parents were on the day you were born? (Mindful of single parents, this might be visualized as a trip to the hospital and so on.) Mary, the Mother of Jesus, was even more excited because she knew how special her child Jesus would be from the long list of her relatives in Matthew's Gospel. Just notice how both Mary and Joseph trusted in God's promise. They not only trusted, but they were excited about this news.

When the preacher ponders a liturgy with a multicultural assembly or even simply a broad congregation, the children are witnesses to the excitement of the whole church on this Vigil; that was Israel's surprise when God promised the chosen people that he would take them as his beloved, his espoused. God never forgets, as every child knows who expects a gift each Christmas. God wants everyone around the altar to make memory in love. So the church is also full of joy this Vigil (Entrance Antiphon) because we are "sought out." If we have been wandering in exile with the chosen people throughout Advent, we are all the more joyful that we have been scooped up into the arms of the loving God, snatching us from alienation and meaninglessness.

We don't have to wait for this joy; it is now (Collect) in God's time. Just look again at the children, who know neither past nor future. They are telling us right now of the joy in the church because Christ is already present at the Eucharist here with his people. God has brought us into this moment in human history for a reason. Think, for a moment, how one child has changed the lives of several people in the congregation. (Include a story here of how children change lives in the present. Perhaps Charles Dickens's *A Christmas Carol* would be appropriate.)

God's child, God's Anointed, will change the whole human family and transform the course of history. We celebrate this with these children this night and in the age to come.

Holy Family of Jesus, Mary, and Joseph

Readings from the Ambo

1 Sam 1:20-22, 24-28; Ps 84:2-3, 5-6, 9-10;
1 John 3:1-2, 21-24; Luke 2:41-52

The beginning of the First Book of Samuel recounts the important event of the birth and consecration of Samuel (in Hebrew: *shemuᵓel*, or "the one who is from God"), who, together with the priest Eli, was the last of the judges in Israel; he will become a major force in Israel's history, especially as a mediator between God and future kings Saul and David. The Hebrew Scriptures single Samuel out as a special child, dedicated as a Nazirite from birth, who will carry out priestly duties later in 1 Samuel (owing to his ties to the Levitical priesthood in 1 Chr 6:26). Yet the emphasis on the selection today in the **First Reading** is not so much on Samuel as on Hannah and her husband Elkanah.

The story of Samuel's parents precedes our selection in the Lectionary, a component of which remains significant for understanding the full impact of the present text. Of particular note is Hannah's mixture of faith and despair. Cursed and shamed because she is childless, Hannah nevertheless strives mightily to bargain with the Lord with a vow: "O LORD of hosts, if you look with pity on the misery of your handmaid, if you remember me and do not forget me, if you give your handmaid a male child, I will give him to the LORD for as long as he lives; neither wine nor liquor shall he drink, and no razor shall ever touch his head" (1:11). The selection we have today from 1 Samuel discloses how Hannah's vow is fulfilled, as she carries out the Jewish customary sacrifice of presenting a bull, "an ephah of flour, and a skin of wine" to the Lord in Shiloh. It is notable that the child given to Hannah and Elkanah belongs to God and not to them alone. As such, Samuel is returned to God. "'Now I, in turn, give him to the LORD; as long as he lives, he shall be dedicated to the LORD.' Hannah left Samuel there." The dynamic of offering back to God the child one has been given may strike contemporary folks as antiquated or even preposterous, but the text emphasizes that God is the origin of human fecundity and that everything belongs to the Creator.

Interestingly enough, the **Gospel** reading for this year finds Jesus moving contrary to what we might expect, but very much in keeping with the tradition of Hannah and Elkanah. If honoring parents is a commandment, then why is Jesus causing his own kin such difficulty? As his mother says, "Your father and I have been looking for you with great anxiety." I think we should avoid strict rigidity in interpreting this passage but recognize the affinity this Gospel has with the First Reading in the reply of the young Jesus. "Did you not know that I must be in my Father's house?" The child Jesus literally belongs to God and so exemplifies the way in which all children come from God and are returned to him. Moreover, Christ's comment bespeaks his commitment to a larger family, as God becomes the Father even for the young Christ, dedicated, like Samuel, to the Lord from birth. That said, the Gospel says that Jesus "came to Nazareth, and was obedient to them." The point then is incarnational: Christ is subject to the Father as Son and to his own family as a human being. They are mediators of the Father as he is obedient to them under the law of Moses, but subject to the Father as the only Son of God.

This incarnate God dwells in us richly, according to Paul, and moves us from mere teaching or reflection on the law to praise, worship, and thanksgiving. The young Jesus moved from his own familial situation to a more universal one when he claimed to be about the Father's business. Christians are moved out of the diaspora of the law into freedom to be children of God, "singing psalms, hymns, and spiritual songs with gratitude" to God.

Connecting the Bible and the Liturgy

There are obvious liturgical reasons why the feast of the Holy Family occurs when it does: it highlights the Nativity by stretching that solemnity out into a contemplative meditation on the mystery of Christ born of a woman in human history. In today's Gospel, we are left to ponder the singular instance in the canonical Gospels in which Jesus as a youth maintains a little dialogue with his parents. In a way, it is all too human—the "lost" boy, the confused and frightened parents, the frustration of a moment not understood. This child must be about his Father's house. What Mary muses on in her heart is also the church's meditation this day as well: the incarnate Lord who has a foot both in the house of God and in our own dwelling. With this particular Gospel we see the incarnation played out in a very everyday moment; it is a sober reminder that all of us are primarily and first of all God's children and must be about that house.

Preface I of the Nativity of the Lord asks us to consider the reality of the Holy Family, albeit in a Christmas context to be sure. But the emphasis is on the visible as a sign of the invisible—which, in a very tangible sense, becomes an incarnational reality in the family itself, a prime mediator of the presence of God among his people. "For in the mystery of the Word made flesh / a new light of your glory has shone upon the eyes of our mind, / so that, as we recognize in him God made visible, / we may be caught up through him in love of things invisible." Christ as center of the family, the human family, mediates the invisible in his visible, indeed sacramental, form. Mary and Joseph's search for their child in the midst of the bustling Jerusalem shows us that Christ is the center of our human desire, often a drama played out in familial relationships. Hannah, though she predates the coming of Christ in the flesh, nevertheless expresses the longing of the human heart for generativity. That longing bespeaks the hidden presence of the Christ yet to come who will renew the whole earth by his divine entrance into our world.

The liturgy today calls us to live at the center of Christ's family —to be in the Father's house in joy. If we participate fully in the gift we have been given, returning the gifts of bread and wine, fruits of the earth and made of human hands, then this eucharistic family looks ahead to "delight one day in eternal rewards" (**Collect**).

Strategy for Preaching

The church has already celebrated the Holy Family in the Nativity itself—Mary's fiat, Joseph's obedience to God in a dream, the infant's humility. This feast today recapitulates what we already know and seeks to bring the reality of the birth of Christ and its implications into the hearts of the faithful even deeper. Unfortunately, preaching today could be a sentimental voyage into idealism and wish-fulfillment, or a diatribe about the loss of family life today. Yet the First Reading sets the tone for a family life that is mixed with bitterness in the midst of intense desire for God and fueled by faith. Indeed the Gospel itself paints a portrait of a family life with questions that go unanswered; Mary is left to ponder these inexplicable mysteries in her heart. In keeping with the Christmas season, I suggest a homily firmly rooted in the incarnation and its manifestation in the life of the human family. So the core homiletic idea for today might be to desire to constantly imitate the Holy Family—that is, any family in which Christ is made visible, even in mystery.

How is Christ visible in our families? Good question. This inquiry might trigger a sober reflection for a family of any kind—whether a single-parent family or a more traditional one. Do we long for the kind of generativity that enkindled Hannah's desire to bear a child? The family is born of fecundity but the system does not stop at the door of the house; it moves out into the world of others and regenerates the Gospel of love in the marketplace. Jesus clearly was stretching the boundaries of the traditional family when he named God as a Father, even at an early age. Do we afford as much respect to the members of the human family as we do our families or is it more the case, as the cliché goes, that blood is thicker than water?

The **Collect** suggests that we practice "the virtues of family life," together with "the bonds of charity," implicating our role of the baptized as all members of the human family. Paul certainly urges mutuality in our relationship with one another. His (rather loaded) expression of submissiveness indicates a certain kind of docility, a virtue that must drive all our relationships, and exemplified by the Son of God's own relationship to his parents on earth. To the extent that we make room for others in our home, we will imitate the Holy Family and make Christ the visible sign of the invisible (Preface I of the Nativity).

The incarnation has made God nearer than we could imagine. Our families are the closest things we have, but even these frail human beings are bridges to the God of love. Can we see a God manifested that close, in the joy of the Father's house?

Solemnity of Mary, the Holy Mother of God (Years ABC)

Readings from the Ambo

Num 6:22-27; Ps 67:2-3, 5, 6, 8; Gal 4:4-7; Luke 2:16-21

The choice gleaned from the book of Numbers occurs at the end of a section in that book dealing with the Nazirites, particularly the laws governing Naziriteship, the most familiar of which to us is Samson's promise to not cut his hair. But the benediction at the end of chapter 6 seems fairly unconnected to the rest of the text and functions something like a coda just before a description of the leaders' offerings commences in chapter 7. In a certain sense, the prayer of blessing is not so much an instruction on proper behavior (contrasting with the specific ones that we have been seeing in the instructions to the Nazirites) than it is God's own promise for a benediction when his name is invoked. Here we might recall the importance of the name in ancient Israel, particularly how Yhwh or the Lord was so transcendent and wholly other that this "G-d" could not be represented, and then only obliquely, in an unutterable, unpronounceable symbol. As far as antiquity is concerned, knowledge of the divine name implies ownership and control. This episode recorded in the **First Reading** is an interesting development when the life of Moses is examined from our own horizon. Indeed, when in chapter 3 of the book of Exodus Moses first encountered the Lord on Mount Horeb, God told the future leader that he would not give him his name (*shem*) in a parlance of what is really the Semitic equivalent to "It's none of your business." In the current passage, though, the Lord is telling Moses that the priestly lineage connected with Aaron (and Moses himself, also traditionally reckoned as a Levite)

41

has access to the name, suggesting the sacred character of the Levitical priesthood (cf. Exod 28:1) and its zeal for God. Additionally, God's granting access to his name for the purpose of a blessing guarantees a future cultic legacy for Israel in its covenant with the Lord. We might speculate that this movement on God's part to grant Moses and Aaron a certain amount of ownership when it comes to invoking the Lord's name suggests a divine willingness to enter even more deeply into a covenant of love with his people.

That sacred bond becomes definitively expressed in the incarnation, of course, a promise that is sealed with the name Jesus. The **Gospel** of Luke here recollects "the name given him by the angel before he was conceived in the womb." The circumcision of the child itself resonates with the Israel's covenant with God and so plunges into our humanity at its deepest level by taking on flesh and being subject to the law of Moses. Mary is the witness of all these things, "reflecting on them in her heart," and so, in some sense, she is the holder of memory of the sacred pact precisely because of her own motherhood. The name given by the angel at the annunciation was whispered to her at the most intimate of maternal moments, a mystery she alone would hold claim. Undoubtedly, in this early reference to the Mother of God, Paul's letter to the Galatians ratifies the maternity of Mary in the **Second Reading**, when he recalls God's pact with humanity and its ripening through the very act of birth: *"genomenon ek gunaikos, genomenon upo nomon,"* or "born of a woman, born under the law." Furthermore, the connection with the Christian community is clearly evident, since we have received the Spirit of God's Son in our hearts, "crying out, 'Abba, Father!'" Thus Mary makes possible our own adoption as God's children, "an heir, through God," even as the church initiates its own children into the maternal womb of baptism.

Connecting the Bible and the Liturgy

The **Preface I of the Blessed Virgin Mary** that is to be used on the feast of the Mother of God is a bit more biblical (and darker) in its references than the previous translation. *The Roman Missal* uses a more direct reference to the annunciation with "the overshadowing of the Holy Spirit," which reflects Luke's use of the verb *episkiazo*, meaning to cast a shadow upon. The emphasis clearly suggests a potentially heavy burden, possibly hinting at Mary's future contemplation of these mysteries in her heart, or the passion of the Lord, which the angel Gabriel fails to mention. The *Sacramentary* uses the expression "the power of the Holy Spirit," also present in Luke, but that rendering lacks the haunting encumbrance implied by the Spirit's power "to overshadow." Moreover, the new translation of the Preface demonstrates, in miniature, Mary's role as mother and an instrument of the incarnation: "For by the overshadowing of the Holy Spirit / she conceived your Only Begotten Son, / and without losing the glory of virginity, / brought forth into the world the eternal Light, / Jesus Christ our Lord." The singing of the Preface places the celebrant and the congregation in the same arena as the shepherds, who are also witnesses to the Christ-event; all return, "glorifying and praising God." Therefore the Preface underlines the praise and thanksgiving of the eucharistic assembly in a very powerful way by invoking the unseen witnesses to the Nativity, the heavenly hosts. "Through him the Angels praise your majesty, / Dominions adore and Powers tremble before you. / Heaven and the Virtues of heaven and the blessed Seraphim / worship together with exultation." These are the same vocal instruments of praise, the angels and shepherds, who, at the birth of Jesus in Luke 2:1-15, some lines earlier than the Gospel for this Sunday, became the first evangelists with "Glory to God in the highest / and on earth peace to those on whom his favor rests." The **Prayer after Communion** emphasizes the congregational response in praise and exaltation when it says that "we rejoice to proclaim the blessed ever-Virgin Mary / Mother of your Son and Mother of the Church." This praise is proclaimed not as a slave crying out to its master, but as a child by adoption speaking its first words of love, "Abba, Father." The Body of Christ, then, expresses the Spirit of Jesus in its heart in praise with the angels and all the heavenly hosts. On the octave of Christmas, we are onlookers and witnesses of the Son, "born of a woman, born under the law" for the sake of our salvation, which made us children of the living God. That is the new and eternal covenant that allows us to call upon God by name, "Abba, Father!" and made possible by the Mother of God.

Strategy for Preaching

This feast figures within a range of Marian celebrations, but its position in the Christmas season guarantees it special prominence. In this celebration of the Christmas octave, the eucharistic assembly has come prepared and visually catechized to ponder these things in their hearts. Images of Mary as Mother abound during the Christmas season: on postage stamps, on Christmas cards, and in mangers large and small. The Mother of God remains without doubt the most represented face in Western art, with the exception of Jesus himself. The reason for this extraordinary phenomenon may well be that the sharing of divine life has reached into the most basic and essential aspect of humanity: motherhood. It may be too obvious to point out, but everyone in the congregation will be touched in some way by a maternal relationship. This most common of experiences draws the assembly intrepidly close to this solemnity. The question for the preacher is how to lend this most sacred image a new life and meaning.

The day is marked also by the secular calendar, which is one of the few times that the liturgical season is underlined by a popular cultural event. Millions of people have celebrated the New Year and the preacher should work this reality into the homiletic arc as a way of unfolding the praise and thanksgiving before us in contemplating the motherhood of God. Indeed, a core homiletic idea could focus on the new life that greets us always as a grace, always in mystery, always in blessing. These three areas could be unpacked as we see them marvelously disclosed in the Christmas season: the grace of God's intervention in history, which granted to Mary, as it does to us, an opportunity to cooperate with God's will, even under potentially difficult circumstances; the mystery of understanding that gift (maybe something like a single mother trying to deal with the difficulties of raising a child alone); and the blessing that may lie beneath whatever God places before us, a blessing because even in the most trying of circumstances God has whispered his name to us in the darkness and is with us in the presence of his Son.

The congregation should leave the Eucharist with a sense of God's continued activity in their lives, something that they share with the Mother of God herself. This is grace in action. As the mystery of the incarnation expresses itself in the **Prayer over the Offerings**, "grant to us, who find joy in the Solemnity of the holy Mother of God, / that, just as we glory in the beginnings of your grace, / so one day we may rejoice in its completion."

Second Sunday after the Nativity
(Years ABC)

Readings from the Ambo

Sir 24:1-2, 8-12; Ps 147:12-13, 14-15, 19-20 (John 1:14);
Eph 1:3-6, 15-18; John 1:1-18

The magnificent beginning of chapter 24 in the book of Sirach for the **First Reading** sets the tone for this Sunday, which is one of awestruck wonder at the power of God. Psalm 147 is a festive response to the celebration of Wisdom, the mysterious presence at God's right hand. The author's exultation of the Wisdom tradition in Israel and its relationship with God reflects the overall concern of Ben Sira in developing a school of thought to wean the Hellenistic Jews away from their Greek neighbors and their growing influence on God's chosen people in the Near Eastern world. In a certain sense, the personification of Sophia as a kind of companion to the Most High suggests the intimate relationship that the transcendent Hebrew God has with the depths of wisdom. That chaste companionship stands in sharp contrast to the mischievous and carnal behavior of the Greek gods. The passage we have here should be read in the larger context of chapter 24 in order to grasp the full force of Wisdom's place as a ubiquitous, abiding presence who announces, "Before all ages, in the beginning, he created me, / and through all ages I shall not cease to be. / In the holy tent I ministered before him, / and in Zion I fixed my abode."

Christians might read Jesus as the personification of Wisdom, with some important differences, which will be clarified in the Prologue of John's Gospel. The Logos was present (though uncreated) at the dawn of time, collaborating in fashioning creation with the eternal Father, and, though like Wisdom dwelling in highest heaven, became flesh. The Word has made his home with humanity. A haunting line in this regard is in verses 6-7 from the book of Sirach (chap. 24): "Over waves of the sea, over all the land, / over every people and nation I held sway. / Among all these I sought a resting place; / in whose inheritance should I abide?"

If we think of the Prologue to John's **Gospel** as a hymn, its contours become more lucid, its insights more penetrating. Clearly, the language in John allows for a kind of resplendent praise augmenting the creation narrative itself in Genesis, one that is now informed by the Word becoming flesh. In contrast to Ben Sira, John substantiates not ethereal Wisdom, but the Word become Light in the world. Moreover, the presence of the Word engages testimony (from John the Baptist), which then lives among us in proclamation even though "his own people did not accept him." The plea from Paul to the Ephesians, then, is for the "Spirit of wisdom and revelation resulting in knowledge of him" (**Second Reading**).

Connecting the Bible and the Liturgy

Like the Scriptures, the liturgy for the Second Sunday after the Nativity emphasizes the sublime mystery of the incarnation and offers the congregation an opportunity to delve into its richness. The **Entrance Antiphon**, even if it is unused in the liturgy itself, is especially evocative for reminding us of the connection between the eternal Word leaping from "heaven's royal throne" at midnight. The **Collect** picks up on the presence of the eternal Word becoming flesh in our world precisely as light, revealing to the world the glory of God "to all peoples by the radiance of [his] light." But perhaps the most available liturgical language for drawing out the scriptural readings remains in any of the three **Prefaces for the Nativity of the Lord**. For instance, **Preface I**, though rather brief, picks up very nicely on the "mystery of the Word made flesh" by echoing John's Prologue and its imagery of light when it says that "a new light of your glory has shone upon the eyes of our mind [*nova mentis nostrae oculis lux tuae claritatis infulsit*], / so that, as we recognize in him God made visible, / we may be caught up through him in love of things invisible." There are notes here of the recognition (*cognoscimus*) and discernment enlightening the mind, which, we might remember, Paul emphasizes in his letter to the church at Ephesus, and a homage to the place of wisdom in gaining understanding. Similarly, **Preface II** emphasizes the Word becoming flesh and dwelling among us, and our response "on the feast of this awe-filled mystery." In fact, most of this Preface might be considered as a theological commentary on the Christmas event, certainly one that fits neatly as a companion to the Prologue. "[T]hough invisible in his own divine nature, / he has appeared visibly in ours; / and begotten before all ages, / he has begun to exist in time." Yet the Preface does not end there but suggests the work of redemption and, as the Prologue puts it, makes us the recipients of his fullness, "grace in place of grace." Our nature has been thus taken up in Christ, "so that, raising up in himself all that was cast down, / he might restore unity to all creation / and call straying humanity back to the heavenly Kingdom." This last section, in particular, discloses the mission of the Word made visible, not simply for our edification but for divine reconciliation. Lastly, **Preface III** focuses on "the holy exchange" implied in the Prologue and in Paul's letter to the Ephesians, the latter of which says that this exchange "destined us for adoption to himself through Jesus Christ." The Preface affirms the same since, "when our frailty is assumed by your Word / not only does human mortality receive unending honor / but by this wondrous union we, too, are made eternal," or as Paul might say, we receive "the riches of glory / in his inheritance among the holy ones."

Strategy for Preaching

With Christmas only a few days beforehand, the homily on this Second Sunday after that solemnity should focus on a concrete theological expression of the incarnation. Most congregations are really waiting for a more searching interrogation of the mystery of God made flesh. That task is not easy, since all the readings, beautiful as they are, speak rather abstractly about Wisdom and its place before all ages, together with the Word present from the beginning and its appearance among us as Light. Even Paul seems a bit like a systematic theologian at times in the letter to the Ephesians. How can the preacher make the Word made visible, really *visible*, to the Sunday assembly? Of all days, it would seem that our task as homilists remains, to paraphrase novelist Joseph Conrad out of context, "to make them see."

That said, I might recommend a combination of catechetical and practical rhetorical strategy for the homily. A prime resource to keep in mind here and elsewhere is the *Catechism of the Catholic Church* (chap. 2, art. 3), which deals with the creedal affirmation, "He was conceived by the power of the Holy Spirit, and born of the Virgin Mary" (456–83 might be particularly useful in addressing that statement). Now the assembly will not hear a tissue of quotations strung along without any force or context, but a homiletic core idea could be posing the question simply as, Why did God choose to dwell among us and how is he re-creating us day by day? The readings and the liturgy help to fill out this theological query because they are full of images of light, "Wisdom sings," "opens her mouth," and ministers before God "[i]n the holy tent." Ironically, John's Prologue seems much removed from the common experience where men and women toil and love, but it is the preacher's responsibility to be what *Fulfilled in Your Hearing* calls "the mediator of meaning" for the assembly and unfold the Word made visible.

So then the issue to confront is simply this: What does John's Prologue look like? Are there appropriate windows into the text? Yes, undoubtedly. The coming of the Word is like opening the window in a dusty attic on a brilliant spring day, or a sudden yank of some heavy and dusty drapes in a room filled with decay. (A good reference might be the closing chapters of Charles Dickens's *Great Expectations* in which the protagonist, Pip, lets in the sunlight on old Miss Havisham's frightful room, where, with mice as her companions, she has sat for decades with her rotting wedding cake for a day that never came.) The coming of the Word is also like a wonderful secret that was first whispered in the dark, but now takes on new life when it is proclaimed. We know the negative side of spreading gossip and rumors, the useless words we throw around every day on our mobile gadgets, but what about good news that travels? This witnessing was what John the Baptist did, even though he was not the Light. His testimony and ours can multiply the presence of the Word among us. The coming of the Word is also like the Word we speak back to God through Christ in the liturgy. This suggestion encourages the assembly to intentionally embrace the language of praise and live inside faith, hope, and love. Since the Preface will soon follow, getting the congregation to listen closely to that text and to own the responses at the **Preface Dialogue** as well as other congregational responses, such as the Mystery of Faith, is an unfailing homiletic tactic that blesses the faithful with the same thoughtful intention contained in the words of Paul: "May the eyes of your hearts be enlightened, that you may know what is the hope that belongs to his call, what are the riches of glory in his inheritance among the holy ones."

The Epiphany of the Lord *(Years ABC)*

Readings from the Ambo

Isa 60:1-6; Ps 72:1-2, 7-8, 10-11, 12-13;
Eph 3:2-3a, 5-6; Matt 2:1-12

The inspiring selection from the book of the prophet Isaiah to celebrate the solemnity of Christ's manifestation among the nations belongs to the larger frame of Isaiah 56:1–66:24, often referred to as "Third Isaiah." The scholarly community generally dates the text somewhere around 520 BCE, marking this section as contemporary with the return of Israel from the Babylonian exile. Generally speaking, Third Isaiah shares some common features with Second Isaiah (some believe the author to be a disciple of his forerunner), and is informed by a somewhat disillusioned reality because the jubilant expectations of Israel have not come to pass. Chapters 56–59 are strikingly strident in their admonitions to Judah after their return from exile in 539 BCE, which include warnings about idolatry, false worship, and injustice.

The current passage for the **First Reading**, however, shows itself to be a bit of an exception to the content and the tone present earlier in Third Isaiah and even includes a promise for rebuilding by foreigners, which is not part of this selection (v. 10). Notable from the first verse is an address to Jerusalem itself and the promise and even the carrier of light. We might mention the importance of the corporate salutation, a feature of community joy and responsibility that will run through all the readings. Third Isaiah is here paying special attention to the homage of earthly powers to God's kingdom of light: "Nations shall walk by your light, / and kings by your shining radiance," specifically Midian, Ephah, and Sheba, all of them from eastern Arabia. From the point of view of the present solemnity, these tributes from the diverse nations become especially evocative, right down to the bearing of "gold and frankincense" imagined in the Isaiah text, an echo of the gifts of the Eastern visitors in Matthew's Gospel. These two texts reveal an interesting little intertextual dynamic at work, but the parallel should not be overdrawn. There is more to tell, especially when it comes to the corporate share of responsibility. Where Third Isaiah represented Jerusalem as the splendor of the Lord, that city is implicated in the **Gospel** by resisting the new light in the heavens, together with its king, Herod, who was *"etarachthe kai pasa Ierosoluma met autou"* ("greatly troubled, and all Jerusalem with him"). Matthew is reminding his hearers that corporate opposition has its associations with the remarkable global call of "the wealth of the nations" brought to the poor. Bethlehem of Judea, then, the least of cities, eclipses Jerusalem as the city of light because God has rested beneath the light; it is now the new light of nations and owns a child as its king.

Meanwhile, Paul is at work with his own reversals in his letter to the Ephesians (**Second Reading**) and begins to sketch out what he reads as God's revelation to the Gentiles, a theological insight that will become one of the dominant threads in the unmatched preaching tapestry. This mission to the Gentiles highlights yet another significant color in the Pauline theological weaving: unity in Christ. A few verses earlier, at the end of chapter 2, for instance, Paul speaks of Christ as the cornerstone that holds the whole dwelling together and into which we are all drawn into participation. So Paul sees the Gentiles as "coheirs, members of the same body, and copartners" and *"sugkleronoma kai sussoma kai summetocha"* in God's unfailing promise in Christ. The call to unity in *sussoma*, the same body, sets up a wider discussion of the unity of the Body in chapter 4.

Connecting the Bible and the Liturgy

This liturgy occasions a Vigil Mass as well as a Mass during the Day; the readings are the same for both. The solemnity is unusual in that it is well integrated in terms of the symbolic structure present in both Word and sacrament, even in its cultural ambiance. As with the Mass during the Night at Christmas, the Vigil Mass for the Epiphany already presents the Christian community with the natural symbols to be accessed for the solemnity: darkness, light, and, of course, the stars. The texts themselves highlight each other as well. The **Collect** for the Vigil implores the "splendor" of the Lord's majesty to "shed its light upon our hearts, / that we may pass through the shadows of this world / and reach the brightness of our eternal home." The coming of the Lord makes this day like a new Jerusalem, where God's light is shining in Christ.

A very interesting (and hard to avoid) parallel exists between the liturgy and the action of the Gospel registered in the **Prayer over the Offerings** for both the Vigil and the day Masses. "[I]n honor of the appearing of your Only Begotten Son," the presider asks on behalf of the congregation that the Lord accept "the first fruits of the nations" (Vigil). The allusion here is to the corporate body, the nations bringing tributes from afar in Third Isaiah, but also the *ethnoi* in Paul who are now incorporated into one Body, one partnership. The Presidential Prayer and the Gospel fit nicely together here. Along these lines, the Prayer over the Offerings in the Mass during the Day transforms this parallel action of the magi and the congregation into a theological statement about the work of Christ: "Look with favor, Lord, we pray, / on these gifts of your Church, / in which are offered now not gold or frankincense or myrrh, / but he who by them is proclaimed, / sacrificed and received, Jesus Christ." The sentence structure is a bit awkward here, but the christological moment should not be lost. Christ is the new gift being offered, who, in receiving them, also proclaims our redemption. The prayer recalls Christ's grace of reconciliation, which fully takes up all gifts preceding it, even as the nations come toward the Light. The **Preface of the Epiphany of the Lord** picks up on this mystery when it says that "when he appeared in our mortal nature, / you made us new by the glory of his immortal nature." That "*nova nos immortalitatis eius Gloria reparasti*" of the great exchange between God and humanity reminds us that the Lord is the true giver of gifts, transforming our own.

Strategy for Preaching

With the solemnity of the Epiphany of the Lord, the readings and liturgical prayers shift the axis of the congregation's worship from contemplation to action. The days after Christmas, including the solemnity of the Mother of God (as well as the Second Sunday after the Nativity), are continued reflections and deep ponderings of the mystery of the Nativity. Now the church has hardly ceased its meditation on the incarnation, but the Scriptures for today bring into focus the implications of God taking on human flesh in a public and, indeed, global way. In this regard, the liturgical pattern from the Nativity to the Epiphany follows Paul's own movement in the Spirit, who tells us that he first received the mystery "by revelation," but has now become a promise to all. The Light that has dawned will not and cannot be encased in darkness. So God's outreach shines even to the ends of the earth, where nations will come streaming. That same light shatters distinctions between Jew and Gentile for Paul.

Preaching on this solemnity, then, has global signification and its symbols have a very contemporary feel. With our instant communication, our own world is itself becoming more and more like a large village. Moreover, this solemnity's corporate emphasis raises the issue of national boundaries, which God has erased. The social implications of following the Gospel become clear from the trek of the magi who "departed for their country by another way." Some, like the magi, may choose to follow the light; others, like "all Jerusalem," may find themselves allied with earthly powers instead of God's kingdom.

A core homiletic idea might consist of challenging the congregation to consider the social realities of God taking on our human flesh. If we are to take the **Preface of the Epiphany of the Lord** at its word, or that we have been made "new by the glory of his immortal nature," then a new star has appeared in our horizon implicating us in God's splendor. Are we willing to see the transformation of our earthly reality into the gift of witness to the incarnation? And if so, what would that testimony look like in the public square? Here, the homily might start to name the contemporary gifts all of us bring to be unwrapped by grace. Needless to say, the more specific we can be in the homiletic text, the better the hearer of the Word will be able to become copartners with the preacher. Some bring gifts of diversity that are golden in their poetic expressions of Hispanic song and praise. Others offer the frankincense of their hard work; after a long day at the accounting firm, they come to offer their time by helping with parish bookkeeping. Still others bring the myrrh of bereavement ministry to their brothers and sisters, by cooking dishes after funerals or spending time with the children of loss. All of these gifts are testimony to the global reach of the incarnate Word into which the Christian faithful have been drawn this season. This witness will have public consequences in and out of the parish. These are specific challenges to ratify the promise God made in Christ, an invitation to enflesh what has already been made incarnate.

The Baptism of the Lord

Readings from the Ambo

*Isa 40:1-5, 9-11; Ps 104:1b-2, 3-4, 24-25, 27-28, 29-30;
Titus 2:11-14; 3:4-7; Luke 3:15-16, 21-22*

The **First Reading** initiates the beginning of a well-known section (40:1–55:13) commonly referred to as Second Isaiah or Deutero-Isaiah, a text known for bringing healing to those in exile in Babylon around 540 BCE. This text is an iconic Advent witness; the selection we have today is used as the First Reading for the Second Sunday of Advent in Year B because of its promise of hope and reconciliation in the midst of despair and emptiness. But this particular portion of Second Isaiah expresses a tone of strength with an undercurrent of profound and abiding comfort from the Lord.

The First Reading also sets the stage for the beginning of Jesus' ministry, a marvelous frame for the Baptism of the Lord and fitting orientation for Ordinary Time. The baptism of Jesus begins, of course, the Lord's public life with God's people and so Isaiah's text, which promises that "the glory of the LORD shall be revealed, / and all people shall see it together," becomes a commentary on Jesus' manifestation among the people of Israel and beyond: "Here comes with power, / the Lord GOD, / who rules by a strong arm; / here is his reward with him, / his recompense before him."

God's manifestation of his power in his Son becomes visible at the Jordan, where "heaven was opened and the Holy Spirit descended upon [Jesus] in bodily form like a dove" (**Gospel**). Luke highlights the baptism of Christ as a trinitarian moment as well; this transformation of the waters of the Jordan by the one who made them reveals a unique relationship among three Persons: "And a voice came from heaven, 'You are my beloved Son; with you I am well pleased.'" The voice of the Father directs itself to Jesus, who, having received the Spirit, now is claimed by God. It is useful to contrast the two other Synoptics here: Mark's representation of the baptism blueprints the same point of view—the Father speaking directly to Jesus. But Matthew's account shows the Father making a kind of public declaration: "This is my beloved Son, with whom I am well pleased" (3:17). In both Mark and Luke, Jesus must own the voice of the Father directed at him and that relationship between the Father and Son, together with the descent of the Holy Spirit, tells us that Christ's baptism is not only a beginning of his public ministry, but the revelation of an utterly unique relationship in the Godhead.

Paul's Letter to Titus, extracted for the **Second Reading** today, makes theological sense for the baptism of Christ in precisely trinitarian terms. Moreover, Paul discourses on baptism for the faithful with the allusion to our salvation "through the bath of rebirth / and renewal by the Holy Spirit, / whom he richly poured out on us / through Jesus Christ our savior." Christ's baptism in the Jordan prepared the way for us. We know that John the Baptist carved out a road for Christ, but Christ prepares the way for us, baptizing "with the Holy Spirit and with fire." Christ's relationship with the Trinity allows him to baptize with the Holy Spirit, comforting and bringing the tenderness God spoke to the exiles in Babylon. Now in the exile of sin, we are brought out into the fold. "Like a shepherd he feeds his flock; / in his arms he gathers the lambs, / carrying them in his bosom, / and leading the ewes with care" (First Reading).

Connecting the Bible and the Liturgy

Most parishes have access to a variety of resources, but some might consider the wellspring of Christian hymnody available even outside such seasons as Christmas and Easter. Why not carry the singing church into Ordinary Time with some suitable texts as well? A perfect point of departure in this regard is today's feast of the Baptism of the Lord. Particularly with the First Reading's selection from Second Isaiah, *Tröstet, tröstet meine Lieben*, composed by Johann Olearius (17th century) and translated by Catherine Winkworth, makes a nice connection. "Tell of all the sins I cover, / And that warfare now is over." Our sins are covered because we are children of adoption born of water and the spirit; as the **Collect** puts it, "grant that your children by adoption, / reborn of water and the Holy

Spirit, / may always be well pleasing to you." Our comfort this day is that we are the Beloved in Christ, made whole by the indwelling of the Trinity. We are covered with the Holy Spirit, beloved of the Father through the river of Christ's mercy.

At the same time, the Baptism of the Lord is also the threshold of Jesus' mission on earth. The baptism of Christ in the Jordan made those waters holy for a reason: so that this sign might become for us the proclamation of the Good News with which we are now emboldened to preach together with Christ. As the **Preface: The Baptism of the Lord** tells us, "by the Spirit's descending in the likeness of a dove / we might know that Christ your Servant / has been anointed with the oil of gladness / and sent to bring the good news to the poor." Christ is anointed as God's Servant, even as the chrism of the newly baptized crowns and seals the neophyte with that same sign. The baptized assembly gather to celebrate the Eucharist and are sustained as they dine at the table of the Lord and move into mission for our brothers and sisters. As the **Prayer after Communion** says, "Nourished with these sacred gifts, / we humbly entreat your mercy, O Lord, / that, faithfully listening to your Only Begotten Son, / we may be your children in name and in truth." The prayer references the Matthean Gospel account of the baptism of the Lord, with the Father's command to listen, but there is something for the baptized to own here as well. If the Father addressed Jesus personally as Son, we are God's children "in name and in truth." Baptism literally gives us a new name, which God continues to whisper as we grow in our commitment to his truth. So it is not only a matter of listening to the voice of Christ but of claiming our relationship with the Trinity that dwells within us at baptism. We have been named God's children, the beloved. So we listen to the Son, our brother.

Strategy for Preaching

To know that we are God's children in name and in truth through Christ's baptism might well be the core homiletic idea for today. Although the feast does not hold sway in the public imagination, its significance should not be underestimated or overshadowed by the (rightly solemnized) Christmas season that precedes it. For the preacher to take hold of this feast means orienting the congregation to the distinct demands of Ordinary Time, which is to say allowing the listening assembly to comprehend their own baptism in celebrating

Christ's encounter with the Father and the Spirit in the Jordan. In so doing, "my beloved" is a name that God has said to us all, now brought into being in the worshiping community redeemed from the darkness of sin and oblivion by the grace of adoption.

A very poignant and useful introduction might be a contemporary reality check: there are millions of displaced children throughout the world, stricken by war, poverty, disease, and hunger. The Red Cross, Catholic Relief Services, and people of every persuasion or religious confession provide temporary relief, but the children of our violence, sin, and neglect are always before us. If we want to know what original sin looks like, this is it.

That sad story holds up a mirror to this day: Christ's baptism brought all of us orphans of sin into adoption (Collect). The fragmentation and meaninglessness of original sin has been covered by the comfort God has offered us, his children. When the author of the book of Isaiah was preaching God's word, the people of Israel were literally displaced from their homeland in Babylon. But they have been yoked back into the promise of a homeland, their anxiety covered.

So, too, the waters of rebirth have made us not only friends of God, but beloved partakers of divine life in the Trinity (Second Reading). Consider the same tenderness with which the Father addresses the Son and the gentle outpouring of the anointing of the Spirit. So were we held by the church and anointed in the sacrament of baptism and welcomed into the Christian community with a new name as the Beloved. (It would be appropriate to briefly sketch out three vignettes of baptismal scenes, each using a specific name.)

How can we resist the Word as it lays claim to us during Ordinary Time? We will travel with Christ in Luke's Gospel each Sunday with a unique perspective through Lent, Easter, and Pentecost. Those ordinary Sundays in Year C will follow the Beloved to the cross on the feast of Christ the King, where, with the repentant thief, we will ask to possess paradise with the Savior. This day celebrates that we are no longer orphans and are called to bring others into our same family. We cannot keep from singing, even in Ordinary Time, where the Trinity dwells deep within us. (As I suggested in the previous section, it may be useful to deploy an appropriate hymn text to underline this point, such as "Comfort, Comfort Ye, My People." The congregation may even be encouraged to stand and sing as a response to their baptism, preparing them to recite the Creed.)

 LENT

First Sunday of Lent

Readings from the Ambo

Deut 26:4-10; Ps 91:1-2, 10-11, 12-13, 14-15;
Rom 10:8-13; Luke 4:1-13

The present selection from the book of Deuteronomy in the **First Reading** comes from a subdivision in the text often entitled "Presenting First Fruits and Tithes," the meaning for which would be more obvious if the passage for today had commenced from the very beginning of chapter 26. The first few verses of this chapter make it clear that when the chosen people come to the Promised Land, they are to offer their gifts; the lines that follow are Moses' own tribute or fruits, if you will, of gratitude to God. The rationale of the great leader is fairly obvious; offerings come from and emerge out of a thankful heart. "When the Egyptians maltreated and oppressed us, imposing hard labor upon us, we cried to the LORD, the God of our fathers, and he heard our cry and saw our affliction, our toil, and our oppression." Memory unlocks the gates of our heart, which opens up in thankful offering to God.

It might be helpful to view the Lukan account of the temptation by Satan in the desert as something like a reminder to the Christian community to be grateful. As Jesus is tempted in a triple seduction by the Evil One, we might remember the fate from which the Savior has delivered us. Christ's resistance to turn stone into bread, or seek power and vainglory, shows us the reach of evil and the depths into which Satan probes humanity. Christ's victory over these temptations is like being brought out of Egypt with a mighty hand and being ushered into a Promised Land of redemption. Our response can only be to remember in thanksgiving such a champion of humanity. Simply put, this is God's action in Christ: our deliverance from Satan's grasp.

So in the **Second Reading** Paul's Letter to the Romans acknowledges this supreme debt to Christ for defeating the enemy through confidence and faith in God—the same faith we ask for ourselves. "For everyone believes with the heart and so is justified, and one confesses with the mouth and so is saved." This particular portion of the Letter to the Romans, interestingly enough, finds Paul quoting Scripture extensively and interpreting it, a dramatic dynamic that will be repeated by both Satan and Jesus in the **Gospel**. Further, the **Responsorial Psalm** is exactly the same passage that Satan deploys to tempt Jesus. The faith that defeats temptation and believes with the heart and so is justified cannot survive simply by quoting the words of Scripture—even Satan can manipulate these passages to his own end. Rather, faith takes us to the world of the interior, where, as the psalmist says, "No evil shall befall you, / nor shall affliction come near your tent, / for to his angels he has given command about you, / that they guard you in all your ways." We have been protected from the Evil One by the angels and God's Angel, Christ Jesus, who has safeguarded our feet from stumbling on sin and bears us up in redemption.

Connecting the Bible and the Liturgy

One of the high hurdles to overcome at the beginning of Lent remains this great season's association with our penitential work to the potential eclipse of Christ's work. Even beyond the benign attitudes of "giving up" something for this time of repentance, we face a subtle diminishment of Christ at the core of the season and a self-aggrandizement of our pious works and prayers (and ironically, falling prey to the vainglory Jesus defeats in the desert). I certainly do not want to nay-say the importance of prayer, fasting, and almsgiving, as long as we recognize that these works of pastoral charity are made possible through Christ's work already in us, because of his triumph over sin and death. At the same time, we are not Pelagians and so if we are capable of doing good, it is only because Christ has sanctified us by his grace and defeated human temptation head-on. If we do not grasp this christocentric feature of the season of Lent, then the Scripture and the liturgy will cease to have much meaning beyond some pious reminders and adages, and our works advertisements for our own religiosity.

What I am suggesting is a First Sunday of Lent that begins with gratitude to God for the gift of Christ. The **Collect** for today invites this christological exploration when it says, "Grant, almighty God, / through the yearly observances of holy Lent, / that we may grow in understanding / of the riches hidden in Christ / and by worthy conduct pursue their effects." So the church asks the congregation to first contemplate "the riches hidden in Christ" *et effectus eius digna conversatione sectemur*—"and by worthy conduct pursue their effects." The understanding that our right-conduct or ability to engage in conversion on the First Sunday of Lent is nothing less than that which Moses advised in chapter 26 in the book of Deuteronomy. The Christian community offers its firstfruits of good works for this season because of gratitude, a virtue impossible in and of itself, if it were not for God's gift. Satan's triple temptation suggests the root sins present in each one of us, all of them undermining gratitude, praise, and thanksgiving. So the **Prayer over the Offerings** asks that we be given "the right dispositions" to make our gift of the just fruits—our hearts disposed to understand the riches of Christ's treasures.

It seems clear that Christ remains the center for this Lenten season as we head toward a celebration of the paschal mystery. He is our example, teacher, redeemer, since "by overturning all the snares of the ancient serpent, / [he] taught us to cast out the leaven of malice, / so that, celebrating worthily the Paschal Mystery, / we might pass over at last to the eternal paschal feast" (**Preface: The Temptation of the Lord**). Like the chosen people, we await the Promised Land at the end of a time of trial and temptation, at the end of which we will bring the firstfruits of our newly sanctified lives in baptism to the Lamb's High Feast.

Strategy for Preaching

Most would agree that it is far easier to get people to engage in some kind of mildly heroic ascetical enterprise than to deepen a sense of gratitude. Yet the preacher's task today, the First Sunday of Lent, is just that difficult: how to remind the congregation of "the riches hidden in Christ / and by worthy conduct pursue their effects" (Collect). This portion of the Opening Prayer makes for an effective two-part structure for a core homiletic idea. If this schema is followed, I suggest an introduction that would set up the first portion of this section of the Collect; it might look something like this:

I. We can only imagine the riches hidden in Christ. This introduction would then proceed to focus on a central image that I recommend may come from the First Reading: "We are apt to forget that like the chosen people of Israel, we sometimes need to be reminded of the work God has done for us." Allusion to the Responsorial Psalm. (Some selected recollection of local events to illustrate.)

II. Another momentous occasion of God's work unfolds before us today, Christ defeating Satan in the desert.

   A. All of us face temptations, even as Jesus' humanity experienced them as part of the mystery of the incarnation.

   B. We have all desired things that chain us down, longed for the appetite of stones turned to bread, or power and pride. But only Christ said no to every one of these. That was an encounter Christ made with the Evil One so that we could live in freedom.

   C. Imagine a moment in which we have resisted a temptation; that was possible because of Christ's gift of grace. (Illustration.)

III. Our response to Christ's gift can only be to aspire to worthy conduct, as our Collect tells us for today. We can offer our lives, change our behavior, and believe the Gospel more fully.

   A. Prayer over the Offerings

   B. Preface: The Temptation of the Lord

IV. Lent is an opportunity to express our self-denial as a way of showing gratitude to God. The Scriptures help us remember; that yields a collective "thanks" from us all.

   A. First Reading (Israel's response to being liberated).

   B. Second Reading (faith comes from the heart).

   C. (Illustrate what it means to remember something and be grateful.)

Second Sunday of Lent

Readings from the Ambo

Gen 15:5-12, 17-18; Ps 27:1, 7-8, 8-9, 13-14;
Phil 3:17–4:1; Luke 9:28b-36

Taken together, these biblical readings for today range from the personal to the theologically speculative; all are windows into the promise expressed by the **Responsorial Psalm**: "I believe that I shall see the bounty of the LORD / in the land of the living."

In the **Second Reading**, Paul's invitation to the Philippians to become imitators or *summimetes* (really, co-imitators, or fellow imitators) of him extends to the contemporary Christian church as well. Paul is not setting himself up as some kind of arrogant gold standard to be followed, but begs the church at Philippi to discover him as a model, an anchor, or a teacher, who loves the community to whom he writes as his "joy and crown." Paul has placed himself, a person convicted "in tears," as a kind of ambassador for the kingdom of God. He is an earthly witness to the things of heaven, forming a living apologetic against the "enemies of the cross of Christ." For he says that "our citizenship is in heaven, and from it we also await a savior, the Lord Jesus Christ. He will change our lowly body to conform with his glorified body by the power that enables him also to bring all things into subjection to himself." In a certain sense, by persuading the Philippians to be fellow imitators of him, Paul is preparing that community for the transformation of their bodies through the power of witness: his own example will help to transform the church even before Jesus transforms their lowly bodies into his glorified body. Paul is a human witness to the divine promise, a reflection of the light of Christ.

Abraham is about to become yet another witness for future generations in chapter 15 of the book of Genesis (**First Reading**). The great patriarch will be an enduring sign for ages to come for the Jewish people. "The covenant that he made with Abraham, / his sworn promise to Isaac" is a living trope of the psalmist in the history of the divine covenant (1 Chr 16:16, NRSV). There would be tragedy underneath this divine covenant for the Jewish people, in a history fraught and scarred with anti-Semitic prejudice and persecution, which would demand a constant recourse to the promise made through Abraham to the chosen people.

Some will invariably be shaken when it comes to the disclosure of the suffering God who, mysteriously, is also the keeper of the covenant. At Tabor, Peter cannot reconcile the glory of Christ with "his exodus," his passion, as a fulfillment of the promise. Yet the Trinity that discloses itself on the mountain is uniquely expressed in the transfigured Christ, as it was at the Lord's baptism in the Jordan. Christ embodies the promise foretold centuries before in Abraham and the Prophets. His exodus will fulfill the Law and the Prophets, Moses and Elijah, who now converse with him. The scene at Tabor is the most intimate of disclosures, but also the most cosmic; it reveals the Son as the face of the Father, while drawing all of us into the cloud of unknowing, a future to be fulfilled by God alone (**Gospel**).

Connecting the Bible and the Liturgy

Preachers who are praying through a homiletic that speaks "through the Scriptures" do well to recall both the personal and the global dimensions of the Lectionary texts used for the Second Sunday of Lent, together with their liturgical counterparts. By "personal" I do not wish to implicate God's radically intimate relationship with the human subject (as exemplified by Abraham and Paul) with our own culture's obsession with individualism. On the contrary, I propose that it is only in seeing through the macro lens of God's covenant and promise that we are able to glimpse our own micro encounter with the Lord. In other words, a taste of the divine promise made with Abraham through the Law and then the Prophets after him becomes intimately accessible to the baptized assembly in the transfigured Lord who has gathered Moses and Elijah to himself. We become witnesses ourselves to the cross and resurrection, in order that, like Paul, we may show forth the Christ in us come to full stature.

Consider, then, the **Collect**, which marvelously positions the assembly as partakers in the cross and resurrection of the Son as Word of God, so we might behold the promise that has been disclosed for us. "O God, who have commanded us / to listen to your beloved Son, / be pleased, we pray, / to nourish us inwardly by your word, / that, with spiritual sight made pure, / we may rejoice to behold your glory." It is the trinitarian relationship disclosed at Tabor that manifests the cross and resurrection—that is, the suffering God rising to new life—the eternal covenant foreshadowed in the promise made to Abraham, Moses, and Elijah. We ought to see Peter as the disciple seeking the ongoing revelation of God in his Christ the Beloved, aptly stated by the **Entrance Antiphon** for today: "*Tibi dixit cor meum quaesivi vultum tuum, Domine, requiram, no avertas faciem tuam a me.*" "Of you my heart has spoken: seek his face. / It is your face, O Lord, that I seek; / hide not your face from me."

As members—or future members of the baptized assembly—this congregation of seekers longs to discover the revelation of God in Christ. As Paul promised in his own testimony, so those gathered for worship see the witness "by the testimony of the law and the prophets, / that the Passion leads to the glory of the Resurrection (**Preface: The Transfiguration of the Lord**). If we are to be co-imitators of Christ, then we must be prepared to face the cross as well, so as to witness to the glory of the resurrection.

Strategy for Preaching

How can the homily disclose the vital axis of God's revelation that is personal and global, intimate and historical? As I have suggested elsewhere, the personal witness of the preacher is a nonnegotiable when it comes to bringing the Word to the Christian assembly. Have you been to the mountaintop and seen the glory of the Father in Christ's cross and resurrection? To spend some time with this question is to invite a personal encounter with the Lord on Tabor. In turn, the preacher initiates the assembly into the text, God's word proclaiming the mysterious cloud of God's irrevocable covenant. So the core homiletic idea for today might be to help the assembly grasp the covenant God made to Abraham, then disclosed in the Law and the Prophets and fulfilled in Christ's cross and resurrection. This seems like a daunting preaching task and it is; thankfully the Scriptures and the liturgy vibrantly accompany the assembly on their journey. Indeed this core idea is nothing more than the Preface of the Transfiguration of the Lord, unpacked for the listener to devour with holy zeal.

The structure of the homily, then, might move from a micro personal encounter to a macro teaching or catechesis of God's revelation at Tabor in something like the following:

The first part of the homily could take its cue from Paul: the preacher's micro story becomes the witness to be imitated. This is a personal testimony for a strategic purpose. Indeed, any story or personal disclosure should be strategic and have an economical purpose in mind. Questions such as these should accompany any personal narrative in the homily: Why am I really telling this story? Where is it going? What is the purpose of it? Here the preacher might briefly account for a personal testimony of the Holy, either in Word or sacrament, or a pastoral encounter with God's people. This is the witness of Tabor: transfigured Christ in us all.

Then a reference might be made to the Entrance Antiphon, which expresses the common experience of everyone—"Seek his face"! I would then advert to Abraham, Paul, and Peter (and the other disciples, James and John) as those who have been the recipients of the covenant given by God, who desires to reveal himself to all humanity in Christ, first in the cross and then in the resurrection.

The last portion of the homily could then move to a unique and definitive disclosure of the Father's face in Christ through the Spirit revealed at Tabor. The Preface for today supports this revelation of divine disclosure, albeit in mystery. We are longing for the fullness of the paschal mystery as we await the Triduum and God's final word: Jesus is risen! For further catechetical gloss, preachers should consult the *Catechism of the Catholic Church*, article 555. This Second Sunday of Lent is a fine opportunity to prepare the congregation for the great solemnity of Easter, the prelude for which is the Passion of the Lord.

Third Sunday of Lent

Readings from the Ambo

Exod 3:1-8a, 13-15; Ps 103:1-2, 3-4, 6-7, 8, 11;
1 Cor 10:1-6, 10-12; Luke 13:1-9

I wonder to whom Jesus is referring in this parable when he speaks of the person who came in search of the fig tree he planted to see if it bore fruit. We know that from the point of view of allegorical biblical references, the fig tree is Israel. In Matthew 24:32-33 the tree's budding may represent an apocalyptic sign. But it is Jeremiah who gives us the clearest parallel between the fig tree and Israel in 24:1-10, a comparison that suggests it is God who expects good fruit to be the faithful of Israel. Since Jesus speaks about the repentance and its urgency (posing as example two recent disasters), it seems clear that Christ has in mind an Israel that has failed to heed the word of God. The passage in the **Gospel** is a wonderful example of Jesus as interpreter of the fate of Israel's history and of the chosen people's literary, allegorical heritage used to provoke conversion.

The parable seems to scream that there is still time to get ready. That's nice to hear during Lent, isn't it? I gather that there is a year of reprieve, thanks to the intercession of the gardener who offers to fertilize and cultivate the tree rather than cut it down right away. The patience of the one in search of fruit has been prevailed upon and so time has been purchased for now. But the time of waiting to repent is soon over. Using our own literary imagination, it is not too much of a stretch to identify Jesus as the one who intercedes, the gardener who offers to "cultivate the ground around" our stubborn hearts with parables like this one to see how long it will take for us to bear fruit. But the time for fruit is limited.

In the **Second Reading**, Paul tells the Corinthians that God also gave them the example of Israel in the desert "as an example, and they have been written down as a warning to us, upon whom the end of the ages has come." The upshot of this for Paul is that this is a God of second chances, as Jesus himself intimates. The **Responsorial Psalm** expresses this kindness and mercy of the Lord when it says, in the words of the psalmist, "Merciful and gracious is the LORD, / slow to anger and abounding in kindness. / For as the heavens are high above the earth, / so surpassing is his kindness toward those who fear him."

Given the passages from Corinthians and Luke's Gospel today, the encounter between Moses and God on Mount Horeb may seem misplaced (**First Reading**). Not so. We might recall that Moses was an outlaw and, in fact, a murderer who was running from Egyptian justice. Moses' secret, buried in the desert sands, is a murdered man and waits to be unearthed. Therefore Moses' response to God at the iconic scene of the burning bush is a call not only to mission but also conversion: Moses himself must take off his sandals in order to stand in the presence of the Holy One. In so doing, he must leave his past behind and move into God's future in order to bear fruit. God's patience exists in endless mercy for Israel's great leader and for the chosen people themselves, waiting for the fig tree to blossom in the desert.

Connecting the Bible and the Liturgy

That we are converted by God's kindness is axiomatic in the history of Christian spirituality and clearly evident in today's biblical and liturgical texts. "Mercy" is positioned at the beginning of the Eucharist, as the assembly is called to repentance as part of the **Penitential Act**. The priest or deacon seems to pierce the darkness with an initial invocation: "Have mercy on us, O Lord." This is the cry that begs a rejoinder as the congregation faces the burning bush, the Holy God, radiant on Mount Horeb. "For we have sinned against you." We might imagine that this call to repentance is the Gardener making the fig tree ready for the year ahead, a chance to bear fruit before this Lenten season comes to an end. The Penitential Act is, of course, in the plural, so that we can see ourselves acting in community as examples to one another. In fact, this call to conversion is just the beginning, for at the conclusion of the liturgy we will be sent forth to bear fruit, as the presider says, "Go and announce the

Gospel of the Lord." Like Moses, we have encountered the merciful God on the mountain in the form of his radiant love, and now go and call others into the freedom of the children of God.

The **Collect** for today underlines the strength of God's compassion for humanity as well, as it acknowledges the mercy of God as a support to carry us through the desert of our Lent. We have all come to the Eucharist as "outlaws," so to speak, in need of God to give us healing. "O God, author of every mercy and of all goodness, / who in fasting, prayer and almsgiving / have shown us a remedy for sin, / look graciously on this confession of our lowliness, / that we, who are bowed down by our conscience, / may always be lifted up by your mercy." Mercy, used twice in this Opening Prayer, is the promise of the parable of the Fig Tree, the renewed covenant of God through Moses and the people of Israel. The immediacy of the kingdom alerts us to the necessary repentance, a conversion offered by the church's public prayer at the beginning of the Eucharist. Furthermore, **Preface III of Lent** recalls what fruits our conversion of heart will yield when it says, "For you will that our self-denial should give you thanks, / humble our sinful pride, / contribute to the feeding of the poor, / and so help us imitate you in your kindness." In the end, this transformation into kindness was what allowed Moses to bring the people out of slavery, a redemption purchased by divine mercy.

Strategy for Preaching

I think that "the God of second chances" would find a sympathetic hearing on the Third Sunday of Lent. The advantage of introducing a somewhat colloquial notion into a theological area is that everyone needs a second chance, which is another way of looking at conversion. Additionally, discussion on conversion tends to concentrate (rightly so) on the human subject rather than the instrument of conversion. But our *metanoia*, our conversion, becomes a possibility only because God keeps renewing the divine covenant from age to age, through the intercession and cultivation of Christ, the fount of mercy. That we receive a second chance focuses on the mercy of God, the patience of the one seeking the fruit from a fig tree that may or may not bear gifts. So the core homiletic idea for today might be to understand the opportunity that awaits us through God's merciful goodness, and to bear the fruit of the kindness.

A strong initial foray into the homily could start with Moses—his murder, flight, and transformation on Horeb. How did an outlaw become God's greatest leader and an instrument of his mercy? Divine kindness. Moses is the first of the children of Israel to whom the Lord has come as a deliverer. The rest will follow as they are liberated from the bonds of slavery and brought into the Promised Land.

Jesus understood this divine mercy since he embodied this love. The parable of the Fig Tree, in a certain literary sense, functions as a kind of autobiographical reference to his own role as the one who patiently intercedes for humanity as a cultivator of the heart. This parable asks us to convert by God's patience. (Illustration of someone who is converted by patience: may be something in the life of the preacher, perhaps; or the story of a parent who patiently endures a teenager's growing rebellion until adulthood; or a middle-aged person who cares for her elderly mother.) The church also invokes us into second chances at every Eucharist (Penitential Act). And we note the God of all mercy bringing us all to conversion at the first moments of the liturgy in our Opening Prayer (Collect).

The Eucharist invites us to change, even as Paul advised the Corinthians not to fall into bad behavior and disordered thinking. The Eucharist reorders us into the now-time of repentance, a corporate conversion as a church, the new Israel (before it is too late), the ripe time that Jesus urged so emphatically in the parable of the Fig Tree. Do we dare to bear fruit, together with the "fruit of the vine and work of human hands," and become a spiritual drink for all?

Fourth Sunday of Lent

Readings from the Ambo

Josh 5:9a, 10-12; Ps 34:2-3, 4-5, 6-7;
2 Cor 5:17-21; Luke 15:1-3, 11-32

The **Gospel** for Laetare Sunday offers us a marvelous reason to rejoice even in Lent: God is about to throw a party for a sinner who has returned (not coincidentally, Jesus shares a table with sinners while he is telling this story of the return of the prodigal and is accused of eating with them). Arguably Jesus' most celebrated parable, the story of the Prodigal Son (or, more aptly, as some have said, The Father with Two Sons) has its roots deep in the sinews of anyone who has run amok, rebelled, or even mildly transgressed, but found the peace of reconciliation. Yet the genius of the parable is not only its content but in its anticipation of the hearer. It positions those very Pharisees and scribes who complain about the Lord eating with sinners as the ones who fail to respond to God's mercy. They are not interested in celebrating the return of the sinner and dining with him, but judging and condemning him. These members of the religious establishment are targets of Jesus' parable when he relates a story about an elder son who refuses to go into his father's house to dine with his brother. In so doing, we might find ourselves, righteous churchgoers that we are, also in the company of those who fall short of including the outsider at our table.

The prodigal and his elder brother have images of their father that inform their behavior. Curiously enough, the younger son must have felt loved enough to so boldly ask for an inheritance and then beg forgiveness later. But the elder son shows his cards unwittingly when he says, "Look, all these years I served you and not once did I disobey your orders; yet you never gave me even a young goat to feast on with my friends." Obey orders. A stern taskmaster. That is the image of the father provided by the elder son who describes a moral universe of bartering for goods, of retribution under which this man lives and that informs his behavior and attitude toward both his father and his brother. The younger sibling may be reckless, but he knew the father would take him back and the old man did so, not as a hired hand, but as a beloved child. For those of us still laboring under a moral universe of retribution, this allocation of a party for the disobedient seems unjust. This is Jesus' point.

To be reconciled to God requires an understanding that we are already loved in Christ. As Paul tells the Corinthians in the **Second Reading**, "the old things have passed away; behold, new things have come." This is not any god but a Father; we are not obeying orders, but embracing the Christ who has reconciled us to the eternal God. God's blessing of peace and reconciliation has been foreshadowed figuratively by embracing the chosen people, rebellious and difficult, into the arms of the Promised Land. God's words to Joshua in the **First Reading** are an invitation to walk in a banquet hall to celebrate a fiesta, a Passover to newness. "Today I have removed the reproach of Egypt from you." Have the Pharisees not heard this carte blanche forgiveness from the God of Abraham, Isaac, and Jacob? The work of the psalmist in today's **Responsorial Psalm** captures the emotions we might imagine stirring around the younger son, the chosen people, and all those who have become "a new creation in Christ." The redeemed are able to go to the party God prepares for those who have returned. "Glorify the LORD with me, / let us together extol his name. / I sought the LORD, and he answered me / and delivered me from all my fears."

Connecting the Bible and the Liturgy

Although Lent is most assuredly about repentance, this Sunday reminds us about the real motivations under *metanoia* and God's joy at our return to God. Indeed the traditional name for this Sunday takes its cue from the first word of the **Entrance Antiphon**: *Laetare Ierusalem, et conventum facite omnes qui diligitis eam.* We rejoice in Jerusalem because we know that our mourning will be at an end; we can "exult and be satisfied at her consoling breast."

Based on what we have seen in the parable of the Prodigal Son, the image we choose to guide our understanding of God will directly shape our response to God, our brothers and sisters, and ourselves. Today the image of consolation has certainly been portrayed in the unusually iconoclastic and forgiving embrace of a shamed father by a rebellious teenager: in a divine meal in the Promised Land; in the new creation of Christ. The church comes to this Sunday aware of God's love in the Eucharist, a banquet provided for us sinners because of Christ's gift of reconciliation. We have entered the doors of the hall where the fatted calf has been made ready, giving us the courage to move to the paschal feast itself. As the **Collect** says, "O God, who through your Word / reconcile the human race to yourself in a wonderful way, / grant, we pray, / that with prompt devotion and eager faith / the Christian people may hasten / toward the solemn celebrations to come."

The Liturgy of the Eucharist could not be further from what the elder son expects from the father—a return for being obedient, a dinner with friends because of compliance to orders. The prodigal had his fatted calf, but the Christian faithful have the Lamb of God, slain for our sake and made ready as food for our journey to the Promised Land. When the priest offers the Eucharist to the people during the **Communion Rite**, he is the servant opening the doors for the congregation of the prodigals, the elder sons, and all those who have become "a new creation." *"Ecce Agnus Dei"* is the call to come back to the feast, to enter the doors of the Holy. "[B]ehold him who takes away the sins of the world. / Blessed are those called to the supper of the Lamb." The love of God rejoices to invite us to the supper he has prepared for us. The table has been set. Everyone wants to go in except the elder son, who is, evidently, too preoccupied with his own resentment and moral outrage to hear those comforting words: "My son, you are here with me always; / everything I have is yours." That is the gift we have been given at the Eucharist: everything. No longer under a law that legislates a code for what we think justice should look like, informing us of a seating plan in the kingdom. The celebration God provides tells us that everything he has is ours.

Strategy for Preaching

When it comes to exegeting the assembly of hearers (and this Sunday represents an exemplary case that this process should always be done for preaching because of the listeners' identification with either the younger or the elder son), I would be willing to bet on several assumptions that should be taken as a given for any preacher this Laetare Sunday, Year C.

I. About three-quarters of the congregation are composed of "elder sons," maybe more; they come to Mass out of dutiful responsibility and are probably pretty devout and have been for a lifetime. If the assembly is made up of younger people, this equation will go down, since many of the forty and younger crowd have had some kind of conversion.

II. The assembly's attitude of obedience and retribution will be related directly to how they image God acting (or not acting) in their lives.

III. They may have one or more "prodigals" in their lives with whom they have an ambiguous relationship around religion.

I think that the target group for the homily for today is elder sons, all of whom are sitting in church, dutifully listening; that crowd was Jesus' audience. I am not nay-saying the potential quarter of the population in church, or those who have come because they have hit rock bottom and returned. But chances are these folks are very aware of the forgiving Father in the parable. The preacher makes a big tactical error when analyzing the congregation if the intended audience is not present; the younger son becomes a kind of illusion or fantasy of someone else. It is always easier to talk about someone else's conversion rather than one's own, isn't it? There is a father with two sons, both of whom he wishes to welcome to a great feast. So the core homiletic idea for today might be this: If we knew that God was welcoming people we could not stand to be around at a feast, would we still come? The question here forces the elder sons or daughters in the community to ponder their relationship with God as a loving Father of all people (particularly that wayward brother or sister, the maverick or black sheep of the family). It interrogates an understanding of religion as retributive justice rather than a community of love and reconciliation of the kind Jesus came to bring: that mercy trumps justice in the language of the kingdom, handed on by the Word made visible, who runs to embrace us all.

Introduction: Let's pretend you are invited to a masquerade party. Everything is going well until the host tells the guests to remove their masks. You find, to your astonishment, that all the people in the room were your social nightmares: the neighbor who never speaks to you, the sister who failed to help you with your dying father, the boss who fired you.

I. God wants us at a party, but we don't get to write the invitations. This is the price we pay for a God who loves everyone as if each were the only one. As the father tells his elder son in today's parable, "everything I have is yours." And we are all God's.

   A. We get some help in coping with the folks in the room from Paul. The new creation we are promised forces us to see with the eyes of another kind of vision, the eyes of the baptized. Instead of wearing a mask, we put on a white garment; there is no illusion in that.

   B. We talk about the chosen people—and that means every one of them. Manna was sent for all without distinction.

II. The Eucharist is this: a table meant for those we may not choose to vacation with, or eat with, or celebrate with (Gospel).

   A. *Ecce Agnus Dei*. We have traded the fatted calf for the Lamb of God.

   B. All come to his banquet because all sinners have been forgiven and welcomed.

III. What is our resistance to joy when we see another accepted into love? Why do you suppose the elder son resented the father welcoming the younger son back? Can we imagine that those who are at this moment running from God—maybe they are still in their warm beds, or reading the *Times* in Starbucks, or taking the kids to a soccer game instead of church—are in need of the Father running toward them in love?

   A. After all God went through with the chosen people, God welcomed them into the Promised Land and provided them with manna (First Reading).

   B. Can we imagine the paschal candle at the Easter Vigil showing us the faces of all those who have disappointed us—or who we think disappointed God? This Laetare Sunday is a reason to rejoice because God loves on his own terms and brought us all back. Because we may one day find even our precious selves looking for forgiveness (Collect; Responsorial Psalm).

Fifth Sunday of Lent

Readings from the Ambo

Isa 43:16-21; Ps 126:1-2, 2-3, 4-5, 6; Phil 3:8-14; John 8:1-11

Referencing last week's Gospel briefly, I wonder what would happen if all the elder sons of Luke 15 got together and started looking everywhere (except at themselves, of course) for retributive justice? Well, we might have something like John 8:1-11. Today's **Gospel** is a masterpiece of narrative reversal in which the accusers become the accused.

To be completely fair, the Pharisees and the scribes are following the law of Moses by bringing the woman forward caught in adultery, although it is interesting that her male accomplice goes unmentioned and unpunished. So, like many rigid legalists, the Pharisees follow the law a la carte, as they pick and choose what they will follow and whom they accuse. Clearly, they are hoping that this woman's transgression will bring Jesus' own teaching to be tested. His response to this test case? Doodling in the ground with his finger. In regard to this somewhat bewildering reaction on Jesus' part, there are, I suppose, numerous conjectures as to what such scribbling in the sand might be all about, including popular expressions such as Cecil B. DeMille's version of this scene in *The King of Kings* (1927), in which the Lord writes the sins of the Pharisees and scribes in the dirt. Be that as it may, I would like to think that John asks his readers to understand Jesus' activity as a rewriting of the law as the law of forgiveness and love—and an irrefutable justice aimed at the inner self. "Let the one among you who is without sin be the first to throw a stone at her." Real justice begins with the inward case, not accusations of other people for their sins. The underlying sword that cuts through all our hypocrisy in this passage is simply the question, who are we to judge? In fact, Pope Francis responded in a like manner when asked about the question of homosexuality: "Who am I to judge?" It is the elders of the scribes and Pharisees who finally figure that they are in no position to cast stones, as they drop their small weapons and accusations and depart. So Jesus leaves the woman with a comfort and challenge: "Woman, where are they? Has no one condemned you?" That is the balm of forgiveness Jesus has offered, but this reconciliation comes with an admonition: "Go, and from now on do not sin any more."

The scene in John's Gospel that liberates the woman from her accusers becomes a freeing moment for all Christians. As Paul puts it in the **Second Reading**, he does not have any righteousness on his own "based on the law but that which comes through faith in Christ, the righteousness from God." It is God's righteousness, Paul will insist, that sets us free. That righteousness is exemplified in the healing power of Christ rewriting a new law of justice and mercy.

In a very real sense, Jesus' righteousness not only protects the woman but restores her lost dignity as well. "Go, and from now on do not sin any more" is a frank acknowledgment that sin has occurred, but that God rewrites—which is to say, "re-rights"—all things by his love. It is possible to start over when one is free from condemnation and reconciled. Such renewal also belongs to Second Isaiah's oracle in the **First Reading** that prophesizes new inroads and an utter erasure of past sins: "Remember not the events of the past, / the things of long ago consider not; / see, I am doing something new! / Now it springs forth, do you not perceive it?"

Connecting the Bible and the Liturgy

When God promises new beginnings, "water in the desert / and rivers in the wasteland / for my chosen people to drink," we look ahead to the Great Vigil of Easter where the springs will gush forth and quench the thirst of those to be baptized. At the same time, though, the Gospel informs the whole church of the justice hidden in God's righteousness, that "Go and sin no more" means renunciation of evil so that God can do a new thing in us.

An interesting collateral liturgical text to use in connection with the biblical readings for today might be some selection from the **Blessing of Baptismal Water** used at the Easter Vigil. As Second

Isaiah envisions God's newness, it is water in the desert—life blood for a nomadic people in exile, waiting to be refreshed. Baptism also refreshes those in exile of sin, who are fated to be accused and found guilty under the law. As the priest or deacon blesses the water (when no one is present to be baptized), he says, "You also made water the instrument of your mercy: / for through water you freed your people from slavery / and quenched their thirst in the desert." That water of God's mercy is Christ himself, who says to us all, "Neither do I condemn you."

But we are also to "Go, and from now on do not sin any more." And with that admonition, so recall our renewal that partners with God's spring, gushing forth in the desert. "Do you renounce sin, / so as to live in the freedom of the children of God?" Yes, this renunciation is about freedom to love as a child of God. It is from such bondage that Jesus releases the woman caught in adultery and, in a strange sort of way, the scribes and Pharisees who accuse her by confronting their self-righteous behavior. The elders among them know their hearts have been read and something new has been written. But it is up to us to continue to renounce sin by standing before God's merciful righteousness in all honesty. The waters of baptism have claimed us, so we might say with Paul that "I continue my pursuit in hope that I may possess it, since I have indeed been taken possession of by Christ Jesus." The whole church has been possessed by Christ but not condemned. That reality is reason enough not only to transform our lives by renewing our baptismal promises, but to stop condemning and acting as judge to those who have transgressed our "law." Christ will rewrite that fiction as well.

Strategy for Preaching

This Sunday offers an opportunity for the preacher and the community to investigate the communal side of repentance. After all, Jesus confronts the Pharisees and the scribes as a group. Indeed, there will be penance services all across parishes and deaneries through this season; this Fifth Sunday of Lent in Year C, with its biblical readings devoted to private sin brought into the communal or public square, allows for a look at how our accountability functions before God and neighbor.

As I intimated in the previous section, an exploration of baptism and its relationship to communal sin, forgiveness, and divine reconciliation form worthwhile linkages with these readings today. So the core homiletic idea for this Sunday could be to deepen the assembly's awareness of personal sin and communal sin, while understanding the depth of divine forgiveness and renewal.

The First Reading can be clearly situated as a point of departure for a look at God's font of new life amid the desert of exile. (A short exegesis would be in order here on Second Isaiah.) Moreover, the offer of cleansing water belongs to the whole Christian community by virtue of our baptism (see Blessing of Water, Easter Vigil).

Yet that overwhelming love of Christ, which casts out our accusers, sanctified through those holy waters, asks from us a renunciation of our bad choices and sinful behavior to "God and sin no more." During a reflective moment sometime this coming week, it may be advantageous for us to list how we have offended the community of love and how we plan to amend. (The preacher should tease out the textual dynamics in the Gospel that accentuate a reversal with the Pharisees and scribes, writing a new law.) Such an activity in corporate accountability is wonderful preparation for any parish for Holy Week.

The Good News is that God does not remember the sins of the past. The renunciation of sin carries with it the hope of faith and new life (refer to Renewal of Baptismal Promises, the Profession of Faith). Paul can be our guide so that we remember we are not judged by the law or our lists of who we think should be perfect or not. It is faith that brings new life, and God's righteousness that brings us redemption (Second Reading). We have renounced sin, not for its own sake but, as the Renewal of Baptismal Promises reminds us, "so as to live in the freedom of the children of God."

HOLY WEEK

Palm Sunday of the Passion of the Lord

Readings from the Ambo

Isa 50:4-7; Ps 22:8-9, 17-18, 19-20, 23-24;
Phil 2:6-11; Luke 22:14–23:56

In preparing to exegete the vast complexities of the biblical readings given in today's Lectionary, a useful point of departure might be to isolate the unique features of Luke's passion narrative as distinct from the other accounts for Years A and B. We would find incidences like healing and forgiveness that should not surprise us in Luke's **Gospel**. For example, what comes to mind in the passion narrative this Sunday in particular is the mending of the ear of the high priest's slave, or forgiving the contrite criminal on the cross. These particulars and instances of the healing Christ could be linked with the other readings for this day, together with the liturgical texts.

Another place to start might be to take a look at the contrast at the beginning of each of the passion narratives. Luke positions Jesus as taking "his place at table with the apostles" and treats these disciples of the Lord favorably throughout, without referencing their cowardly flight from the Master. The implication is that Jesus' arrest, trial, and execution in Luke becomes entwined with discipleship and its responsibilities and accountability. His betrayer, Judas, is named by Jesus and the moment of handing over is dramatically highlighted because the one who has handed him over has fallen from the role of disciple. So a point of departure leads us into a discussion on discipleship.

In light of the discipleship that must endure the weight of the passion, Isaiah's Suffering Servant son (**First Reading**) makes a fitting rejoinder. The Servant is submissive in his humiliation: "I gave my back to those who beat me, / my cheeks to those who plucked my beard; / my face I did not shield / from buffets and spitting." Similarly, Paul describes Christ as one who "humbled himself, / becoming obedient to the point of death." This paradigm of kenosis or self-emptying will set the pattern for the true disciple as we will see in the book of Acts. As the Lord has given himself over as the healer and redeemer, humbling himself on the cross, Acts will follow the disciples like Peter and Paul, healing in the name of Jesus, "which is above every name, / that at the name of Jesus / every knee should bend, / of those in heaven and on earth and under the earth, / and every tongue confess that / Jesus Christ is Lord, / to the glory of God the Father" (**Second Reading**). The Lukan passion narrative offers a special opportunity to prepare for the book of Acts, the unfolding of which will occur during Paschaltide, where discipleship will be transformed by the risen Lord.

Connecting the Bible and the Liturgy

One of the great Gregorian plainsong chants is the centerpiece for this day and traditionally sung before the Gospel, a selection from the Philippian hymn (Second Reading). *"Christus factus est pro nobis obediens usque ad mortem, mortem autem crucis . . ."* The verse encapsulates the Servant Son of Isaiah in the First Reading, as well as the passion narrative itself. In particular, the Lukan passion narrative lays stress on the (lack of) humility of the disciples as they follow the Master precisely as the Suffering Servant. To the extent the worshiping congregation owns their identity as disciples who are weak but forgiven, sinners yet redeemed, will be the extent to which they embrace the unimaginable power of this day. The Lukan Jesus desires that his death be an example to others and that the apostles will do the same for each other. He tells them to take the cup "and share it among yourselves." As if foretelling of the Peter in Acts, he reveals to Peter that Satan has demanded they be sifted like wheat, but he has "prayed that your own faith may not fail; and once you have turned back, you must strengthen your brothers." Even the Gentile centurion sees Jesus suffering unto death as an example and glorifies God, saying, "This man was innocent beyond doubt." Even in death, Jesus draws disciples and future disciple together, converting one of the criminals who was crucified beside him. Discipleship does not end with the death of the Lord but begins its most exciting and exacting period of service; it is a Spirit-filled era in which we are still living.

Shortly after Jesus establishes the new covenant, which will be the promise of the kingdom of God, "an argument broke out among them about which of them should be regarded as the greatest." (Note that this statement is omitted in the short form.) So then Jesus tells the disciples not to lord it over those under them but "let the greatest among you be as the youngest and the leader as the servant . . . I am among you as the one who serves." This is Christ the servant leader and teacher who requires the same from his disciples. The **Collect** emphasizes for the contemporary disciple in the assembly the model of Christ as servant of all and the model of humility: "Almighty ever-living God, / who as an example of humility for the human race to follow / caused our Savior to take flesh and submit to the Cross, / graciously grant that we may heed his lesson of patient suffering / and so merit a share in his Resurrection." Yet, the Lord is infinitely more than an example for the disciple, but the very door to disciple-ship. Christ's saving work has been able to accomplish more than we could possibly do, so we are disciples by virtue of our redemption. As the **Prayer over the Offerings** says, "Through the Passion of your Only Begotten Son, O Lord, / may our reconciliation with you be near at hand, / so that, though we do not merit it by our own deeds, / yet by this sacrifice made once for all, / we may feel already the effects of your mercy." The Suffering Servant has humbled himself for the sake of us all and "accepted unjust condemnation to save the guilty" (**Preface: The Passion of the Lord**).

Strategy for Preaching

The homily for this day may be understandably brief, yet it is a crucial moment to reach an unusually large number of congregants—both the "part-time" churchgoers and the devout. Additionally, this Sunday prepares the worshiping community for Holy Week, which lies ahead, giving them an understanding of the Lukan account of the passion and death of the Lord, so as to grasp the coming solem-nities more fully and with greater complexity. So the core homiletic idea for today is the Gospel verse itself, taken from the Second Read-ing, albeit in a condensed and modified form: Christ was obedient unto death on a cross, and so his disciples carry his name always on our lips. Preachers will note the emphasis on discipleship here, which, as I have suggested earlier, makes Luke's passion narrative a unique hearing for the assembly in Year C.

The first portion of this sentence ought to be emphasized at the beginning of the homily once, twice, three times in various ways. We tend to take it for granted, as if the Philippians hymn were so hum-drum that we have ceased to be held under its sway. But as disciples, Christ has given us an example and a definitive lesson of humility (Collect). A short reflection on contemporary discipleship involving sacrificial servant leadership might be appropriate, taken from either personal experience or history (e.g., Dietrich Bonhoeffer, Mother Teresa). The account of Jesus in Luke's passion narrative will test the limits of discipleship, the living expression of a relationship with the Lord when everyone has been put to the test and found wanting (who is greatest?). Jesus healed, he challenged, he gave of himself completely so that we might be freed (Servant Song).

When the so-called "Christ Hymn" or Philippian Canticle in the Second Reading speaks of the exaltation of Jesus' name, we see the legacy of the apostolic witness in what is to come. Acts will tell us about the power of the name and how his disciples will use it to heal and forgive and carry on the work of preaching. We carry the legacy of his name as a reminder of our justification through him (Preface: The Passion of the Lord). Throughout this week, our own discipleship might be read against the drama of the unfolding passion we have seen displayed before us: the search for power, even by Jesus' most trusted disciples, the condemnation of the innocent for political and religious purposes, the betrayal of the Teacher. How does our own discipleship hold up against the backdrop of the humble God who became obedient unto death?

Thursday of the Lord's Supper
(Years ABC)

Readings from the Ambo

*Exod 12:1-8, 11-14; Ps 116:12-13, 15-16bc, 17-18;
1 Cor 11:23-26; John 13:1-15*

The first half of chapter 12 in the book of Exodus deals with the Lord's instructions to Moses on the specifics of celebrating the Passover and the feast of Unleavened Bread. There is a little shift beginning in verse 21 when Moses tells the elders how to carry out these divine instructions. Although our passage is concerned only with what God says to Moses, the section in which Moses transmits God's orders to the elders suggests the emerging institutionalization of Passover: not as a private revelation to Moses, who was unique among men, but as a liturgical feast with which the elders were charged to carry out and repeat through *zikaron*, memory.

The keeping of Passover as a memorial of the passage out of Egypt cannot be emphasized enough, since its celebration clearly represents a moment of life and death for Israel. Later generations would recall God's deliverance from the tenth plague and the meal that ushered in the exodus from Egypt as a renewal of God's promise to the people of the covenant. Among the many noteworthy features of the Lord's instructions to Moses is a divine reordering of the calendar: "This month shall stand at the head of your calendar; you shall reckon it the first month of the year" (**First Reading**). This would be Nisan, the first of months in which the Passover meal would commemorate the great work of God for Israel.

In a certain sense, Paul's First Letter to the Corinthians in the **Second Reading** recalls the very dynamic divine presence with Moses in the book of Exodus concerning divine instruction and its institutional transmission. "I received [*parelabon*] from the Lord what I also handed on to you." The verb that Paul uses for "handed on" is *paredoka*, which can also mean "passed on," even "passed over or delivered to." I am not suggesting that Paul had this in mind, but there is a kind of "passover" going on when he *paredoka* (or "handed on") to the Corinthians the tradition of the Lord's Supper. Furthermore, the connection of the Passover in Egypt is further established by a meal commemorated through memory. "For as often as you eat this bread and drink the cup, you proclaim the death of the Lord until he comes." This is the *anamnesis*, the remembrance of the saving event of Christ, his Passover, when he was handed over for us.

Jesus' final meal with his disciples is both a Passover and a Passing-on in John's **Gospel**; it is a transmission of how to treat one another. As is well known, John does not include the institution of the Eucharist on the night before Jesus' passion as the Synoptics do. For a variety of reasons, the eucharistic theology of the Fourth Gospel would extend into the symbolic reaches of the whole gospel (such as the "Bread of Life discourse") and not be limited to the night the Lord was handed over. Nevertheless, there is a *paredoka* going on between Jesus and his disciples. The act of love is replicated by a footwashing, which in first-century Palestine was the province of a slave or servant to offer guests upon entering a household. The tradition of footwashing was probably ubiquitous in many cultures and was recorded in the Hebrew Scriptures prominently in the book of Genesis and elsewhere. Christ was taking on the role of the servant at the meal, then, and demonstrates this behavior *sui generis*, having received no instruction: the Lord's service emerges directly from him, and he passes it on, like his farewell Passover with the disciples in the Synoptics, with the instruction for *anamnesis*. "If I, therefore, the master and teacher, have washed your feet, you ought to wash one another's feet." Humility and hospitality, then, are "institutionalized" as ritual actions, as virtues to be observed in the Christian community. Modeling divine hospitality and humility all take on the role of a servant in service to one another in a kind of passing over from the selfishness of this world to the light of God's grace. Humility and hospitality are integrally related to the celebration of the Passover of the Lord and are virtues upon which the Johannine community, the community of the Beloved Disciple, built its eucharistic theology of table fellowship.

Connecting the Bible and the Liturgy

It is significant that the church has chosen chapter 13 of John's Gospel for Holy Thursday, which has as a fulcrum the footwashing scene. The emphasis on the Servant Christ who handed himself over to death for the sake of many is replicated symbolically by the church's own reenactment of the footwashing after the homily at the Liturgy of the Lord's Supper. In addition, the readings, the Presidential Prayers, and Preface for the day speak poignantly of the way that Jesus' great act of love was institutionalized in the Eucharist.

Consider the **Collect**, which not only draws an emphasis on Christ's being handed over, but on delivering *himself* unto death. *Morti se traditurus* is a reflexive action, translated by *The Roman Missal* as "when about to hand himself over"; the implication here is that Jesus freely gave himself in love (the lavish footwashing scene in John shows this divine hospitality) and "entrusted to the Church a sacrifice new for all eternity, / the banquet of his love." But there is more. We know that this is a night of being handed over as well, "[f]or he knew who would betray him; for this reason, he said, 'Not all of you are clean.'" So we are dealing with Christ's freely giving himself but also a human agency acting to betray him. The Roman Canon (**Eucharistic Prayer I**) picks up the double meaning of the verb *tradere* by simply leaving it ambiguous: "Celebrating the most sacred day [*quo Dominius noster Iesus Christus pro nobis est traditus*] / on which our Lord Jesus Christ / was handed over for our sake." The word "Canon" accurately captures the Johannine Jesus: the one who was betrayed but who also freely handed himself over.

For our sake: this is the other, necessary half of Christ's eucharistic offering of love, the self-surrender in service unto death. We are drawn into this Eucharist by the God who has called us to participate in this most sacred Supper "that we may draw from so great a mystery, / the fullness of charity and of life" (Collect). The eucharistic meal, then, is a purifying one, granting the assembly *plenitudinem caritatis* in this work of redemption. As the **Prayer over the Offerings** makes clear, our very active participation in the Eucharist becomes a memorial of the sacrifice itself and "*opus nostrae redemptionis exercetur*" ("the work of our redemption is accomplished"). That liberation occurs in the sacrifice of Christ's blood on the cross, an *anamnesis* repeated and institutionalized in the Eucharist. If Jesus named the betrayer as not clean, we hope to find our sins washed away in Christ's blood. As the **Preface: The Sacrifice and the Sacrament of Christ** says, "As we eat his flesh that was sacrificed for us, / we are made strong, / and, as we drink his Blood that was poured out for us, / we are washed clean."

Strategy for Preaching

The homily for Holy Thursday may emerge from a number of different fonts, flowing from the same source: divine service, freely given. The institution of the Eucharist, the call to serve in priestly ministry, the community of the beloved all stream from the initiative of Christ's hospitality and mandate to keep his memory in love. The challenge for the preacher will be to center the homily on *one* homiletic core and to develop an idiom that speaks to contemporary culture about a mystery that appears so difficult to comprehend. Jesus' service to his disciples appears clear enough in John's Gospel and so is his commandment to do likewise. But do table service and footwashing speak to a fast-food culture with very little sense of hospitality and driven by individualism?

A core homiletic idea will allow the congregation to explore their experience of hospitality and encourage them to serve the community in grateful response. These expressions of welcome and selfless giving mediate God's own surrender of himself for our sake. By naming this grace, the preacher anticipates Jesus' own gospel injunction to serve.

Here is an organizational structure naming some tactics to engage the assembly along the lines of hospitality that might open a window into an understanding of Christ's own self-sacrifice.

I. Who opened a door for us in our life's journey? Was it a parent or a teacher or a friend? Where would we be today without that gesture of love?

- A telling example of service that opened a door for countless poor is Dorothy Day and the Catholic Worker. There are Catholic Workers in cities all over that extend the eucharistic table Jesus began this night. The altar of sacrifice becomes our table of service for the poor as we hand ourselves over to them and all those in need in service.

II. Christ was handed over as the Paschal Lamb for our Passover from sin and death to new life. Exodus illustrates the lamb that saved the people; our exodus from sin comes from the Paschal Lamb.

- Christ offered himself for our sins and at the Last Supper anticipated the free offering of his life (see *Catechism of the Catholic Church*, 606–11).

III. There is no service without a surrender of power: that is true humility and hospitality. As we partake of the memorial of this sacrifice, we remember Christ as he remembered us. "The work of our redemption is accomplished."

- We are mindful of our mission to love, having been loved ourselves and remembered. Name the particular instances in which grace will unfold in my life in the future. Whose feet will I wash in grateful service?

Friday of the Passion of the Lord
(Years ABC)

Readings from the Ambo

Isa 52:13–53:12; Ps 31:2, 6, 12-13, 15-16, 17, 25;
Heb 4:14-16; 5:7-9; John 18:1–19:42

The selection from Second Isaiah is the fourth and longest of the Servant Songs, and arguably the most powerful; it is a fitting icon for Good Friday of the Lord's Passion. The Song is a description of vicarious suffering: "[I]t was our infirmities that he bore, / our sufferings that he endured." The reading places itself at the center of the community as a highly relational text, offering the Suffering Servant as one who purifies the people from their sins. In the experience of the exile, Second Isaiah is well in the tradition of attributing mediated sacrifice of the one for the sake of the many. Indeed, the scapegoat was part of Israel's cultic ritual, and the prophets Jeremiah and Ezekiel also endured pain for the sake of the community's redemption. Moreover, the Suffering Servant is not only an individual but the community of Israel itself, the suffering people in Israel who endure sorrow and loss for the sake of the future revealed by prophetic oracle.

The passage in this **First Reading** is framed by a haunting presence that opens and closes the Servant Song: "my servant shall prosper" the passage begins; and "I will give him his portion among the great," near its closing. This is the language of the Lord guaranteeing his presence to his Beloved, even in the midst of anguish. Moreover, the last portion of the passage in particular offers hope by way of fruitfulness and new life for the many: "If he gives his life as an offering for sin, / he shall see his descendants in a long life, / and the will of the LORD shall be accomplished through him . . . / through his suffering, my servant shall justify many, / and their guilt he shall bear." The promise from God is that his chosen people remain close to him and find expiation through exile.

The imagery alone would guarantee this fourth Servant Song a place on Good Friday, with its language associated with a servant of God being "raised high" and a man "of suffering," "pierced," "like a lamb led to the slaughter," he "opened not his mouth." The passion narratives will find their own narrative interpretation of this fourth Servant Song in the Person of Jesus, of course, as does the Letter to the Hebrews, which is a kind of theological, christological gloss on the work of Christ the Servant and his priestly sacrifice for the sake of many. Some might claim that the passage here is a bit tough to absorb, but when juxtaposed with Second Isaiah's Servant, the letter to the Hebrews unfolds its riches for the Christian community. The author wraps the mystery of the incarnation (one who is able "to sympathize with our weaknesses") around a cultic expression of priestly atonement: "In the days when Christ was in the flesh, he offered prayers and supplications with loud cries and tears to the one who was able to save him from death" (**Second Reading**). In so doing, Hebrews helps us to understand how Christ's suffering became redemptive, a purifying offering because "Son though he was, he learned obedience from what he suffered; and when he was made perfect, he became the source of eternal salvation for all who obey him." The writer of this very rich text's last observation allows the community to participate in the offering of Christ through their own obedience.

The first two readings provide a crucial antechamber for our passage into John's passion narrative in the **Gospel**, with its rejection of the Servant, his being led to the slaughter like a lamb, but also his glorification. The high christology present in the text contrasts to varying degrees with the Synoptic texts proclaimed on Passion Sunday: John's account of the passion repeatedly alludes to a Jesus aware of his fate, as when the Lord says to Peter, "Shall I not drink the cup that the Father gave me?" That Christ is brought to slaughter and pierced at precisely the moment of the day of preparation for the Passover links Jesus to the Lamb brought to sacrifice for the sake of liberation for the community. The numerous allusions to the Hebrew Scriptures during John's passion narrative also remind us of the fulfillment of a plot greater than the one that is transpiring before us, with God as the author and the one who will vindicate his Son and raise him to glory, even as "he shall be raised high and greatly exalted."

Connecting the Bible and the Liturgy

The striking entrance of the celebrant and his assistants with a full prostration at the beginning of the liturgy suggests that this is one day that the church is without words, all the more to underline the Letter to the Hebrews in which Jesus himself "offered prayers and supplications with loud cries and tears." The silence that troubles this day acknowledges the Lamb that is dumb before the slaughter. The opening **Prayer** breaks the silence with a plea from the whole church that this assembly of the presanctified enters the protection of God's mercy to "sanctify" his servants, "for whom Christ your Son, / by the shedding of his Blood, / established the Paschal Mystery." The use of the word *famulos* (servants) aligns the congregation with the role of Christ himself as Suffering Servant, who was obedient unto death. As servants of God, we find our "source of eternal salvation" precisely as servants—"for all who obey him," as the letter to the Hebrews suggests. Moreover, as servants, we are helpless before God, urgently begging his mercy.

The unusual ritual that accompanies this day highlights the work of Christ's passion like no other, and the readings climax to the moment when the Suffering Servant is offered up on the cross. The crucified Christ has an exalted place in the Fourth Gospel as a disclosure of God's glory. And the **Solemn Intercessions** place a special emphasis on the mediation of the cross for the sake of all humankind, from the church itself to those of every nation and religion, from the faithful to the unbeliever. Each of the prayers that follow the orations has specific allusions proper to the intention, but the first one, "For Holy Church," seems to set the tone for the rest of these supplications when it says, "Almighty ever-living God, / who in Christ revealed your glory to all the nations, / watch over the works of your mercy." The reach of Christ's intercession is as unfathomable as God's mercy and so we can only adore the one in gratitude who pleads for us by the wood of the cross, the instrument of our salvation and redemption.

Strategy for Preaching

The advantages of preaching on Good Friday are many, since the assembly will be comprised of the devout members of the congregation seeking to understand the mystery of the Lord's passion and death in a deep and meaningful way. The liturgy itself is a kind of homily, with the cross as its center, and so the preaching forms something of a companion piece to a mysterious disclosure, giving voice to the profound articulation of the Word voicing its "loud cries and tears." Along these lines, a theological explanation of the sacrifice of the cross is certainly in order, but it would be useful if it occurred in a way that allowed the listening assembly to feel and experience the event in an immediate, rather than abstract, way. After all, the sacrifice of Christ on this day is a purifying event, and so the closer the homily approaches a catharsis for the congregation, the more the preaching approximates the liturgical action of which it is a part.

One creative way of approaching a homily on Good Friday is by way of an indirect theological expression through a monologue, in this instance an eyewitness report of the events surrounding the passion. The monologue is something along the lines of a dramatic retelling of an event from one person's perspective. A monologue on Good Friday would pull out a character from the passion narrative in John's Gospel and relate the events from the perspective of that character. What would the garden in the Kidron valley and the events of the betrayal look like from the point of view of one of the participants, say Malchus, the high priest's slave? Or how about the gatekeeper who had an encounter with Peter in the courtyard? Mary, the mother of Jesus, or the Beloved Disciple at the foot of the cross? We already have a popular gospel song suggesting witness: "Were You There when They Crucified My Lord?"

Here are some of the advantages of the monologue homily:

I. A subjective point of view allows the hearer to participate in a very affective way the events of the Gospel, from which he or she might be otherwise separated by a cultural distance. This separation might be particularly true when we consider the events of the cross.

II. Holy Week should offer a variety of modes of preaching, and the monologue homily for Good Friday allows for an intimate, vivid expression of an interior witness that is particularly suitable to the Johannine Gospel.

III. This is a chance to problematize the way we view and judge characters. If we are quick to assign blame to Peter or even Judas, granting them a "hearing" fills the picture out a bit more on this day when God's compassion is boundless.

IV. This style of homily could also lead the congregation to further meditation on the passion of the Lord, particularly imagistic prayer of the kind Ignatius Loyola encourages his retreatants to engage in in the *Spiritual Exercises*.

Easter Sunday
of the Resurrection of the Lord

The Easter Vigil in the Holy Night
(Years ABC)

Readings from the Ambo

Gen 1:1–2:2 (First Reading); Ps 104:1-2, 5-6, 10, 12, 13-14, 24, 35
or Ps 33:4-5, 6-7, 12-13, 20 and 22

Genesis's first account of creation (Priestly writer's) is a story of origins, a fitting initiation to the Liturgy of the Word for the Easter Vigil. The Liturgy of the Word begins with a familiar text, underneath which is a brave and simple faith: *"Bereshit bara Elohim et hashamayim ve'et ha'arets"* ("In the beginning, when God created the heavens and the earth"). The root of the first word of the Hebrew Bible, *bereshit*, is from *rosh*, meaning head or chief, underlining this story of origins. In contrast to the second reckoning of creation (Yahwist writer's), this passage reveals a lofty and mysterious maker of the cosmos whose *ruah* or spirit hovers over the waters and permeates the corners of all created things, breathing into the nostrils of humankind the breath of life. The story climaxes with the creation of human beings, made in the image of God. This *imago Dei* becomes a key theological term that will underlie Christian anthropology for centuries and continue into the present day. With the proclamation of this reading at the celebration of the passion, death, and resurrection of the Lord, the recognition of the human subject as *imago Dei*, crystallizes the gift of our redemption purchased for us in Christ, now restored.

Gen 22:1-18 (Second Reading); Ps 16:5, 8, 9-10, 11

The story of Abraham and the *Akedah*, or Binding of Isaac, is a heartrending moment in salvation history, which the patristic fathers would seize as an allegorical representation of God's surrender of his own Son unto death. Needless to say, the violence of a text in which God asks the first patriarch of Israel to sacrifice a child can only strike the hearer as barbaric. Yet, as some have argued, this may be a story that rails against human sacrifice, since God prohibits Abraham's actions and finds a ram in his stead. Still, the violence is hard to ignore. Benjamin Britten's *War Requiem* (1962) renders the ferocity of the sacrifice of Isaac palpable when he retells the story: Abraham ignores the angel's intervention and slays his son anyway. The story as Britten refashions it locates the violence to kill in the heart of the human subject, stretching back to antiquity. That iconoclastic reading notwithstanding, the raw emotion present in the text as we have it here points us to an emblematic example of unflinching obedience to God's command, even at the expense of one's dearest love. It is that white-knuckled emotion that is meant to wash over us, singling Abraham out as the father of our faith.

Exod 14:15–15:1 (Third Reading); Exod 15:1-2, 3-4, 5-6, 17-18

The selection from the book of Exodus catches the chosen people at a climactic moment on their journey from Egypt to the Promised Land, when a definitive boundary has been crossed and their ruthless pursuer has been eradicated. With the crossing of the Red Sea, as with many key moments in the Hebrew Scriptures, the patristic authors would find a christianized allegorical reading. Origen, for instance, would discover a profound symbolic connection between the crossing of the Red Sea and Christian baptism, which allegorizes Pharaoh as the power of Satan drowned in the waters of new life in Christ. Therefore the response of the people of Israel and the newly baptized is the same: "I will sing to the LORD, for he is gloriously triumphant." This text, then, gathers the community of Israel and the Christian faithful on the side of the same sea, all of us waiting to cross into the Promised Land of our redemption. In addition to an allegorical interpretation informing Christian baptism, this passage has been a hermeneutical blueprint for those kept in bondage awaiting freedom from the 1960s civil rights movement to apartheid in South Africa.

Isa 54:5-14 (Fourth Reading); Ps 30:2, 4, 5-6, 11-12, 13

In the last of the Zion oracles, Second Isaiah speaks to the exiles of a God who will never give up on the chosen people: the promise will endure forever. Beginning in verse 1, Isaiah uses a series of spousal images that vividly bring to light God's covenantal love. At the same time, the immanent presence of the Lord contrasts strikingly with the transcendent God of the universe: "The One who has become your husband is your Maker; / his name is the LORD of hosts." Like some powerful images in the Bible, these metaphors can be somewhat troubling and patriarchal for contemporary hearers. Are we to take the Lord, calling back Israel during the exile, as "a wife married in youth and then cast off" or in a "brief moment . . . abandoned" and "[i]n an outburst of wrath" faced a God who hid his face? To understand the "enduring love" expressed by the biblical author we may have to suspend modern sensibility for a moment and lean into the historical presence of the text that desires to convey a God of mercy and pity. Interestingly, there is another side to this God, infinitely more complex than we imagine. The portrait of the Lord given by Second Isaiah is of a repentant God, who likens these days of exile to the time when he renewed a covenant with Noah, which became an eternal promise. The passage's overriding intention asks us to see a God of unconditional love, remembering with some sentiment, a covenant of peace.

Isa 55:1-11 (Fifth Reading); Isa 12:2-3, 4, 5-6

One way of understanding this passage is to see the text precisely as a kind of rejoinder or companion piece to the previous reading. Having testified to a steadfast covenant in which justice and peace will be established in foundations and battlements of precious stones, God now prepares a banquet for his people. This festive meal is extended to everyone without cost, a fitting celebration from the God who loves unconditionally. Yet alongside this promise of water to the thirsty and grain for the hungry, there is also the plea for conversion, to heed God and eat well, to "Seek the LORD while he may be found, / call him while he is near." Once again, we face a God who is both merciful and powerful. These two seemingly irreconcilable characteristics converge in God's *dabar*, the word that, like "seed to the one who sows / and bread to the one who eats," achieves its proper end and does not return to God "void." God's power is accomplished in the very act of intending goodness, which is mercy and abundance—watering the earth and making it both fertile and fruitful. From a Christian perspective, the baptismal imagery and invitation to conversion and renunciation is clear enough: all are invited to renew themselves in God's saving waters and at the table of God's endless mercy. The Lord's banquet gathers the lost, even as God's memory of the covenant assured to David identifies his descendants as precious. In the response that follows, taken from First Isaiah, that promise is reified: "You will draw water joyfully from the springs of salvation."

Bar 3:9-15, 32–4:4 (Sixth Reading); Ps 19:8, 9, 10, 11

Speaking to Israel in a time of captivity, Baruch presents God's wisdom and commandments as the anchor of salvation. Although Israel has rejected "the fountain of wisdom," Baruch offers a return to prudence as a pathway back to the Lord. "Turn, O Jacob, and receive her: / walk by her light toward splendor." The underlying virtue embedded in Baruch's admonition to Israel is hope, since when we know where prudence, strength, and understanding abide, then we will also know "where are length of days, and life, / where light of the eyes, and peace." The advice Baruch has for Israel is echoed in the psalm response: "Lord, you have the words of everlasting life." The word of God and the precepts of the law are the building blocks for faithful and virtuous living in the land of exile. In a sense, Baruch has to rearticulate a whole tradition to a people who have lost everything, including their sense of direction, as it were. Which way is home? He speaks to Israel of a wisdom tradition in order to refound a people in the midst of exile and darkness. It is the Lord God who has found these precious people and gives them direction. In Baruch's hands, wisdom becomes the arbitrator of life, a handmaid of the Most High, the law that can be returned to over and over again: "She is the book of the precepts of God, / the law that endures forever." This rebuilding for Israel will be a pathway lit by the splendor of wisdom, a light that will never go out, even in the midst of the diaspora.

Ezek 36:16-17a, 18-28 (Seventh Reading); Ps 42:3, 5; 43:3, 4 or, either Isa 12:2-3, 4bcd, 5-6 or Ps 51:12-13, 14-15, 18-19

Ezekiel's utterance is both a rebuke and a promise. The Lord recalls the reality of Israel's transgressions and the penalty they paid—scattering and dispersion among the nations. Most of all, it is for the sake of God's holy name, which has been profaned in exile, that the Lord has relented and will redeem his people by sprinkling clean water upon them to cleanse them from their impurities and idols. A central image that focuses on this redemption is a promise of transformation: "I will give you a new heart and place a new spirit within you, taking from your bodies your stony hearts and giving you natural hearts." The spirit of the Lord will also inhabit this new Israel, even as that same spirit will give life to the "dry bones" in the valley the prophet encounters and records in 37:1-14. God guarantees new life to those in exile, since those who have been lost will be gathered. Like Second Isaiah, the water imagery is a baptismal mystic bath when seen from a Christian perspective. When the catechumen dies to sin in baptism it is then that a new life begins in Christ: that is the coming of the Spirit that animates the hearts of those who have traded their stony hearts for ones made of flesh. Christians have been gathered in from sin, that place of reckless and unruly exile, and have been brought under God's re-creative vision.

Rom 6:3-11 (Epistle); Ps 118:1-2, 16-17, 22-23

Paul finds himself in the company of Isaiah and Ezekiel as he also promises newness of life, once we are dead to the power of sin and alive in Christ Jesus. In a certain sense, Paul's theological discourse on baptism and its connection to the death and resurrection of Christ forms something of a commentary for all those who have listened to Isaiah and "come to the waters" and have found "new life." This newness of life has been purchased by Christ's own death and resurrection, freeing us from being "in slavery to sin." Paul makes it abundantly lucid that all those who are baptized participate in Christ's work, since they are "dead to sin and living for God in Christ Jesus." The liturgical context of this reading of the epistle from Paul shifts the tone of the vigil rather dramatically, since after the last reading from Ezekiel the presider will intone the *Gloria in excelsis Deo* and then acknowledge that the Lord has made holy "this most sacred night . . . with the glory of the Lord's Resurrection." Paul's words to the Romans, then, are blooming with the reality of new life brought by Christ and the place baptism holds for Christians, since "[w]e were indeed buried with him through baptism into death, so that, just as Christ was raised from the dead by the glory of the Father, we too might live in newness of life."

Luke 24:1-12 (Gospel, Year C)

Luke has a fondness for angels, whose presence signal wondrous occurrences in his narrative. The striking threshold with which we enter the Lukan account of the resurrection is kept vigil by two men who stand in dazzling clothes before the awestruck women. Identified later as "angels" (24:23), they provide a mirror image of the heavenly hosts who announced the news of Jesus' birth in Luke 2:13-14. The witnesses to the joy of the Good News come from heaven itself, reassuring those of us who are trembling with doubt and fear. Giving testimony to the risen Lord was an essential aspect of the kerygma of the early church; Luke suggests that it is the angels themselves who are the first of these witnesses. Two men in white will also appear in Luke's account of the Lord's ascension in Acts 1:10. They remind the disciples who are gazing heavenward that this same Jesus will come again, even as he has ascended. We are all called into that space we call divine hope, once we have rolled back the stone of our own doubt. And so we respond at the Eucharist to the proclamation of the Mystery of Faith in a joyous ascent of love. With the angels we say, "We proclaim your Death, O Lord, / and profess your Resurrection / until you come again."

Connecting the Bible and the Liturgy

The opportunities to make connections with the Scriptures and the liturgy for the Easter Vigil are almost too many to enumerate, to say nothing of doing so in such a short space. But from the perspective of unique opportunities, the *Exsultet*, that ecstatic announcement like no other, certainly presents a panorama of salvation history filled with emotion that will find its echo in the sweep of the scriptural readings. Indeed, the bringing of the light of Easter to the earth echoes with the excitement of Prometheus unbound as the fire radiates, "ablaze with light from her eternal King." The Genesis text will bring to our horizon the Creator who first created that light that now finds its benediction as Easter fire. Indeed, the coming of the light is also the brightness brought to the exiles, led out of Egypt and given the good news of hope by Isaiah and Ezekiel. When it comes to the **Blessing of Baptismal Water**, this text rehearses the primal waters fashioned by the Creator from the beginning and now made new in Christ. The freedom from bondage, "set free from slavery to Pharaoh," expressed in Exodus now celebrates the gift of living water offered in gratuitous largesse from the God who invites all to "come to the waters" that have no price.

Additionally, at the Easter Vigil there is a wonderful opportunity to connect the Scriptures with the liturgy in the **Prayers after the Readings**. The global reach of the readings to all people is highlighted in the prayer after Genesis 22:1-18, for instance, when the presider begs God to pour out "the grace of adoption / throughout the whole world / and . . . through the Paschal Mystery / make your servant Abraham father of nations." The prayer makes the obedience of Abraham so astonishingly vivid in the Scriptures that there ensues an immediate invitation to the liturgical assembly to do likewise in their own (sometimes painful) call to do God's will: "grant, we pray, / that your peoples may enter worthily / into the grace to which you call them." Similarly, after the reading concerning Israel's passage through the Red Sea, the parallel with the congregation is once again established between the two worlds: "grant, we pray, that the whole world / may become children of Abraham / and inherit the dignity of Israel's birthright." In fact, the prayer makes it clear that the Lord has not ceased from doing such wonders, since this is a God *"cuius antiqua miracula etiam nostris temporibus coruscare sentimus"* ("whose ancient wonders remain undimmed in splendor even in our day"). Needless to say, asking God that in *Abrahae filios et in Israeliticam dignitatem totius mundi transeat plenitudo* in the current political climate is a bold claim, but the connection between the people of Israel and the Christian community ought not to be overlooked, or its interfaith relations go underappreciated—especially during the Easter Vigil. With the catechumens crossing the Red Sea into baptism and the Christian community renewing their baptism by renouncing the slavery to the pharaoh of Satan, the liturgical assembly and the people of Israel are deeply united, and, in this very recognition, God's promise of liberation becomes clear from age to age, even as Abraham has become the father of faith and of many nations.

Strategy for Preaching

The lavish richness and the deep breadth of the readings and the liturgy for the Easter Vigil present the preacher with a formidable task: how to capture the incredible panoply of texts, scriptural and liturgical, which encompass this night in a homily that is less than ten minutes in length. We have just watched salvation history being retold before our eyes. That makes the Easter Vigil a unique preaching experience. Indeed, the homilist should not make the mistake of thinking that preaching for the vigil is identical with that which will be proclaimed at the liturgy during Easter Day. The character of the Easter Vigil will mark a homily that understands the sweep of salvation history, the gift of baptism, and the place of the resurrection in the life of the Christian community.

Below are three practical tactics for preaching on this night of nights, all of which may be expanded or diminished as needed.

The arc of the homily can first be sketched by attending to all of the readings and identifying *one* characteristic in each of them during a session of *lectio divina*. I am recommending one characteristic so that these features might be resources when the homily is shaped— First Reading: Gift; Second Reading: Obedience; Third Reading: Liberation; Fourth Reading: Covenant; Fifth Reading: Rebirth; Sixth Reading: Hope; Seventh Reading: Redemption; Eighth Reading: New Life; Ninth Reading: Faith.

I. After the characteristics are identified, use the orations following the readings to enter into a prayerful dialogue with how you understand the text. What do you want to ask of these texts based on the liturgy that responds to each of the scriptural selections?

II. After this process, see what homiletic core emerges. This core might look like the following: This is the night when God has brought us out of the darkness of sin and death and liberated us in the waters of redemption. Given the multiple combinations of readings and liturgical texts, there are any number of core homiletic sentences that might surface in the course of a prayerful encounter before the homily is preached.

III. After the core homiletic idea is established, introduce the variety of dialogue partners to start organizing the homily. There are the scriptural texts that will broaden the core homiletic idea. In the case of the core just recommended, the readings from the vigil such as Exodus, Isaiah, Ezekiel, Paul, and Mark all help to establish credibility to the focus or core homiletic sentence. Lastly, the liturgy for the vigil provides further text to establish a dialogue such as the *Exsultet*, the baptismal liturgy, the Preface I of Easter, and the proper Presidential Prayers for the eucharistic liturgy.

Based on this strategy, a possible outline for the homily could be organized in this fashion:

I. Introduction (leading into the homiletic core sentence).

II. This is the night when God has brought us out of the darkness of sin and liberated us in the waters of redemption.

    A. Exodus 14:15–15:1.

    B. Prayer following this reading.

    C. *Exsultet.*

    D. Blessing of Baptismal Water.

III. But we tend to live in exile, away from God, unaware of the covenant that has endured forever.

    A. Ezekiel 36:16-17a, 18-28.

    B. Isaiah 54:5-14; 55:1-11.

    C. Prayer following the reading.

    D. Preface.

IV. So it will take faith to live the experience of the resurrection.

    A. Mark 16:1-7.

    B. Luke 24:1-12.

    C. Romans 6:3-11.

    D. Baptismal promises.

    E. A story (short) illustrating a discovery of new life. This may be a secular story or a religious one illustrating making alive what once was dead.

V. Conclusion (closing off the core idea). We are united this night with the children of Abraham as we are freed from our bondage, even as the earth shakes us loose into God's kingdom of his Christ.

Easter Sunday
of the Resurrection of the Lord

At the Mass during the Day (Years ABC)

Readings from the Ambo

Acts 10:34a, 37-43; Ps 118:1-2, 16-17, 22-23;
Col 3:1-4 or 1 Cor 5:6b-8; John 20:1-9

The **First Reading** from Acts is a fitting summary leading up to the moment of Jesus' resurrection. Peter's address to the centurion Cornelius and his household recapitulates the life, ministry, death, and resurrection of the Lord for the Gentiles. The rising of Christ from the dead is a message that is meant for all. As Peter begins his speech (not included in the selection from Acts here), "In truth, I see that God shows no partiality" (10:34b), or more graphically in the Greek text, *prosopolepsia*, meaning to lift up someone's face, showing favorites. As Paul would say in 1 Corinthians, this message of the resurrection is the good news that allows us to celebrate the feast of the paschal lamb with a little yeast that "leavens all the dough." Therefore Jesus himself showed no partiality but "went about doing good and healing all those oppressed by the devil, for God was with him." After Peter's speech, Acts 10 will conclude with the Holy Spirit falling upon all who heard the Word in the house of Cornelius. The Spirit falls without partiality as well but comes to those who hear the Word.

While the Good News is meant for all, Jew and Gentile alike, there are certain demands placed on the receivers of the Word. Like Peter, Christians proclaim and witness to the life, death, and resurrection of Jesus. Like Cornelius and his household, the invitation is to hear and believe. Hearing the Word opens those present to the eschatological moment of the coming of the Holy Spirit; that is as true for those who hear Peter's preaching as it is for the assembly of the baptized gathered for Eucharist on this first day of the week on Easter morning in the twenty-first century.

In a very different context than Acts, in the **Second Reading** Paul writes to the Colossians in prison, encouraging them to be hearers of the Good News of the resurrection of the Lord. Throughout the letter to the Colossians, Paul stresses the authority granted to Christ through the power of the resurrection, which has rescued them from death and pagan practices and *metestesen*, or transferred, us into the kingdom of his beloved Son. Paul, himself in chains, is conscious of being transported by "what is above, not of what is on earth," longing for Christ to appear with him in glory. So the source of Paul's encouragement is abiding in Christ, which is accomplished in baptism because the Christian's "life is hidden with Christ in God."

The selection from John's **Gospel** brings about closure in so many ways. Having run to the tomb where Jesus once lay, the Beloved Disciple "saw and believed." The story of the resurrection is something like the last piece of a puzzle that has gone unsolved until the final ecstatic moment. In John's Gospel, Jesus has performed signs from the wedding at Cana to the cleansing of the temple, until he himself became the definitive sign of God's glory on the cross. Now, at last, the disciples who were closest to Jesus put the missing and jagged piece into its place to complete the picture. The astonishment of the resurrection now begins a new age and a new *kairos* of creation: the first day of the week. The site of the empty tomb yields to an acknowledgment of profound understanding of the Scriptures and Jesus' teaching concerning his place in salvation history. In Luke, two other disciples will have a similar moment of faith, but its revelation comes not from the empty tomb, but from Jesus himself in the Scriptures, the breaking of the bread, and the prayers.

Connecting the Bible and the Liturgy

With the dramatic events in John's Gospel close at hand, a poignant phrase in the **Collect** to recall is this: "O God, who on this day, / through your Only Begotten Son, / have conquered death / and unlocked for us the path to eternity." As described by the author of

John's Gospel, the tomb is locked, and then Mary Magdalene came there and "saw the stone removed from the tomb." She at once proclaimed to the disciples, as the **Sequence** says, "The tomb of Christ, who is living, / The glory of Jesus' resurrection." Moreover, the writer is at pains to describe a race on the path to see if what Mary said was true, as Peter and "the other disciple" ran and made their way to Jesus' empty tomb. They arrive, breathless, to a new discovery of life and resurrection. Therefore God has literally helped us to beat a pathway to the gates of eternity, or *aeternitatis nobis aditum*. The image of the disciples running at the proclamation of Mary Magdalene is also the remarkable beginning of the transmission of this Good News of eternal life: the Word has begotten the Word, which leads quite literally to the *resurgens* of new life. Additionally, Paul's situation in writing to the Colossians is a memorable connection here as well. As we pray in gratitude to God who has "unlocked" the gates of eternity, so, too, does Paul urge the Colossians to seek the Christ who is above, now glorified at the right hand of God. It is Christ who has trod that pathway to eternity and made it clear for all those who have died in him; they now have a life that is hidden, or *kekruptai*, in God.

Depending on whether or not the presider chooses to ask the congregation to renew their baptismal promises after the homily, the **Collect** provides a fitting prelude to these prayers when it prays that as we keep the solemnity of the Lord's Resurrection we may, "through the renewal brought by your Spirit, / rise up in the light of life." With the **Renewal of Baptismal Promises**, a catechetical moment for the assembly awaits them, as the assembly recognizes the presence of the risen Christ's spirit in their own renewal; it is an invitation to remind the assembly that "we have been buried with Christ in Baptism, / so that we may walk with him in newness of life."

Finally, if the Roman Canon (**Eucharistic Prayer I**) is used, there are the Proper Forms of the *Communicantes* that hearken back to the readings and provide yet another catechetical moment, as it begins, "Celebrating the most sacred night (day) / of the Resurrection of our Lord Jesus Christ in the flesh." This doctrinal moment concerning the resurrection should not be passed through lightly, since the resurrection of the body is a seminal article of faith and, appropriately enough, is part of the **Gospel** narrative and its clues. When Peter sees the empty tomb, the burial clothes are in separate places, an important indication that Jesus' rising was not based on a hysterical vision or some kind of a spiritual rising, but a corporeal one. The very bodily resurrection of Jesus will be taken up again in next week's Gospel as John recounts Thomas's encounter with the risen Lord and his wounds.

Strategy for Preaching

Who would disbelieve the sight of the risen Lord? As hinted to earlier, the popular imagination has cultivated any number of episodes concerning the resurrection that are not entirely biblical in their origin and representation. This first day of the week, when it is still dark, Mary Magdalene, Peter, and "the other disciple" Jesus loved face a far more existential encounter than a vision of the Lord; they face the empty tomb and must interpret its consequences. We know that in John's Gospel Jesus will make himself known as a risen body in a variety of ways after this initial moment—appearing to Mary Magdalene in the garden, revealing himself to the disciples in the locked room and by the Sea of Tiberias. But this Easter Sunday faces the Christian assembly with deep questions of faith, baptismal renewal, and the search for Christ amid the darkness of despair. The homiletic core idea is literally a matter of life and death. The question for this Easter morning for the Sunday assembly might be shaped around this: How do we understand the empty tomb as a call to believe God's promise for eternal life?

A good preaching plan for developing this question is to help the congregation come to the same conclusion as the Beloved Disciple. "He saw and believed" should be the goal toward which the homiletic arc is moving. To this end, the preacher might consider a kind of "retelling" of Jesus' life and ministry, death, and resurrection along the lines that Peter proclaims in the house of Cornelius. According to John's Gospel, the site of the empty tomb triggered in the Beloved Disciple is an insight, *pisteuein*, "he believed." If we are to take the Beloved Disciple as the first witness of the resurrection, we might consider his witness value to the works or signs of Jesus as a way into understanding and believing. That strategy does not mean a repetition of the whole gospel, but helping the hearer to unlock the mystery of God's gift of eternal life.

Consider one such sign early in John's Gospel: the cleansing of the temple (2:13-25). This is an important episode in the life of Jesus and the disciples precisely because verse 22 makes a specific reference to the activity at the temple and the recollection the disciples have after Jesus rises from the dead. " 'Destroy this temple and in three days I will raise it up.' . . . Therefore, when he was raised from the dead, his disciples remembered that he had said this, and they came to believe the scripture and the word Jesus had spoken" (2:19b, 22). The preacher might begin by asking the assembly to ponder what it would be like if the very building in which they were worshiping might vanish. What would they have? The Johannine community faced the destruction of the temple and Jesus himself seems to peel off the layers of external temple practices early in John's Gospel, seemingly to replace it with himself as the new temple that is raised up. When all is taken away from us—even the security of institutional religion—and we stare only at an empty tomb in the dawn of the morning, do we see the Lord before us?

A courageous story of faith is the episode immediately following this passage (John 10–18) in which Mary meets Jesus in person. She was with him to the end—right up to the cross and came to the (empty) tomb to care for him. That is the faith that begins with love. The homily could build on this premise and use other contemporary stories of the strong relationship between love and faith. It is probably not an accident that the Beloved Disciple reached the tomb first because of this love and also, he was the first witness to believe in the resurrection. Stories that show love as the gateway to faith and trust will underline the devotion of the Beloved Disciple to love and believe: standing at the foot of the cross and racing to the tomb has born the fruit of testimony—the Gospel itself.

In the end, the buildings we come to adorn with our Easter lilies and spring flowers are wonderful places, but nothing substitutes for the temple of the risen Lord. Like the disciples, we come to the Lord, running with all we have and find ourselves witnessing to his rising from the dead. The Eucharist allows us once again to recognize him in the garden that the church has invited us all to dwell in on this fragrant Easter morning.

EASTER TIME

Second Sunday of Easter

Readings from the Ambo

Acts 5:12-16; Ps 118:2-4, 13-15, 22-24;
Rev 1:9-11a, 12-13, 17-19; John 20:19-31

When taken as a whole, the readings for this Sunday represent an experience of God in two vastly different ways. The Acts of the Apostles and the Gospel of John disclose God's presence in community, while the book of Revelation shows us a picture of Christ driven by a wondrous vision, an ecstatic glimpse of "the first and the last, the one who lives." In a certain sense, when these passages are taken together they form a continuum of the ecclesial post-resurrection community: those who discover the risen Christ mediated by community on the one hand and the prophetic or visionary on the other.

The attributes of the risen Lord in community are fairly obvious in the **First Reading**, where there is a swelling of the ranks of believers, "more than ever, believers in the Lord, great numbers of men and women, were added to them." This is the community in which "[m]any signs and wonders were done among the people at the hands of the apostles." The simple gathering of all together in one place (much like Pentecost itself in the upper room) in Solomon's portico allows for wonders to be accomplished. The risen Christ is mediated by his disciples. "A large number of people from the towns in the vicinity of Jerusalem also gathered, bringing the sick and those disturbed by unclean spirits, and they were all cured." One senses here that this sanctification and healing is not about human agency but divine power. Indeed, Peter's shadow manages to cure those who are sick and their healing suggests that this is even less something the apostle does than who he mediates. These events are expressions of witness of the risen Lord, disciples preaching the Word of God, which cannot be chained.

In the **Gospel** the disciples gather in one place as well, but this time it is locked by fear. Jesus makes his wonders felt by his own presence and breathes peace and reconciliation; he also uncovers his wounds. For the community gathers in order to explore doubts and to probe the nail marks in the hands and side of the Savior. As the First Reading intimates, we are in the presence of the risen Christ, the one who comes to heal the community with love so that his followers might find peace, healing, and reconciliation. Thomas may be a doubter but he has also yet to risk the fate of one who dares to live in the presence of the crucified, now risen from the dead. When the disciple does so, exploring the wounds of the Lord, he is ready to witness, "My Lord and my God!"

By contrast, John's revelation confronts the Son of Man in all his fullness because he has looked on the risen One in faith: "Once I was dead, but now I am alive forever and ever. I hold the keys to death and the netherworld." In the Gospel, Jesus intends to give those keys to the disciples who have gathered, but John claims a vision that reminds us that the One who calls himself the Alpha and the Omega alone is able to set us free. So the mission for John is not so much a witness in the public square as a prophetic register of the wondrous Christ who tells him, "Write down, therefore, what you have seen, and what is happening, and what will happen afterwards."

Connecting the Bible and the Liturgy

The peace that comes to the apostles gathered in the locked room is given to the church, not only in the wonders of faith proclaimed by believers, but also in sacrament, particularly the Eucharist, which reconciles and heals. When those gathered in faith proclaim the death of the Lord and his rising from the dead—even when they doubt—Christ administers his peace. As the presider prays in the Order of Mass at the **Communion Rite**, "Lord Jesus Christ, / who said to your Apostles: / Peace I leave you, my peace I give you," these words echo the Lord's farewell to the apostles but also his welcome.

Christ's gift is peace and that is also what we bid for one another. Indeed, Christ's moment of peace becomes simultaneous with his gift of reconciliation. "Receive the Holy Spirit," he says to the disciples after he breathes on them. "Whose sins you forgive are forgiven them, and whose sins you retain are retained." The Lord does not offer what St. Benedict refers to in his Rule as a *"pacem falsam"* (RB 4:25), but a genuine moment of graceful reconciliation. So, too, the presider at the Eucharist says, "look not on our sins, / but on the faith of your Church, / and graciously grant her peace and unity / in accordance with your will." Therefore, as the Lord gathers us in, even those who harbor deep fear are healed of sin and division—and, as we learn from Thomas, unbelief.

Thomas's exploration of the wounds of Christ becomes the occasion for his own reconciliation and ours as well. "Blessed are those who have not seen and have believed." In a certain way, the believing Christian assembly is not unlike those who are swelling the ranks of the early church. We are blessed in our belief, but also in our very gathering and witness to one another of the risen Lord. The prophetic witness of John allows us to cast a shadow of healing on one another at the Eucharist so that we "write" what we have seen in the book of our heart and pass this peace on to others. *"Pax Domini sit semper vobiscum. Offerte vobis pacem."* We are truly reconciled by an exchange that heals and forgives before we prepare to see the Lamb slain for our sake. The exploration of Christ's wounds becomes more dramatically enhanced in the Fraction Rite, in which the presider breaks the host over the chalice and places a small piece in that cup, saying quietly, "May this mingling of the Body and Blood / of our Lord Jesus Christ / bring eternal life to us who receive it." Here is wounded Christ unfolding in the Eucharist whose wounds are disclosed, the Lamb of God "who takes away the sins of the world." We can only echo what the Lord said to Thomas: "Blessed are those who have not seen and have believed."

Strategy for Preaching

Most of the homilies I have heard from students for the Second Sunday of Easter could be entitled something like "Doubting Thomas and Us" or "We Are Doubters Too." Fair enough: Thomas becomes a way of identifying the congregation's growing edge of faith. But the real power of these biblical texts, in my estimation, comes from grasping the power of the risen Lord to bring peace and reconciliation into a locked room that was filled once with fear, mistrust, and doubt on the part of all those gathered. Similarly, the other biblical text for this Sunday evinces the transformation of Peter, who even in his shadow mediates the presence of the Lord and John of Patmos transmitting a vision for all to behold. Christ comes to the eucharistic assembly alive and filled with the joy of peace and forgiveness. So the core homiletic idea for today might be this: the risen Lord brings peace to us who have believed and we are witnesses to that transformation in community and personal prayer.

An introduction might account for the emotional impact of Christ's death on the disciples, visually drawing implications as to why they would be so fearful—and one of them doubtful and incredulous. In light of this beginning, we might ask, what is our room of fear and doubt? (Name a variety of contemporary fears.) These are realities of the present world or of our own making into which Jesus brings peace. Note the contrast in an underdeveloped homily that would presume that "we are all doubters." (That presumption of ascribing emotions or feelings or lack of faith to a congregation is not uncommon and does not do justice to the gathered assembly who are not blank texts to be written on but a vibrant listening community waiting for the Word.) The homiletic strategy I am describing allows the listening assembly to lean into their fears so that the risen Lord might come and visit them with his peace, his eucharistic peace. This peace of Christ is not some kind of panacea or a drug of denial but a deepening awareness of his crucified presence in the midst of our pain. Here is where Thomas the Doubter fits in: we are invited to explore the wounds of God's mercy; that is, the healing presence that unfolds before us in Word and sacrament, in vision and community.

It is our faith in the presence of fear and difficulty that sustains our longing for Christ. The Eucharist promises the peace of Christ— "my peace I give you," he says. This is the invitation to reconciliation, which is the doorway to peace and faith. We cannot ignore the connection between reconciliation and peace—Christ brings both into a locked room. And that goes for this room as well, where we have all gathered as a church. (Reference the Communion Rite; the Sign of Peace.) Peace is contagious and we caught it from the risen Christ—and the apostles; we are in Peter's shadow of healing, which has stretched out in our direction (First Reading). This transmission is, after all, the power of the Word. Remember: "Peace I leave you, my peace I give you." Peace comes to meet us in the Eucharist as it came to John on the island of Patmos: nothing halts God's mercy and we see those wounds, even as they once were revealed to Thomas in the upper room and to the Polish nun St. Faustina, given to us radiant as a sign of God's enduring love and divine mercy.

Third Sunday of Easter

Readings from the Ambo

Acts 5:27-32, 40b-41; Ps 30:2, 4, 5-6, 11-12, 13;
Rev 5:11-14; John 21:1-19

If last week's selection from the Acts of the Apostles focused on the power of the risen Lord set loose among the disciples to cast a shadow of healing in the ever-increasing throng of believers, this week's **First Reading** reveals the consequences of faithful ministry: persecution. The second half of chapter 5 in the book of Acts finds the Word unchained and ready for proclamation in the temple (vv. 19-21), but the apostles face the wrath of the chief priests, the Sanhedrin, and the elders of Israel. Not unlike the Lord himself, the Word of God faces a confrontation with institutional religion that wants to harness its divine power and twist its prophetic contours into its own image.

The emphasis in the present selection, however, is on the power of the "name," which the institution desires repressed. In order to underline the importance of obeying to God rather than pleasing human beings, note how Peter confronts the Sanhedrin with the recent historical data: God raised and exulted Jesus, who was slain, and granted Israel reconciliation; and the apostles are witness to these things. What is missing from today's Lectionary selection, unfortunately, is the passage that alludes to the integrating presence of the wise rabbi Gamaliel, who defends the potential God-given charism of this new movement of followers of Jesus. I take this stance of the teacher to mean that the name of Jesus may be God-honored, rather than disdained, as it was by the Sanhedrin.

The importance of the name of Jesus in this section of Acts cannot be overestimated. How to carry on the work of the Lord becomes a lightning rod for this passage and for all the biblical texts today. The power of name must endure. Peter must deal with his past as a disciple who said, "I do not know the man." The famous **Gospel** scene at the Sea of Tiberias, in effect, undoes the threefold denial with Jesus' plea for agape love (in the end, the Lord settles for brotherly friendship) for the sake of the sheep. In a way, this haunting presence of the erstwhile disloyal disciple confronts the internal conflict of all those called into mission. Yes, there are the external efforts of the Sanhedrin among us who would like to shut down the efforts of the Way. But there are also the inner voices that attempt to dismantle the mission we have been given by raising the specters of sin and guilt. Here, among the disciples, we carry on the name of the one who came to reconcile Israel and all humanity and the historical remembrance of the work of God in Christ raised from the dead.

That remission of sin and guilt, which enables the prophetic voice of Peter to utter the name of Jesus, is reason to rejoice: it liberates us from prison for the sake of the Word made visible. John's vision of the Lamb and all the heavenly hosts is a celebratory victory over the forces that would halt the Word—both the inner and the external voices. We have only to join those choruses to recall the only word that matters to all who would hear: Jesus.

Connecting the Bible and the Liturgy

In some respects, the biblical readings and the liturgical texts challenge us with a single question: How will we respond to the provocation of the risen Lord? The **Entrance Antiphon** answers that particular and direct question with *Jubilate Deo, omnis terra*, "Cry out with joy to God, all the earth; / O sing to the glory of his name. / O render him glorious praise, alleluia." This psalm (66) recognizes the wonders God has done in Christ Jesus and is ready for mission, a response in service with love. This call to feed the lambs becomes clear in Jesus' encounter with Peter: Do you love me? Feed my sheep. Free to serve in love is the response of a grateful people. Peter in Acts reveals the exultation that passes through the prison of the shamed inner self—then through a physical prison until he is no longer the disciple who betrays and denies, but the friend who loves Jesus more than anyone else.

Not coincidentally, then, the **Collect** prays for a profound ability to rejoice at the Eucharist during Paschaltide, to be renewed in virtue and a lively faith. "May your people exult for ever, O God, / in renewed youthfulness of spirit, / so that, rejoicing now in the restored glory of our adoption, / we may look forward in confident hope / to the rejoicing of the day of resurrection." There is a blue note of reparation in these lines, as we sing of the "restored glory of our adoption," perhaps as an echo of that same loss and restoration granted by the Lord to Peter on the shores of the Sea of Tiberias. Moreover, the **Second Reading** suggests that the exultation we ask for is already present in the heavenly creatures and elders who sing around the throne. (These worthy blessed contrast with the Sanhedrin and the assembly of the unjust in Acts.) Like the Entrance Antiphon, the cry in heaven is ubiquitous praise: "Then I heard every creature in heaven and on earth and under the earth and in the sea, everything in the universe, cry out: / 'To the one who sits on the throne and to the Lamb / be blessing and honor, glory and might, / forever and ever.'" Now the name of Jesus is at last honored and exulted.

That eternal praise belongs to the eucharistic assembly gathered for worship and reinforced as a living Body as the presider prays the **Prayer over the Offerings**: "Receive, O Lord, we pray, / these offerings of your exultant Church, / and, as you have given her cause for such great gladness, / grant also that the gifts we bring / may bear fruit in perpetual happiness." This gift of perpetual happiness remains the Shepherd's gift to the sheep in love, the Eucharist as the food for mission, as we are sent forth to preach the name.

Strategy for Preaching

The buoyant person of John the Evangelist, visionary on Patmos, presents the preacher this Sunday with a somewhat lofty, but nevertheless inspiring, image for joyful proclamation of the Good News. Indeed, in the tradition of the prophet Ezekiel, John preserves for the church the role of the herald, to capture the ecstatic sight of the Eternal City, now bejeweled and with the choir of elders and others giving praise and worship to the Lamb. Like John, the preacher catches fire with the name of Jesus and burns with zeal for the Word and makes him visible in order that the listener might join their voices to those before the Lamb. Therefore, the core homiletic idea is much like the question I raised in the previous section: How will we respond to the provocation of the risen Lord to love and mission for his sake?

Note that this interrogation does not concern the preacher's provocation, but Jesus', which I regard as a crucial distinction in the face of Jesus' specific challenge to Peter to feed the sheep. While the function of the preacher as a "mediator of meaning" is certainly normative in most common examples of Christian liturgical preaching, the herald has its origins in the prophets of the Hebrew Scriptures, John the Baptist, and John the Evangelist. John the Baptist's well-known saying that "he must increase, I must decrease" is applicable this Sunday as the preacher acts as a transparent instrument for the risen Lord, probing the congregation to respond to the Lord, even as Peter did at the Sea of Tiberias: "Do you love me?"

The preacher might do well to begin with a visual connection with the vision of the Lamb, connecting it with the Entrance Antiphon: All the earth cries out with joy. This rhetorical tactic is an invitation to the congregation to imagine what we and the blessed are called to in the presence of the Lamb. That vision is where we are most alive and made new by God's reconciling and peaceful presence (Gospel, which repairs Peter at the Sea; the Collect's emphasis on restoring our "youthfulness"). This church is the place where we are most fully alive because we are most loving, capable of responding to service, and self-giving as "one body, one spirit in Christ."

So we bring this love of Christ to mission by feeding his sheep. (Specific lived examples taken from everyday life.) We will face disappointment and setbacks but, like the apostles before the elders, we await the presence of the Word, which we know is of God (Acts). We have the name of Jesus to which we cling. (An example of a contemporary person who does not yield to discouragement, disappointments, or difficulties.) That is why we rejoice in the presence of the Lamb.

Fourth Sunday of Easter

Readings from the Ambo

Acts 13:14, 43-52; Ps 100:1-2, 3, 5; Rev 7:9, 14b-17; John 10:27-30

In one way or another, the Good Shepherd is at the center of the biblical readings this Sunday. The **Gospel** for Year C is the shortest of the selections taken from John 10; it completes the one used for Year A (10:1-10) and Year B (10:11-18). Jesus deploys various images in chapter 10 in order to showcase his relationship with his followers, beginning with the figure of speech *ho poimen ho kalos*, the Good Shepherd, who has an instinctual relationship with the sheep—in contrast to the stranger, from whom the sheep flee.

The role of the shepherd, or the Good Shepherd as Jesus identifies himself in John 10:11ff., has various nuances throughout the chapter. Year A underlines Jesus' role as the "gate for the sheep." Year B focuses on the adversarial relationship with the hired hand who works for pay versus the sacrificial role of the Good Shepherd. At the same time, Year C succinctly points us to the subject of eternal life given to the flock by Christ, who has been given them by the Father and "is greater than all, and no one can take them out of the Father's hand." Drawing on his own relationship with the Father, Jesus brings the passage to its conclusion with a point of his own unique identity: "The Father and I are one."

Listening to the voice of the Shepherd, then, grants the sheep access to the Father and eternal life. To hearken back to the early portion of chapter 10, Jesus calls himself the "gate of the sheepfold." From the beginning of John 10, however, the Pharisees "did not realize what [Jesus] was trying to tell them" (v. 6). The Pharisees become the outsiders, the strangers, who work for hire, in contrast to the charismatic Shepherd who has a unique invocation of the sheep. That relationship between sheep and Shepherd becomes clarified in the **First Reading**, in which a new flock of sheep, as it were, the Gentiles in Antioch, are singled out. Moreover, Paul and Barnabas show themselves to be faithful followers of the Shepherd, despite jealousy and persecution. They are a "light to the Gentiles" in the same way that the Lamb becomes a lamp for the blessed. In the **Second Reading** John makes the Lamb also the Shepherd of sheep, as if to synthesize the Gospel and his own perception of the Apocalypse. "For the Lamb who is in the center of the throne / will shepherd them / and lead them to springs of life-giving water . . ." Although John had something more visionary in mind, Paul and Barnabas are reminders of the ones who have survived the time of the great disaster, the time of the marauders who would capture and kill the sheep, and "follow the Lamb wherever he goes" (Rev 14:4).

Connecting the Bible and the Liturgy

The liturgy for today is surely oriented toward identifying the assembly with those who hear the voice of the Lord. As Jesus says, "I know them, and they follow me. I give them eternal life, and they shall never perish." The **Responsorial Psalm** reinforces this relationship of the congregational sheep with the Lord as Shepherd in the refrain: "We are his people, the sheep of his flock." The Responsorial Psalm may be especially noteworthy today because of the Gospel's emphasis on the sheep hearing the Shepherd's voice. Indeed, verses 1-2 of Psalm 100 make it plain that we are responding precisely as a baptized, liturgical assembly with one voice to the call of the one Shepherd, leading us through the gates of the Eucharist: "Sing joyfully to the LORD, all you lands; / serve the LORD with gladness; / come before him with joyful song."

The **Collect** offers an opportunity to see through a lens of the Shepherd calling after the sheep. The gift of eternal life promised by the Shepherd as a gift flows from Christ, offering himself as the Lamb; his followers "have washed their robes" and made them white "in the blood of the Lamb." Therefore we pray in the Opening Prayer, "Almighty ever-living God, / lead us to a share in the joys of heaven, / so that the humble flock may reach / where the brave Shepherd has gone before." The Prayer presumes that the congregation is willing to be led through Christ the Gate. We have had a snapshot of where that Shepherd has gone before us in the Second Reading, with John's vision of the Lamb. Moreover, we know the obstacles that the sheep face from those who would persecute the flock of Christ. Nevertheless, Christ has promised eternal life to his flock and "no one can take them out of the Father's hand." So, too, the baptized assembly has been led into the waters of baptism, from which no one can take us. That mystic bath has enjoined us to follow the Lamb and to renew ourselves day after day through conversion.

Our redemption, which was purchased by the Good Shepherd when he laid down his life for his sheep, leads us to the heavenly homeland, together with the blessed with whom we sing praises to the Lamb. This praise before the Lamb unfolds before us in the Eucharist, the Lamb of God we behold who takes away the sins of the world. Appropriately enough, the **Prayer after Communion** says, "Look upon your flock, kind Shepherd, / and be pleased to settle in eternal pastures / the sheep you have redeemed / by the Precious Blood of your Son." Those who hear the Shepherd's voice will follow the Lamb wherever he goes. He went to death for the sake of his sheep, and we follow him now with our baptismal robes, white because of his red blood.

Strategy for Preaching

There is something paradoxical about what is sometimes known as Good Shepherd Sunday. On the one hand, we are (at least in the modernized West) far from the world of shepherds and sheep. There are some urban dwellers who have never laid eyes on a sheep let alone a shepherd, except in a zoo. At the same time, the message Jesus asks us to attend to his voice, appropriate for a society that needs to cultivate its attention to what is important: the gates of eternal life.

Over the years of teaching homiletics to seminarians, I have found that the preachers who have the most success with the readings on the Fourth Sunday of Easter are those who come from developing countries, especially Africa. That reality alone should remind those who are native to this country that our immigrant brothers and sisters are a blessing to us and provide us with new ways to uncover the Gospel message. When it comes to the homily for this Sunday, these foreign-born preachers can engage the rest of us with clear examples of real shepherds and real sheep that serve as models for what Jesus has in mind. There is no substitute for life experience, strategically placed and well thought out in a homily: it provides access to an alternative world we might imagine. What is it like to listen to a shepherd and to be owned by him, or for him to lay down his life for his sheep? I finally learned the import of Jesus' image from a seminarian from Kenya who talked about shepherds in his country who purposely dress in red to ward off wild animals from their flock. So the core homiletic idea for today might be, how does the community of faith hold fast to the voice of the Shepherd, bathed in blood, who comes from the Father for the sake of the sheep?

For those preachers from our own culture, I have a point of departure. It might be useful to begin the homily with a reflection on communal singing, or why we raise our voices in song to both secular and sacred circumstances, and how such rejoicing (or lamenting) is so ubiquitous in many different cultures. Communal song may be the only time we are actually joined together as one, despite race, religion, or way of life.

That introduction leads into the reflective refrain: we are his people, the sheep of his flock. We are responding to the First Reading, of course, in which Paul and Barnabas gather in the fold through the proclamation of the Good News. We have come to do the same, with our white garments, thanks to the blood of the Lamb. (The Collect could be referenced here.)

Christ's voice in the eucharistic liturgy is speaking to all of us gathered for worship; he has opened the gate to eternal life because he is that gate. (All of chapter 10 might be briefly referenced. As far as an image is concerned, the Divine Liturgy of the Orthodox Church is a wonderful illustration of what the Gospel draws out for us. After the Creed, the call goes out: "The Doors! The Doors! In wisdom, let us attend!" Do we dare to follow Christ into the gates of life? That is what we profess. Such faith will involve a risk, as it did for Paul and Barnabas. We may face doubts, even persecution, but this road comes from following Christ in a very deliberate way. We take our courage from the word of God in the Gospel where Jesus tells us that no one can take us out of his hands. If we believe this to be true, we will settle with him "in green pastures" now at this Eucharist, as we go through the gates and taste the heavenly vision of the Lamb of God seated on the throne.

Fifth Sunday of Easter

Readings from the Ambo

Acts 14:21-27; Ps 145:8-9, 10-11, 12-13;
Rev 21:1-5a; John 13:31-33a, 34-35

The **First Reading** from the book of Acts gives us a whiff of the aroma of collaboration in the early church, which will be more fully expressed in chapter 15 (next week's reading) and its details of the famous Council of Jerusalem. There are three elements in the First Reading that seem to point to this collaborative Spirit unloosed on the early church. First, Paul and Barnabas "strengthened the spirits of the disciples and exhorted them to persevere in the faith." This support is not without its realist and frank appraisal of hardships that must be endured in order to enter the kingdom of God. Secondly, they "appointed elders for them in each church and, with prayer and fasting, commended them to the Lord in whom they had put their faith." Trust in God allows the elders a share in the ministry of Paul and Barnabas and as this relationship begins to unfold, its dynamic will have an important role to play in the upcoming Council of Jerusalem. Thirdly, after arriving in Antioch, "they called the church together and reported what God had done with them." The work of Paul and Barnabas does not dwell in silence, but makes itself known among the larger body of believers.

This collaboration among the various members of the church was possible only by a new vision of the risen Jesus and the possibility of a new heaven and a new earth, as we see in the book of Revelation (**Second Reading**). Far from some kind of pie-in-the-sky utopia, the revelation of God to humankind comes as the incarnate Word; that living Word has taken up residence in the church, a Spirit that moves freely so "[h]e will dwell with them and they will be his people and God himself will always be with them as their God." If the church loves one another as Christ loved us—in shedding his blood—then the church will continue to be the visible presence of Christ on earth. That mission, then, requires servant leadership of the kind Paul and Barnabas were willing to engage in their own ministry. The obvious implication for the contemporary church is that collaboration and service must be the order of the day, allowing the Spirit to move freely among elders and the young alike. Just as the elders provided pillars of wisdom in the early church, the coming together of older members of men and women provide a coherence of the tradition for the rest of the faith community. These dynamics not only adhere to the contemporary world of dialogue and mutual respect for all people (as envisioned by the Second Vatican Council), but find their origin in the early church and the Council of Jerusalem.

Connecting the Bible and the Liturgy

In these days after Easter, when the book of Acts plays such a prominent role in the biblical readings during the liturgy, we might focus on the spiritual dimension of the church's ministry in a special way, particularly in regard to the sharing of Jesus' own unique, peaceful presence through the "new commandment" to love one another.

That the church is ever new, *semper reformanda*, yet grounded in tradition and apostolic witness is surely a legacy of the Council of Jerusalem. The act of corporate change and sharing of ministry we see in the book of Acts bears witness to the "new heaven and a new earth" unfolding before us. Indeed, the church recomposed and reordered simply by virtue of the newly baptized brought about in the celebration of the Easter mysteries. As the **Collect** expresses this newness, "Almighty ever-living God, / constantly accomplish the Paschal Mystery within us, / that those you were pleased to make new in Holy Baptism / may, under your protective care, bear much fruit / and come to the joys of life eternal." Note that the newness we ask for is quite internal in its orientation, implicating the members of the church in accountability for conversion, a *reformanda* or, as Pope St. John XXIII termed it when he called the Second Vatican Council, *aggiornamento*.

That call to allow the paschal mystery to be constantly accomplished in us—*"semper in nobis paschale perfice sacramentum"*—means setting aside our own ego for the sake of Christ's ministry among all peoples of goodwill. And, above all, for the sake of love. That is what love is: to give as he himself gave, distributing ourselves equally among the Body, the church, making possible a new vision. In so doing, the new heaven and the new earth has come already and "God's dwelling is with the human race." Indeed, Christ's sharing of his love is also a substantial encounter with his redemptive power. As the **Prayer over the Offerings** says, "O God, who by the wonderful exchange effected in this sacrifice / have made us partakers of the one supreme Godhead, / grant, we pray, / that, as we have come to know your truth, / we may make it ours by a worthy way of life." It is *"per huius sacrificii veneranda commercia"*—the wonderful exchange itself that we are able to become *"divinitatis participes"* or partakers of God's very life and power. In a word, God is collaborating with his people by sharing himself with us. This partaking of the supreme Godhead is nothing less than the unfolding of the early church in its love and respect for each other, and the active and full participation of the baptized in the eucharistic celebration. Our celebration of this sacrament of unity brings about the effect Christ has desired for us in shedding his own blood: "[L]ove one another. As I have loved you, so you also should love one another. This is how all will know that you are my disciples, if you have love for one another."

Strategy for Preaching

When a Jesuit cardinal archbishop from Argentina was elected pope in March of 2013, few could have predicted the transforming power of Pope Francis on the church. We knew that collaboration with the people of God was foremost in the new pope's mind when he asked the large crowd to give him their blessing. Since then, the pope has appointed his own council of elders, eight cardinals from across the world, as a kind of advisory board, representing various opinions and constituencies in the universal church. *Ecclesia semper reformanda*. Newness does not require revolution, but it does mean letting go of the old order in order to make way for a new vision of heaven and earth. This "holy indifference" or detachment concerns not so much previous ways of doing business than it does our own ego, which may be attached to that agenda. To love as Jesus loved us invariably demands a sharing of our power, even as God shared himself.

The preaching for today allows for Christ's greatest commandment to come alive in an already established order and to take root and blossom. If we were wondering what it means to love one another as he did, we need look no further than the Acts of the Apostles. I suggest using the three characteristics of the First Reading that I identified in the earlier section to structure the homiletic core idea, which might be constructed like this: Jesus asks us to love one another as he did and that means supporting one another, being mutually obedient, and sharing our gifts together. As always, the liturgical texts buttress this scaffolding that the biblical readings provide today.

An introduction might be something other than what Jesus refers to as true discipleship. Unfold for the congregation another kind of *commercia*, then, a commerce or exchange or trafficking in a world of retail sales, commercial enterprises, and competition, or anything that might accentuate a dog-eat-dog mentality that runs counter to the Great Commandment to love one another. The tactic here is a wake-up call by contrast. So follow this vivid illustration of secular competition with, "As I have loved you, so you also should love one another."

I. Christian communities share and support one another (Acts 14) in love and encouragement.

   A. Liturgy: as witness of faith.

   B. Reforming ourselves in newness (Collect).

   C. Illustration: a married couple challenging each other as an invitation to newness and conversion.

II. We accomplish this support, as the Collect suggests, by the grace of our baptism and by being docile to those who carry legitimate authority for the sake of the whole Body, the church.

   A. Obedience to elders means being open to the word of God, but also sacrificing our own ego for the greater good. Such docility also means being open to church teaching. But this docility remains also part of being radically open to others in our midst, a kind of mutual obedience.

B. Illustration: soldiers in wartime serve as example of sacrifice for others, even when it means disagreeing with an order.

III. So we show our love to our brothers and sisters as Jesus loved in the day-to-day surrender of ourselves in faith and love and collaboration.

A. Pope Francis and a new vision for the church.

B. New heaven and new earth discloses not the future but now (Second Reading).

C. Prayer over the Offerings: we partake of God's power, who shares himself with us at the Eucharist. So we mission forth to do the same.

Sixth Sunday of Easter

Readings from the Ambo

Acts 15:1-2, 22-29; Ps 67:2-3, 5, 6, 8;
Rev 21:10-14, 22-23; John 14:23-29

The Council of Jerusalem, recorded for us in the Acts of the Apostles, chapter 15 (**First Reading**), was a defining moment for the early church. As is well known, the church, on its way to including Gentile converts, had to face obstacles as to the admittance of non-Jews into a movement that was clearly of Jewish origin. Should the Gentiles have to observe circumcision and dietary restrictions according to Jewish law before they were into the church? We know where Paul stood on the issue. The Council of Jerusalem would ponder this question and its related complications with a collaborative body and the aid of the Spirit.

It did not have to go this way. The church, led by Paul and Barnabas, could have reserved such decisions for themselves instead of being part of a collegial movement of representatives "who have dedicated their lives to the name of our Lord Jesus Christ." Additionally, the church might have devolved into a small sect with legalistic requirements, making initiation near to impossible for Gentiles. But instead, the council came to a decision, "not to place on you any burden beyond these necessities, namely, to abstain from meat sacrificed to idols, from blood, from meats of strangled animals, and from unlawful marriage." Lastly, the church could have become a kind of ecclesial senate, which carried representation but ignored the role of the Holy Spirit in the decision-making process. It did not. Instead, the deliberation became a matter of discernment through the Holy Spirit when the apostles and elders say, "It is the decision of the Holy Spirit and of us." The Council of Jerusalem accomplished its work as a model of collaboration with God and human beings and provides a window into mutual dialogue and respect in the church for the purpose of missiology and beyond.

If we asked where one of the places the Holy Spirit was most obviously active in the early church, it would be at the Council of Jerusalem. As Jesus tells his disciples in the **Gospel**, "The Advocate, the Holy Spirit, whom the Father will send in my name, will teach you everything and remind you of all that I told you." The elders and apostles deliberating in Jerusalem are a snapshot of the indwelling of the Trinity, the labor of the Spirit, a Spirit-filled work sent by the Father and in the name of the Son. In some sense, then, we might see this moment in Acts 15 as an earthly manifestation of "the holy city Jerusalem coming down out of heaven from God" (**Second Reading**). Its gleaming stones were the faithful, the elders, the apostles, all of whom spoke by the labor of the Holy Spirit; there was no need of a building or even a sacred edifice to hold such a divine presence, for "its temple is the Lord God almighty and the Lamb." Sharing the church's ministry with the Spirit gives testimony that the triune God longs to be among us. In union with the Father and the Spirit, the Son promises that we "will come to him and make our dwelling with him."

Connecting the Bible and the Liturgy

The memory of Jesus' promise of the Holy Spirit acting in the name of the Son must have been uppermost in the minds of those deliberating in Jerusalem in the first century. The church was, after all, the dwelling of the Trinity and so its members were actively discerning the presence of the Lord in their midst as a guiding voice in regard to the future, the formation of its membership. The **Collect** for today's liturgy keeps the contemporary church ever-mindful of the memory of the Lord Jesus, that "[w]hoever loves me will keep my word, and my Father will love him, and we will come to him and make our dwelling with him." The worshiping community gathers precisely to keep memory of the Lord, and proclamation of the Word and the breaking of bread become the indwelling abode of the Trinity filled with the Spirit of the Lord: "Grant, almighty God, / that we may celebrate with heartfelt devotion these days of joy, / which we keep in honor of the risen Lord, / and that what we relive in remembrance

/ we may always hold to in what we do." The phrase "what we relive in remembrance," or *"quod recordatione percurrimus,"* certainly pertains to the church's witness, keeping the memory of the Lord Jesus through *anamnesis* in the Eucharist. The congregation is now invited to recall that very promise of the Spirit. But we also recall that the church always invariably proceeds—through Christ—in the movement of the Trinity in our gathering: "Through our Lord Jesus Christ, your Son, / who lives and reigns with you in the unity of the Holy Spirit, / one God, for ever and ever." The Body is the temple of the triune God, speaking a voice of praise and thanksgiving in the Eucharist back to the Father by the gift of the Holy Spirit.

With the promise of Christ to send the Spirit among those who keep his word in mind, the Eucharist proclaims his passion, death, and resurrection until he comes again. We who gather do so as a church of elders, representatives—all those who have come, not with heavy burdens but to keep his memory. So as a church that prays through the Spirit we offer our gifts: "May our prayers rise up to you, O Lord, / together with the sacrificial offerings, / so that, purified by your graciousness, / we may be conformed to the mysteries of your mighty love" (**Prayer over the Offerings**).

Strategy for Preaching

The events recorded in Acts 15 become a wonderful lens with which to view the optimal working of the Spirit in the lives of men and women inside and outside the church. Preachers will note the inclusion of "outsiders" in this description because it would seem to be topical, indeed necessary, to understand the work of the Spirit with all of creation, and not just the church. After all, the Council of Jerusalem dealt precisely with the outsider becoming one Body through the work of the Spirit. To this end, the role of hospitality becomes a centerpiece in welcoming the triune God in our midst, while not "requiring anything burdensome" to those who may cross our path. I take it that the new evangelization is new because it welcomes a larger range of God's people, maybe unimagined before. Dialogue and openness are, therefore, operative words, as God takes a dwelling place in the midst of the assembly. Discernment of the Spirit is considered normative in the Christian community and part of ongoing communal and personal reflection. So a core homiletic idea for today may be something along these lines: Christ's promise of the Trinity comes with the risk of trusting the Spirit and one another, even the stranger among us.

As far as beginnings go, the church as a place of hospitality might be a good place to start. I am thinking of the heroic ways in which the church has, over the centuries, provided "sanctuary" for those persecuted by hostile and unstable political regimes. Or, perhaps more down-to-earth, soup kitchens, welfare agencies, shelters for battered women and children, homes for pregnant women—to name just a few—have been the refuge of the marginalized over the years.

Then the body of the homily: The church is also the home of historical memory, which keeps the remembrance of the Lord Jesus (Collect) and his words (Gospel). The community of faith holds the living memory of God's action in the world, particularly the life, death, and resurrection of Jesus. In so doing, those who speak the Lord's memory at the Eucharist become members of the household of God, both conformed and welcomed by the triune God (Prayer over the Offerings).

But such an abidance in the Trinity would not be possible unless we make a home for another in our hearts, without "requiring anything burdensome." The Council of Jerusalem widened the boundaries of regulations in order to absorb the Gentiles (First Reading). This welcome was part of the way of collaboration of the early church, sharing power, the very power of God in the Spirit. (Some examples of contemporary collegiality might follow.) The early church provides us with a model for making room for God dwelling among us, even in ways we could not have imagined. We love one another. So we can become the new Jerusalem, the city of love. (Illustration: the partisanship of the earthly Jerusalem, war torn and violent, contrasts with the heavenly one. Contemporary illustration of polarization in religion and politics.) Is it possible that we can make our love for one another shine like jewels in that new city? If love is that strong, if hospitality that great, if welcome is that open, there is no need for light, because the Lamb of God has come and made his dwelling, as he does here at this Eucharist when we acclaim, "Behold the Lamb of God, / behold him who takes away the sins of the world. / Blessed are those called to the supper of the Lamb." There is always one more place at that table for our brother or sister.

The Ascension of the Lord

Readings from the Ambo

Acts 1:1-11; Ps 47:2-3, 6-7, 8-9; Heb 9:24-28; 10:19-23;
Luke 24:46-53

Year C for the solemnity of the Ascension of the Lord presents us with two accounts in Luke-Acts of Christ's return to the Father. There is one scene in the **Gospel** that speaks of the Lord leading the disciples "out as far as Bethany . . . and was taken up to heaven." And the other, more elaborate narration of the Lord's heavenly passage in Acts (obligatory for all three years in the Lectionary cycle) is complete with angels addressing the men of Galilee with their provocative inquiry and promise of an apocalypse: "[W]hy are you standing there looking at the sky? This Jesus who has been taken up from you into heaven will return in the same way as you have seen him going into heaven" (**First Reading**). When compared to the other Synoptic writers' version of the ascension, Luke alone pictures Jesus blessing his disciples before he is taken up into heaven. Matthew's account is really more of a commissioning to baptize all nations and a promise that Jesus will be his disciple "until the end of the age." Mark's so-called "longer ending" is probably a third-century addition, bringing together elements taken from other narratives.

Luke's vision of Jesus at the end of his time with his disciples is very much in keeping with his portrait of the Lord from the start. He is teacher to the last, explaining the meaning of the Christ to the disciples as drawn from tradition: "Thus it is written that the Christ would suffer and rise from the dead on the third day and that repentance, for the forgiveness of sins, would be preached in his name to all the nations, beginning from Jerusalem." Jesus used similar words to interpret his own activity just previous to this episode on the road to Emmaus, when he once again explains to the disciples all about the Christ in the Scriptures.

The Lord is careful to underline the very point of his mission on earth to suffer, die, and be raised up and that repentance for the forgiveness of sins would be preached in his name. The ascension, then, provides a kind of coda for the Gospel of Luke, giving us Jesus the interpreter, one last time. In the **Second Reading** the Letter to the Hebrews dramatically emphasizes the role of Jesus as the High Priest, to "take away sin by his sacrifice." By comparison, Christ in Luke leaves with a blessing and then the disciples "returned to Jerusalem with great joy, and they were continually in the temple praising God." There, they await the great High Priest over the house of God to pass into the heavenly sanctuary. One senses the Lukan community gathered in prayer and worship while they were looking up to heaven and waiting for the return of the Lord. Not a bad model for the contemporary church, this vigil of prayer and waiting for the Lord to return to us in the same way as he departed to return to the Father. And the Letter to the Hebrews adds a rejoinder: "Let us hold unwaveringly to our confession that gives us hope, for he who made the promise is trustworthy."

Connecting the Bible and the Liturgy

The solemnity of the Ascension as it is celebrated according to the Roman Missal has both a Vigil and a Mass during the Day. The **Entrance Antiphon** for the Mass during the Day is uniquely situated for positioning the eucharistic assembly as joining the activity related in the Acts of the Apostles: *"Viri Galilaei, quid admiramini aspicientes in caelum?"* Indeed, the angels seem to be asking the congregation of worshipers to attend to the reality of this solemnity, but to remember the Lord's return as well. *"Quemadmodum vidistis eum ascendentem in caelum, ita veniet, alleluia."*

This *admiramini aspicientes*, or gazing in wonder, begs for an interpretation, which Jesus has already given to us in the Gospel and which the author of the Letter to the Hebrews glosses still further: If the church stands in vigil waiting for the Lord to return as we gaze at the heavens in awe, we know that Christ enters that sanctuary "that he might now appear before God on our behalf." According to Jesus, "Thus it was written that the Christ would suffer and rise

from the dead on the third day and that repentance, for the forgiveness of sins, would be preached in his name to all the nations, beginning from Jerusalem." The hope of reuniting with Christ is based
on the promise of the two men dressed in white who tell the disciples
that Jesus will "return in the same way." But until then, Christ offers
intercession for the church that prays at Vigil, since he has entered
into the sanctuary once and for all. So Christ tells his disciples that
the promise of the Father will come upon them and to "stay in the
city until you are clothed with power from on high." Jesus sets the
stage for chapter 2 of Acts, in which the power of God in the Spirit
will clothe the vigilant disciples with heavenly gifts.

Yet this hope expands to one day joining Christ precisely because
of the promise that he will return in glory. In the **Collect** we pray
that "where the Head has gone before in glory, / the Body is called to
follow in hope," to be reunited as our earthly nature dissolves and
our divine immortality that has been clothed in baptism is taken up
in Christ completely. As the **Preface I of the Ascension of the Lord**
says, "he ascended, not to distance himself from our lowly state /
but that we, his members, might be confident of following / where
he, our Head and Founder, has gone before." Until then, we await the
Lord in praise and thanksgiving as a worshiping community of Christian faithful. Here again, Luke's Gospel joyfully anticipates the disciple's own worshiping experience as they keep vigil. So the beginning
of the Collect begs God to keep the church full of joy until Christ's
coming again. The Latin is quite strong in its insistence that the
Christian community need their hearts to be gladdened. *"Fac nos,
omnipotens Deus, sanctis exsultare gaudiis,"* which is to say, make
us, almighty God, exult with holy joys (translated in the Roman
Missal as, "Gladden us with holy joys, almighty God"). In the end,
the congregation asks to be remade as those who keep vigil in joy
and praise. The solemnity of the Ascension reinforces the power of
God to live inside his people as we worship, since Christ has entered
the sanctuary as our intercessor and "[m]ediator between God and
man, / judge of the world and Lord of hosts."

Strategy for Preaching

The ascension of the Lord places some very heavy faith proposi-
tions before the Christian community. We take it as a creedal formula,

of course, that Christ ascended into heaven and is seated at the right hand of the Father. Additionally, this same Christ, we believe, will come again even as the men of Galilee saw him go up to heaven. Finally, where he has gone, we hope to follow, "confident of following / where he, our Head and Founder, has gone before" (Preface I Ascension of the Lord).

Preaching on the ascension can be lethally abstract so that the congregation, already awash in theological speculation and the profession of faith, really wonders what this has to do with them here and now. We could answer that by saying that the ascension is about the future where we hope to follow. But I would suggest pushing the envelope just a bit on this solemnity. The ascension is not a celebration of a creedal formula but the triumph of Christ and his power to intercede on behalf of humanity. The ascension harbors an outrageous promise of redemption and eternal life if we only dare to believe. That is the core homiletic idea for today, in my estimation. The Lukan Jesus is in a particularly good position to help us, with his blessing, interpretation of his role as the suffering Christ, and promise of return. "Thus it is written that the Christ would suffer and rise from the dead on the third day and that repentance, for the forgiveness of sins, would be preached in his name." The ascended Christ continues to intercede for the church and the world, but in the meantime, we gather to praise God and wait for his return in glory. The ascension is the embodiment of hope—for what has been, what is, and what is to come.

The Eucharist uniquely offers a sanctuary of hope, into which Christ has entered and where we hope to follow (Second Reading; Collect; Preface I Ascension). It might be useful to ask the congregation at this point a rhetorical question: What did they come hoping to find here at the liturgy? The Eucharist functions as a window into eternity by the revelation of Christ through the proclamation of his passion, death, and resurrection. We gaze into this window until he comes again. The image of the window might be a good one to draw out. What do we see in that window we call praise and thanksgiving? Do we see Jesus ascending and coming again? Something else? In a sense, the preacher is allowing the Lukan Jesus to unfold, interpreting the events of Christ as we await him.

To draw such an image for the congregation begins to get at the pivotal question related to the core idea: What, then, are we hoping for? The dazzling promise of everlasting life and eternity. By my reckoning, we do not preach enough about eternal life, so here is our chance to draw from everyone from St. Paul to St. Augustine to Dante. Our praise and thanksgiving offer us a clue as to what eternal life will look like; we do not have to resort to stories about the clinically dead, seeing light streaming from a welcoming tunnel. The baptized have already been buried with Christ, and so long to be with him, a foretaste of which is with us even now at this Eucharist.

Seventh Sunday of Easter

Readings from the Ambo

Acts 7:55-60; Ps 97:1-2, 6-7, 9; Rev 22:12-14, 16-17, 20; John 17:20-26

As we could anticipate, these readings for the Sunday between the Ascension and Pentecost catch us paused between the now and the not yet. Most poignantly, perhaps, Jesus' prayer to the Father in chapter 17 of John's **Gospel** also positions him between his sharing himself in the present moment with his disciples, and the awareness that his "hour" is still to come. Jesus seems to utter this very unique stance between the Father and the disciples when he says, "I have given them the glory you gave me, so that they may be one, as we are one, I in them and you in me, that they may be brought to perfection as one, that the world may know that you sent me, and that you loved them even as you loved me." This portion of John's Gospel functions as Jesus' priestly prayer because he stands in the breach between the Father and his disciples, offering himself to the Father's glory for the sake of those he loves.

The deacon Stephen also finds himself straddling heaven and earth in chapter 7 of the book of Acts (**First Reading**). The passage is rather jarring in its contrast between the brute force of Stephen's persecution and death by stoning and the proto-martyr's vision of heaven: "Behold, I see the heavens opened and the Son of Man standing at the right hand of God." We know as well that Stephen's death is an echo of the Master's when he says, "Lord, do not hold this sin against them." As Stephen is taken up into Jesus, the martyr's prayer becomes Jesus' cry to the Father as well, interceding for all humanity on the cross. The passage not only suggests the way in which the early martyrs became conformed to Christ's own death, but invites us to consider how their deaths were taken up into Christ's own offering of himself to the Father.

The *maranatha*, the begging of the Lord Jesus to come at the end of time in the finale of the book of Revelation, shows us, albeit in a triumphal way, a lofty moment between heaven and earth. Having spent the entire book in a kind of visionary trance of the future, the coming of the Lord seems quite immanent to the ecstatic John on Patmos: "Behold, I am coming soon. I bring with me the recompense I will give to each according to his deeds" (**Second Reading**). Indeed judgment itself seems to be pressing in. All John can do is shout as he longs to be swept away from the present and gathered into the heavens. He imagines the immediacy of reunion to capture his own longing: "The Spirit and the bride say, 'Come.' Let the hearer say, 'Come.' Let the one who thirsts come forward, and the one who wants it receive the gift of life-giving water." This is the unfolding of the almost-but-not-yet as the church awaits the gift of the Bridegroom.

Connecting the Bible and the Liturgy

Almost-but-not-yet seizes those gathered for worship as well. This Sunday really is unique insofar as it captures the congregation in an existential longing, a liturgical moment ripe for the coming Spirit. Christ has ascended and we who remain anticipate his return as if we are glimpsing the end time, or the kind of vision John saw or the Stephen beheld before his death.

The personal nature of God's face in Christ for which we yearned and which was expressed for us by John and Stephen, is relived for the eucharistic assembly in the **Entrance Antiphon**: "*Exaudi, Domine, vocem meam, qua clamavi ad te.*" "O Lord, hear my voice, for I have called to you." "*Tibi dixit cor meum, quaesivi vultum tuum, vultum tuum Domine requiram: ne avertas faciem tuam a me, alleluia.*" The Antiphon accentuates the alliterative *vultum tuum, vultum tuum.* "[M]y heart has spoken: Seek his face; / hide not your face from me, alleluia." Those who have gathered acknowledge in hope the ascended Lord and long for his face by expecting his coming, even as the angels told the men of Galilee as these followers of Christ looked up to heaven. So the **Collect** recognizes the faith community as the church of believers who wait in hope, live in promise, and pray without ceasing in joyful anticipation of what is not yet. Jesus has given his word in which we abide while his disciples await him in Spirit and in truth: "Graciously hear our supplications, O Lord, / so that we, who believe that the Savior of the human race / is with you in your glory, / may experience, as he promised, / until the end of the world, / his abiding presence among us." The Opening Prayer picks up again on the *Exaudi, Domine* of the Entrance Antiphon, as if to underline the needs of the community, here and now, waiting for God.

The Roman Missal says that any of the Prefaces for either Easter or the Ascension would be suitable for today, but I recommend using **Preface IV of Easter** because its language nicely holds us in its grasp in restating the work of Christ, leaving us longing for his presence: "For, with the old order destroyed, / a universe cast down is renewed, / and integrity of life is restored to us in Christ." Christ Jesus has vanquished the "old order" of sin and death, and *"renovantur universa deiecta"* by which a fallen world has been refashioned. That universe has been remade, but not completely, for we await its completion when Christ will hear the groanings of all creation and liberate us from our bondage to decay. It is then that, *"vitae nobis in Christo reparature integritas."* We will be complete when the Spirit and the bride say "Come." Until that time, we will not be left orphans, as the **Gospel Antiphon** reminds us, but will be returned to the Head, as the Bridegroom comes for his Bride, the church.

Strategy for Preaching

Although the majority of dioceses in the United States celebrate Ascension on this Sunday, rather than the previous Thursday, those who do follow the Seventh Sunday of Easter have another opportunity to evangelize, another perspective to offer before Pentecost Sunday in a unique way. The dramatic martyrdom of Stephen, the passionate vision of John for the face of Christ, and, most significantly, the person of Jesus himself mystically disclosing his incarnate presence for his disciples are crucial touchstones in faith. If we ask the people of God to long for Christ and prepare for his Spirit, then here are texts that the preacher may deploy to his advantage. So the core homiletic idea for today could be something like this: to be a Christian means to long for Christ's coming and he desires to return to those he loves. This core idea not only signals the congregation to the now and not yet reality of the church, but prepares them for the upcoming feast of Pentecost, where the Spirit, the Comforter, will console those who wait with gifts from God.

I think that the structure of the preaching for this Sunday works out well by using the three major Lectionary readings together with liturgical texts as an armature. Note here a strong caution: I am not suggesting that the preacher simply go through the readings and provide a commentary on each one independently. This "method" simply glosses over the readings and may provide some interesting observations, but does not provide an organic narrative homily for the listener. So I will highlight the first sentence of each of the following paragraphs, sections that will be linked to the readings, but also cohere to a more or less unified text.

I would begin with a strong initial first sentence, reminiscent of the biblical texts themselves: Christian discipleship is a matter of life and death. We take our lives as Christians for granted, usually performing good works and attending what we are supposed to do. (This can be expanded.)

Some Christians encountered life at the moment of death. Take Stephen, for instance. He was the first martyr (First Reading). We hear this reading at another time of the church year as well. When we are still in the afterglow of Christmas, and maybe have yet to kiss the last guest good-bye, on December 26, we see what true witness is all about. It is a matter of life and death. (Illustration: contemporary people who give their lives in service to the church or other causes for the sake of others.)

But we don't have to be martyrs to long for Christ—just sacrifice all we are and all we have to express our great longing for him (Second Reading). Saint Stephen was granted a vision of the heavens being opened; the face of Christ was in his sight, even forgiving his murderers as our Lord did his own slayers. Yet John also had a vision and he lived to a long, old age. John's exile on the island of Patmos probably taught him to yearn for Christ, to continue to seek him in solitude and in his Spirit-filled longing. This is possible for us as well, even as we long for the Spirit to come at Pentecost. (Name some graced moments of waiting for God.) That is what our Entrance Antiphon tells us today as well. We long to see Christ who has departed from us in the ascension. And where he has gone, we are to follow. Where the Head has gone, so too the Body (Collect).

That is because Christ was one of us, incarnate of the Virgin Mary, and loved us to the end (Gospel). Can you imagine that kind of love? Jesus tells the Father that we are his gift? On the contrary, Lord, you are our gift! We have been made sharers of his life, so how can we remain separate from the one who came to live among us (Preface IV of Easter)? We wait in vigil for his Spirit, which longs to rush through us and re-create us and keep us ever joyful, thankful, and full of praise until that day when our Blessed Lord comes back for his friends.

Pentecost Sunday
Mass during the Day

Readings from the Ambo

Acts 2:1-11; Ps 104:1, 24, 29-30, 31, 34;
Rom 8:8-17 (1 Cor 12:3b-7, 12-13); Seq., Veni, Sancte Spiritus;
John 14:15-16, 23b-26 (John 20:19-23)

The Spirit of the Lord has come and is neither timid nor shy. The **First Reading**, taken from the book of Acts, paints a vital picture of the manifestation of the Spirit as aggressive and powerfully energetic: windy, fiery, and, yes, intimately personal. "Then there appeared to them tongues as of fire, which parted and came to rest on each one of them." We are apt to miss this little detail, but it is as if the Spirit is parsing himself out on the individual members very uniquely, having come first on the entire group of those who have gathered together in one place. This gift of the Spirit first of all seems to suggest that the particular person partakes of the whole and shares that life intrepidly and in grace. It seems to me that at least one way of understanding the mystery of the Pentecost event, of those who were suddenly able to comprehend one another, despite their diversity, is that language is no longer a barrier when it comes to mutual self-giving and communication of the mighty acts of God. That Spirit has shared himself with the whole community as one and in very particular ways.

Along these lines, Paul tells the Corinthians (**Second Reading, First Option**), "There are different kinds of spiritual gifts but the same Spirit; there are different forms of service but the same Lord; there are different workings but the same God who produces all of them in everyone." The point Paul is making is that the Holy Spirit gives unity and peace; he utters Jesus is Lord. This Spirit, though diverse, is not the engine of disunity and fragmentation; that is the spirit of wickedness and has its origin in Babel, with its overreaching tower of madness and willful power. Again, in the Letter to the Romans (Second Reading, Second Option), Paul says that living according to the Spirit means being possessed by Christ, who animates the Body. "For you did not receive a spirit of slavery to fall back into fear, but you received a Spirit of adoption, through whom we cry, 'Abba, Father!'"

When we consider the **Gospel** for today in the context of the other readings in the Lectionary for Pentecost, it is this spirit of adoption with which Jesus commits to companion the disciples when the Lord promises that the Spirit "will teach you everything and remind you of all that I told you." If the Spirit is crying out "Abba, Father," it is the voice of Christ that calls out to God, a wondrous and mysterious unfolding of the Trinity. The backdrop to such an utterance is the cross, where the faithful Son uttered loud cries and was heard by the One who loved him. That same Spirit, dwelling within us and in the church, unifies through the love of Christ and makes his dwelling among those who keep the commandments to love as he taught us.

Connecting the Bible and the Liturgy

As we might expect, the Pauline metaphor of adoption finds its way throughout the liturgy of Pentecost. It is fitting, then, that the liturgical language of adoption—so crucial to our understanding of Christian baptism—closes out the Easter season. With the extinguishing of the paschal candle we are reminded that the light that Christ brought us at Easter still remains in our heart or, indeed, like a tongue of fire over our heads. Christ has set us free from fear and division and brings us into the unified kingdom of God's peace, which only the Spirit can bestow upon us. The **Preface: The Mystery of Pentecost** draws heavily on Pauline theology when the text says, "For, bringing your Paschal Mystery to completion, / you bestowed the Holy Spirit today / on those you made your adopted children / by uniting them to your Only Begotten Son. / This same Spirit, as the Church came to birth, / opened to all peoples the knowledge of God / and brought together the many languages of the earth / in profession of the one faith."

Needless to say, our very presence at the Eucharist celebrating Pentecost can only remind us of how the Spirit has drawn us together. Indeed, we are one with the one bread and one cup, not only with those with whom we are gathered, but with the church throughout the world and those who have gone before us "marked with the sign of faith." If the presider uses the Roman Canon (**Eucharistic Prayer I**), then in the Proper for Pentecost of the *Communicantes* he says, "Celebrating the most sacred day of Pentecost, / on which the Holy Spirit / appeared to the Apostles in tongues of fire, / and in communion with those whose memory we venerate, / especially the glorious ever-Virgin Mary, / Mother of our God and Lord, Jesus Christ . . ." The Spirit's fire extends to all the church, those gathered on earth and those in heaven.

Finally, the liturgy accesses the biblical dynamic that lays claim to the Pentecost event as both a communal and personal experience. Indeed, the Spirit has filled the whole church, but each member, though diverse, partakes in the Spirit in order to profess the Creed: "I believe." (Formerly, of course, this beginning of the **Profession of Faith** was "We believe." With the current translation, each individual must stand up and be counted among the many, expressing the "Abba, Father," crying out by virtue of his or her baptism. Yet, the Creed is expressed aloud in one voice and common unity of gesture.) Moreover, the **Collect** nicely summarizes the working of the Spirit; this prayer asks almighty God to sanctify the "whole Church" as well as "the hearts of believers." The presider says, "O God, who by the mystery of today's great feast / sanctify your whole Church in every people and nation, / pour out, we pray, the gifts of the Holy Spirit / across the face of the earth / and, with the divine grace that was at work / when the Gospel was first proclaimed, / fill now once more the hearts of believers." The Opening Prayer is a mirror of that fateful moment when all of them gathered in one place: "Then there appeared to them tongues as of fire, / which parted and came to rest on each one of them."

Strategy for Preaching

Preaching at Pentecost should be as vibrant as the Spirit that animates all Christian preaching and who caught the disciples in rapturous tongues of fire; it is a homiletic directed at the whole church, yet personalized as if it rests in the hearts of the individual believers. So the core homiletic idea for today may be that the Spirit has given birth to the whole church, but that same Lord calls each of its members individually to adoption.

To get right to the center of the homily is to express no timidity this day, but to gather the congregation together in one place and set them ablaze with a common experience of language and imagination. Perhaps give some visualization of what might be festive occasions for gathering. The book of Acts shows the disciples waiting in vigil, while Jesus gathers his disciples and asks them to keep his commandments and promises the Spirit. The Gospel for Year C (first option) brings the disciples together in fear, which Jesus dispels with his life-giving breath. In truth, people come together for a variety of reasons—support, common interests, grieving, worship—and they leave knowing that they are one mind with someone else, or at least have begun to understand the perspective of another through listening and dialogue.

That is a gift of the Spirit, which has given birth to the church in faith, hope, and love. We profess the same faith and confess one baptism for the remission of sins; the creed unites us, the bread we share brings us together in Christ. This unity is the comfort of Christ's promise to send "another Advocate to be with you always." The church was born out of the spirit of Jesus' love and desire for unity.

But all of us are also in possession of the Spirit in a different way, even if we cry "Abba, Father" here at this Eucharist together (Second Reading; Rite of Communion). If we were able to take a roll call of the congregation, we would see a very different and diverse group of people! (Image: recall for the congregation a classroom roll call and describe in detail the different personalities as each one was called. Five or six examples should make the point clear.) Yet all of these gifts are the common language of God, the Creator. The Word made flesh is part of that language, joining us to the Father, making us adopted sons and daughters of God (Preface: The Mystery of Pentecost).

We return to our homes knowing that the Trinity has come to abide in our dwellings in love. The promise of the Advocate to be with us always and for all time has been given by the one whose trust is beyond measure. Let us remind ourselves of the life-giving Spirit that will teach us everything and help us remember the fire the Lord has given each one of us to burn in our hearts.

 # ORDINARY TIME

Second Sunday in Ordinary Time

Readings from the Ambo

Isa 62:1-5; Ps 96:1-2, 2-3, 7-8, 9-10; 1 Cor 12:4-11; John 2:1-11

Both the **First Reading** and the Gospel concern weddings—of a very special sort. Isaiah speaks of the Lord espousing the land of Israel in one of three oracles or poems (the others are 60:1-22; 61:11) in the context of a larger collection of visions taken from text that spans 56:1–66:24; it dates from shortly after the exile. Therefore the promise of an espousal union of the Lord with his people is imminent: "For the LORD delights in you / and makes your land his spouse. / As a young man marries a virgin, / your Builder shall marry you; / and as a bridegroom rejoices in his bride / so shall your God rejoice in you."

The prophet himself increases the expectation of God's salvation from exile when he seems unable to contain his speech concerning the coming liberation of Israel: "For Zion's sake I will not be silent, / for Jerusalem's sake I will not be quiet, / until her vindication shines forth like the dawn / and her victory like a burning torch." Similarly, the beginning of Jesus' public ministry recorded in today's **Gospel** also suggests an espousal: Christ will transform the old water for ritual purification into the new wine of the kingdom that will be imbibed by the church, the people of God. This new ministry of Christ will bring those who have been in the exile of sin into the bridal shower of God's mercy, in union with the Bridegroom. Parenthetically, it is interesting to note the prophetic role Jesus' mother plays in interceding for the couple who have run out of wine. This provocation to action, a reminder much like Isaiah's urgent speech that cannot be silent or contained, suggests the dynamic role of Jesus' ministry that will soon unfold. The transformation of the lives of the couple at Cana becomes not only a relief from shame and embarrassment, but a sign of God's glory through Christ. This, the "beginning of his signs at Cana in Galilee," will serve as a touchstone for God's compassionate espousal love for those whose well has run dry throughout the Gospel of John (as we will see with the Samaritan woman at the well shortly). So we are able to celebrate with the **Responsorial Psalm** and Isaiah, "Proclaim his marvelous deeds to all the nations."

In a sense, the gifts Paul speaks of in the **Second Reading** become articulations emerging from the wonders we have beheld at Christ's mystical wedding between the Bridegroom and the church. The Spirit of that unity shouts and cannot keep silent because "there are different workings but the same God who produces all of them in everyone." For the Lord calls out to those who have been scattered and fragmented in thick darkness to drink of the Spirit, who draws us into Love's embrace.

Connecting the Bible and the Liturgy

If Isaiah and Mary perform a powerfully prophetic role in their own way, uttering a newness for Zion and the future church, then the **Collect** takes on a pleading role for the worshiping community as well. Indeed, note how the Opening Prayer seems to call the Almighty into a reminder of his compassion for his people: "Almighty ever-living God, / who govern all things, / both in heaven and on earth, / mercifully hear the pleading of your people / and bestow your peace on our times." In some sense, the church pleading for intercession and mercy takes its identity from the Mother of God who intervenes for the couple at the wedding at Cana. Now the church asks for a transformation "on our times."

Along these same lines we might ask what the new wine might be for which we ask; or again, what do we ask of the Lord to transform as our well runs dry? Simply put, what are we begging to be changed, together with the Bread of Life and the cup of salvation? The Collect answers us: "bestow your peace on our times." Christ's peace becomes the wine of peace, the new wine of peace, because God has taken us as his spouse and has not forgotten the people he loves. We recognize this transformation into the spouse about to drink the wine of peace in the Communion Rite, of course, during the moment of the exchange of peace. *"Pax Domini sit semper vobiscum."* We sense that the gift of the Spirit has been poured out, making us one. Those gathered for worship have many gifts, but the Spirit calls forth peace and the unity of the Body. As Paul tells the Corinthians, "one and the same Spirit produces all of these, / distributing them individually to each person as he wishes." The sign of peace offers a gesture of reconciliation before the assembly is invited to taste the new wine of the kingdom at the wedding feast.

Finally, the **Prayer after Communion** highlights the possibility for peace and reconciliation for "our time" when the oration says, "Pour on us, O Lord, the Spirit of your love, / and in your kindness / make those you have nourished / by this one heavenly Bread / one in mind and heart." This communion with the Lord has accomplished something. It has made us one Body, sharing the same Spirit. This is the peace that has been bestowed on our times. Our transformation into the espoused of the Lord allows us to remember our oneness with all humankind. We who have supped at the wedding feast go to the marketplace to say, "The peace of the Lord be with you always." The Body of Christ has become a living sign of Christ's action in the world, the life-altering—or life-*"altaring"*—momentum that has invigorated us into new life. We have been freed from shame and given a share in the divine life as the spouse, the Beloved of God.

Strategy for Preaching

The preacher would do well to seize the opportunity to make connections between the First Reading and the Gospel, as the Lectionary seems to imply. I find it hard to resist the connection between the espousal invitation to which Israel, the couple at Cana, and now the church are called. This is a wedding that brings us out of the exile of sin and into the new land that flows with the new wine of the kingdom, God's peace and compassion. So the core homiletic idea for today might be something along these lines: God calls his people to live in covenant with him and to be nourished with the new wine of Christ's banquet.

Although we know that formal weddings are becoming less and less popular in our culture in the West, it is all the more reason to draw on an illustration of a wedding for an introduction in order to highlight the biblical associations with covenantal love. Those gathered for worship have come to respond to God's call to be fully engaged in the love of Christ, to come out of our exile into full worship (First Reading). We have been brought out of exile of sin and ask for God's mercy to be transformed (Collect).

But what is that new wine that Christ renders sanctified? We are being drawn into a covenant with God and the Spirit—making us one with each other in a bond of peace. This is the one bread and one cup from which the Bride will drink. (Illustration: a wedding.) Paul tells us it is the same Spirit that gives each of us different gifts (Second Reading). (Second illustration: a family that has several children, all of whom contribute to the well-being of the whole, but have differing talents.)

That unity is the covenant of peace we extend to one another every time we celebrate the Eucharist (Communion Rite). When we drink of the new wine of the kingdom, Christ is offering us a wedding cup. This is the Bridegroom gifting the church with his own Blood. That relationship is unconditional and espoused by God. We live in unity and bring peace to one another and the world (Prayer after Communion).

Third Sunday in Ordinary Time

Readings from the Ambo

Neh 8:2-4a, 5-6, 8-10; Ps 19:8, 9, 10, 15;
1 Cor 12:12-30; Luke 1:1-4; 4:14-21

Chapters 8, 9, and 10 of the book of Nehemiah show us how the author understands the relationship between the law and the people of Israel. Chapter 8 depicts a kind of liturgical gathering outside the temple precincts, which would have allowed full participation of all the lay hearers. Chapter 8 also shows how much the word of God claimed the people since they are described as weeping (though told to be joyful). Having heard the law, then, there followed a general confession, followed by Ezra's narrative of gratitude for God's provident care. Finally, there is a signing of the covenant naming Nehemiah, the governor, together with priests, Levites, and leaders of the people. This day later became Rosh Hashanah (or Tishri 1), the first day of the seventh month of the new moon and the most important month of celebrations in Israel.

The passage we have excerpted for us in the **First Reading** is a remarkable moment in proclamation history in which "Ezra read plainly from the book of the law of God, interpreting it so that all could understand what was read." As I understand it, that was a moment of great clarity for the hearers who gathered in a square opposite the Water Gate at the eastern side of the city. Without need of mediation, a whole people—without regard to clerical status—were able to make sense of the law such that they came to repentance.

There is a wonderful unity expressed in the hearing of the law, a convergence, as it were, of the whole assembly, the whole body in a response to God's invitation. Paul, once named Saul, was a defender of the law but became a champion of the Spirit. At the same time, however, that same Spirit draws hearers together in the "square" of the baptized assembly, an invisible space of all who gather to respond to God's word. The unity of the Body in no way diminishes the uniqueness of the individual subject. "As a body is one though it has many parts, / and all the parts of the body, though many, are one body, / so also Christ" (**Second Reading**).

Christ's presence in the Body becomes beautifully expressed in Luke's **Gospel** account of Jesus at the threshold of his public ministry. "Jesus returned to Galilee in the power of the Spirit." As he teaches in the synagogue, he is praised by all and, in Nazareth, is revealed to be not only a teacher of the law, but its prophetic fulfillment. After reading the scroll of Isaiah, he announces, "Today this Scripture passage is fulfilled in your hearing." Not tomorrow, but now. The Word becomes the immediate occasion of *"glad tidings to the poor"* and *"liberty to captives."* This is the power of the Word, which in the days of Nehemiah promises, "Do not be saddened this day, for rejoicing in the LORD must be your strength!" But as we will see at the end of chapter 4, the people become very sad indeed: the unity that is expressed liturgically in the First Reading by the listening assembly has not such fate in the synagogue in Nazareth. The word of God in its personified embodiment in Christ Jesus is summarily rejected.

Connecting the Bible and the Liturgy

The **Entrance Antiphon** immediately orients the liturgical assembly to be hearers of the word—indeed, to celebrate God's presence among them with joy as in the days of Nehemiah—with a *Cantate Domino* of Psalm 95: "O sing a new song to the Lord; / sing to the Lord, all the earth. / In his presence are majesty and splendor, / strength and honor in his holy place." Indeed, the biblical readings suggest that *sanctificatione eius* may take place inside or outside the sanctuary, or anywhere when the word of God is fulfilled in our hearing.

That fulfillment is reason to rejoice and be glad on this day that is holy to the Lord, "for rejoicing in the LORD must be your strength!" The **Collect** gives the congregation gathered for the celebration of Word and sacrament a further encouragement as it petitions the Lord to guide us to his "good pleasure." That the Lord himself rejoices in his creation suggests a fulfillment when we ask God to "direct our actions according to your good pleasure" (*in beneplacito tuo*), "that in the name of your beloved Son / we may abound in good works." It is Christ who allows our fulfillment as children of God to unfold and allow God to rejoice in his creation, so that we "will not walk in darkness, / but will have the light of life" (**Communion Antiphon**).

The "good works" that emerge from the Christian faithful suggest a ratification of the covenant made at baptism, a conversion because of Christ's revelatory proclamation in the Gospel of liberty for those held captive by sin. This freedom, we know, is the new life of grace into which we participate as we rejoice in the Eucharist. So the **Prayer after Communion** reminds the assembly of the gift, the Giver, and the life of celebration that comes from thanksgiving. "Grant, we pray, almighty God, / that, receiving the grace / by which you bring us to new life, / we may always glory in your gift." To glory in your gift (*in tuo semper munere gloriemur*) can only mean a life spent in thankful praise, fulfilled in our hearing, not only on this day that is made holy to the Lord, but each day of creation.

There is a caveat to hearing this joyful news, however. It is well to remind ourselves that despite the fact that news of Jesus went throughout an entire region "and was praised by all," these words did not adhere to the lives of the men and women in the synagogue, making them abound in good works. Jesus was praised one minute and driven out with hostility the next. There appear to be many ways of receiving the Word, but not all of them are welcome as a fulfillment of God's "good pleasure" or make us "abound in good works."

Strategy for Preaching

Jesus' movement into public ministry in Luke 4:16ff. at the synagogue in Nazareth is an iconic moment in Christian preaching and its fulfillment in the lives of the hearer. The Word himself has become the immediate cause for the fulfillment of salvation history. In a sense, Jesus now becomes the Law and the Prophets fulfilled, an aural vision, as it were, even before we get to the resplendent wonder of the transfiguration, of Moses and Elijah whispering in his ear. Ezra read the law and the people converted; they were moved into a ratification of the covenant. Jesus now comes to the synagogue ignited by the power of the Spirit, waiting for a new hearing in the lives of men and women, a diverse group in the Spirit. Like Jesus himself, the preacher announces the Good News to be fulfilled in our hearing, a phrase from which the USCCB would draw in order to make their position on liturgical preaching known in 1982. So the core homiletic idea for today might be a simple focus question for the congregation: How is the word fulfilled in our hearing? This might be a dangerous question, because the listening assembly may respond, "With difficulty!" or "Rarely!" These responses reflect the failure of preaching to reach the ears of the assembly, either because the preaching has been ineffective or because the congregation has chosen to reject the message, the messenger, and the text from which both find its origin. From what we can tell from the Lectionary readings today, it is precisely the word falling on one congregation (Nehemiah and Ezra) that brings new life and a ratification of the covenant, while Jesus' word in the synagogue brings hostility to the other in Nazareth.

A good introduction may point out the various ways in which we engage listening. Our society does a lot of shallow listening (examples may follow) but not a whole lot of deep listening.

But we come to the liturgical assembly to hear and be converted by proclamation of the Good News of the love of God in Christ Jesus. Such listening invariably draws us together in Christ (Second Reading). The character of the liturgical/listening assembly is docile before the Word, as we can see from the First Reading. That openness leads to an awareness of joy as well as conversion. The reception of the Word changes us and brings us new life. We live life as the community of ancient Israel: as a Rosh Hashanah—the first day of the year, a celebration.

We must also remember that simply because we show up at the liturgy does not guarantee our engagement. I have sat next to many churchgoers who read the parish news in the bulletin or text their friends during the readings. Luke tells us that news of Jesus traveled and he was praised. But as we shall see at the end of chapter 4, the living Word was rejected. Jesus intends to fulfill the Law and the Prophets by liberating captives like us and bringing Good News to the poor. Are we really ready for that? He does so as incarnate Word, waiting to be heard. He waits for a response to this wonderful invitation for us to sing a new song to the Lord. (Entrance Antiphon; an illustration might follow with a sketch of someone hearing good news—the birth of a child, the safe arrival of a loved one.)

This hearing can only bring us the new life of grace: he waits to be fulfilled as he knocks on the door of our hearts, to guide our actions (Collect; Prayer after Communion). That new life opens to us who, like Mary, hear the word of God and keep it.

Fourth Sunday in Ordinary Time

Readings from the Ambo

Jer 1:4-5, 17-19; Ps 71:1-2, 3-4, 5-6, 15, 17;
1 Cor 12:31–13:13; Luke 4:21-30

The selection taken from the book of Jeremiah for the **First Reading** clearly indicates its essential meaning to be a vocation call. But the brief excerpt here only tangentially touches on the powerful engagement God makes with Jeremiah in all of chapter 1. We might recall that this is not a brief vocational dalliance, but rooted in a vital historical context. Verses 1-4 indicate that Jeremiah was from a priestly family and served as prophet for the Lord from the thirteen years of King Josiah (627 BCE) until the seventh year of Zedekiah (587 BCE). That makes forty years, in which Jeremiah will prophesy about the destruction of Judah and Jerusalem and the immanent invasion of Babylon. In turn, God also warns Jeremiah of his own impending rejection when he tells him that he will prophesy "against Judah's kings and princes, / against its priests and people. / They will fight against you but not prevail over you, / for I am with you to deliver you, says the LORD."

Like Jeremiah, Jesus' vocation has come "from the womb" and appointed to the nations. Both Jeremiah and Jesus will be rejected by their own people. The scene at the synagogue in today's **Gospel** continues last week's lighter side of chapter 4. The revelation of Jesus' mission at Nazareth shows the reality of this "new Jeremiah," preaching not only to Israel but igniting liberation to all captives and all who are blind. Ironically, even though Jesus' hearers from his hometown summarily reject him, they are fulfilling exactly what the Lord said to Jeremiah: "They will fight against you but not prevail over you." Indeed the light to those in darkness will provoke in many not thanksgiving but disdain. Despite Jeremiah's warning, Judah and Jerusalem will meet with defeat and exile in steeling themselves against God's word, but the Son of God's rejection yields not a dark fate, but the reconciliation and forgiveness of the cross. That is Jesus' unique vocational call in God's messianic plan for redemption in which rejection is transformed into divine love.

Paul addresses the Corinthians in a stunning section on the spiritual gifts in the celebrated first 13 verses of chapter 13 in 1 Corinthians; it becomes a divine witness for love all its own. With the First Reading and the Gospel holding prophetic vocation for both Jeremiah and Jesus, the church in a sense holds out a universal vocation plan for all in the **Second Reading**: to love. Some saints, such as Thérèse of Lisieux, in her autobiography, read this particular passage of 1 Corinthians and came to a profound vocational call—just to love the "Little Way" of doing everyday things with great love. At the same time, Paul is not unaware of the difficulties of loving; love is tough, for "we know partially" and perhaps not everyone has put away "childish things." Still, the greatest of the theological virtues is love because it is in this gift that we are fully known—known from the womb and knit together by God. Whatever our vocation may be, all are called to love.

Connecting the Bible and the Liturgy

Both Jeremiah and Jesus will endure wrath and rejection from their own people and it is difficult to avoid the contrast with the Second Reading. Paul invites universal vocation in the contemplation to love, but, symbolically speaking, that celebration of the highest of the virtues will fall flat on Jeremiah's persecutors and Jesus' murderers. The **Entrance Antiphon** seems to capture the inner voice of the prophetic vocation when it is seen through the lens of the thwarted prophet. "*Salva nos*," "Save us, O Lord our God! / And gather us from the nations, / to give thanks to your holy name, / and make it our glory to praise you." Psalm 106 implies that our true home cannot be contained inside any national boundary, but lies only in the loving presence of God, who knows us all from the womb and has fashioned us there. True freedom begins when we stop pretending that liberty consists in the nation-state and come to the reality that our ultimate vocation is being children of God, called to witness to the divine will in our lives and the lives of others. We work this out by loving one another in Christ. The nation and the home country are fickle and easily swayed, as we see in the lives of Jeremiah and Jesus; they murder the prophet in their midst. But the steadfast hope is the Lord, as we hear in the **Responsorial Psalm** refrain: "I will sing of your salvation." Vocation call is intimately linked with service to the nation, and will sometimes conflict as they did with Jeremiah. "For you are my hope, O Lord; / my trust, O God, from my youth. / On you I depend from birth; / from my mother's womb you are my strength." But God's covenantal love, of recognizing that we are his even before we would be part of the woman who bore us, draws us back into our true selves, the persons we were meant to be from the beginning.

The **Collect** invited the community assembled for worship to embrace their own vocation—not in some political way, but in recognition that love is "a still more excellent way." The Opening Prayer is simple and direct, but the challenge is great: "Grant us, Lord our God, / that we may honor you with all our mind, / and love everyone in truth of heart." This prayer captures the greatest commandments, the spine of the Judeo-Christian community. But loving God to the painful exclusion of all things that are not of God will cause us pain. Being true to the word of God even in the midst of struggle is difficult, to say nothing of our ability to "love everyone in truth of heart." That is the rub, if you will, embedded in the love commandment. It will be tempting to think of Paul's celebration of love as something we can do if we just "smile and move on," as some would say. But on the contrary, this passage is perhaps the most regularly chosen Scripture selection for weddings because it signals the deep commitment to love as a vocation, to endure until the end with patience and steadfast hope in God, who has loved us unreservedly.

Strategy for Preaching

When I was a young teenager during the Vietnam War, many of us were radicalized by what we thought were the absurd claims of the right-wing "hawks" who seemed to take an extreme position on national identity and purpose. One famous bumper sticker read, "My country right or wrong." Really? Do we sell our ethics for a stake in national identity? To do so would be to ignore the intimate relationship the Creator maintains with his creation, forming for each one of us a womb for his will. We are very good at compartmentalizing, saying one thing at the Eucharist and putting another sticker on our car or pin on our lapel. How can we possibly read 1 Corinthians 13 and talk of war in the same breath? The Collect enjoins us to "love everyone in truth of heart." So preaching today is going to challenge what we hold most dear—our false selves, our false consciousness about our personal and national identity—and bring us to the brow of the cliff: to recognize that our true vocation and identity come as a baptized Christian following God's will as it is revealed in Christ. To grasp the freight under this reality, we are challenged to speak a core homiletic idea that might run something like this: our true vocation is to love God above all things and love one another—without reservation.

It is without reservation "that we may honor you with all our mind," which could form one hinge in this homily, and to "love everyone in truth of heart" could be the other. These two coordinates, taken directly from today's Collect, draw out the core homiletic idea fairly directly. As far as an introduction goes, as always, it will be necessary to get right to the center of things with a strong initial statement, bearing in mind the trajectory to come: there is really only one vocation in life—to follow God's will; that is going to play out in a million different ways with as many people. (Illustration: Jeremiah and the call of the prophet; Jesus in the Gospel with his return home to difficult circumstances.) For so many of us, the journey we are asked to make may have some unexpected bumps and difficult turns (First Reading). But that is the story of vocation. And of God's will in our lives.

We find our true vocation in the discernment of what God has in mind for us, mediated in prayer and through others. The commitment to love all people brings us into contact with the God who emptied himself for his people. This single-minded, incarnational love shows us how to love God—with all our heart, mind, and will. Paul knew this when he told the Corinthians that without love, "I am nothing." (Contrast this "gift" with more transitory "gifts" we might like for ourselves. Perhaps even some good gifts in contrast to love.)

The following of the will of God and loving one another fully may hurt; in fact, I can promise you that if we "love everyone in truth of heart" as the Collect tells us, we will be in pain at some point. We may find ourselves in conflict with family, friends, and even the nation and its values (or lack thereof). We are pro-life, fighting for the rights of the unborn and an end to capital punishment, and promoting life that draws to its natural conclusion in God's time, not ours. Our country is not interested in preserving these values, by and large. That is not a reason to condemn, but a reason to love. That is tough. But we don't love our values; we love each other. We may face rejection when we bring others liberation and insight. But that is what it means to follow a vocational call.

Fifth Sunday in Ordinary Time

Readings from the Ambo

Isa 6:1-2a, 3-8; Ps 138:1-2, 2-3, 4-5, 7-8;
1 Cor 15:1-11; Luke 5:1-11

The **First Reading** last week detailed the prophet Jeremiah's understanding of his vocation; today it is Isaiah's turn. The contrast between the two prophets is striking and hearkens back to their image of God. Jeremiah's contemplative reflection on his summons to ministry is based on his understanding of the Lord as one who has knit him together in a preconscious manifestation of the divine will. God thought of Jeremiah even before he was conceived. On the other hand, Isaiah's vision of God—transcendent, lofty, unapproachable in his holiness, except through angels—is much more in line with the vision of Ezekiel (1:3-11). God dwells in Jerusalem for this eighth-century prophet and the Lord's otherness demarcates himself from all other entities, especially all that is unclean, a factor that brings Isaiah up short, gasping for air: "For I am a man of unclean lips, / living among a people of unclean lips; / yet my eyes have seen the King, the LORD of hosts!"

There is a kind of cognitive dissonance at work here that will inform Isaiah's conversion. The prophet is amazed that despite the gulf between sordid humanity and the Holy Lord God, he has beheld that same God in a vision. And even further, this transcendent Other calls the prophet into mission. The marvelous image of the burning ember is a liturgical gesture, since this purifying element has been taken from the altar. The response from Isaiah is bold and unequivocal: "'Here I am,' I said; 'send me!'" It might be interesting to contrast Moses' encounter with the burning bush in Exodus chapter 3 with the present passage, particularly in regard to the mediated presence of the angels and the liturgy as an agent for sanctification. Although coming from another literary tradition, Israel's great leader removes his sandals because he is "on holy ground," and then receives the encounter with God and call to mission. Isaiah is also purified, albeit in a more elaborate, liturgical way. But both of these great figures in Israel are sanctified before they go on to mission.

There is a rather significant echo in the dynamic between God and Isaiah repeated in Jesus' call of the disciples, particularly Simon Peter. In the **Gospel** Peter must face the Christ who renews and builds and sanctifies in the context of his own bareness and sterility. It is God's goodness in Christ that causes Simon Peter to say, "Depart from me, Lord, for I am a sinful man." And much like the God who calls Isaiah into ministry, Jesus invites Peter, a wounded reflection of creation, into his circle of trusted friends and disciples. "Do not be afraid; from now on you will be catching men."

In the **Second Reading** Paul puts his own unworthiness at bay in order to do whatever the risen Lord has called him to do when he tells the Corinthians, "Last of all, as to one born abnormally, he appeared to me. For I am the least of the apostles, not fit to be called an apostle, because I persecuted the church of God." Paul reckons his own apostleship precisely from being born outside of history, or in Greek, the noun in question is *ektroma*, which literally means "an abortion." The Spanish translation of the Greek text typically uses this term (*el aborto*), which represents a fascinating contrast to Jeremiah's articulation of being divinely comprehended before conception. What does this make Paul? We might say, in a word, *born again* with an encounter with the risen Lord. Indeed, the recognition of personal unworthiness and being called to holiness and mission will be a dynamic that only an encounter of faith can rectify. It is as if Paul is making a complete break with the past (new name after all) and his vocation comes not from tracing his origins, or a liturgical sanctification, but a complete break, by virtue of the risen Lord.

Connecting the Bible and the Liturgy

The Entrance Antiphon (Psalm 95) and the Collect present the Christian community with contrasting images of God, not unlike the way Jeremiah and Isaiah understand their own relationship with the Lord. "O come, let us worship God," begins the **Entrance Antiphon**, *"et procidamus ante Dominum"* (let us bow low before God), *"qui fecit nos quia ipse est Dominus Deus noster"* (who made us, for he is the Lord our God). I imagine this Antiphon as a kind of prelude to Isaiah's experience with the Lord of Hosts at his vocational calling in the First Reading; he sees the all Holy One before whom he bows and acknowledges his own creaturehood and sinfulness. We might say that Simon Peter is also in here as well, as the faltering man who understands his own sin and the magnitude of the one who stands before him, bringing in fish where once there was nothing.

At the same time, though, the **Collect** pictures God as a pastoral Caregiver of the human family, protecting humankind in love. "Keep your family safe, O Lord, with unfailing care, / that, relying solely on the hope of heavenly grace, / they may be defended always by your protection." The words *"familiam tuam"* (your family) and *"continua pietate custodi"* (with unfailing care) have a gentleness, especially when reinforced by *"tua semper protectione muniatur"* (defended always by your protection). This is a portrait of a Father with *pietate*— dutiful and religious, a very moving way to think about the living God—as truly living indeed! Such a description might have been invented by the likes of Jeremiah recognizing his vocation as coming from the Lord who knew him from the womb and guided him by the divine will and power to move the prophet into mission.

The **Prayer over the Offerings** brings these two realities, the transcendent God and the *continua pietate* custody of the Father, into focus: "O Lord our God, / who once established these created things / to sustain us in our frailty, / grant, we pray, / that they may become for us now / the Sacrament of eternal life." The prayer acknowledges God, the Creator and sustainer, and also our frailty and the need to be sustained. Surely underneath this text we can hear the Simon Peter at the feet of Jesus, saying, "Depart from me, Lord, for I am a sinful man." Indeed, our frailty has been named by prophets like Isaiah who saw for himself that he lived among unclean people and was himself one of unclean lips. Yet still we have been given sustenance to help us in our fragility because God has "willed that we be partakers / in the one Bread and the one Chalice." So despite our sin, we are invited to the table of the Lord. Even though we may think that the Lord should depart from our midst, you and I are called into mission—to be fishers, so that "we may joyfully bear fruit / for the salvation of the world" (**Prayer after Communion**).

Strategy for Preaching

The marvelous and often overlooked spiritual dynamic present in the biblical and liturgical readings today present the congregation with a recognition of God's transcendence, together with his care and love as the eternal Father. Running through this awareness of the Holy is our own sense of contingency and sin. And it comes in precisely this order: like Isaiah we sense the awesome God and then understand our own sinful life against the backdrop of the Holy. Some of the most disastrous preaching forces a congregation into a sinful category of moral misbehavior from the start and then may eventually get to God, maybe not. This kind of moral harangue runs something like this: "We are sinners and the world drags us into its terrible life that ignores God." Such a statement may very well be true (although whatever the so-called "world" is can be anyone's guess or personal dislike at the moment), but Isaiah and Peter and the apostle Paul recognize their own personal frailty and sinfulness (in Isaiah it is also the people of the world) by first encountering God's holiness. Isaiah sees the overwhelming *contrast* of the Lord of Hosts with his own unclean society and even his own unclean lips. Peter senses Jesus' wonders in the depths of the sea and recognizes his own inability to imagine hope. Paul had to encounter the risen Lord before he could understand what conversion meant outside of zealous followers of the law. It is not enough just to say we are sinners; it has to be sensed in the context of what we are lacking compared to the infinite holiness and love of God. So the core homiletic idea for today might follow this twofold "punch": We stand in the presence of the Holy as we gather, yet despite our frailty and sins we are called to eat at the same table with the Lord in love and mercy.

For those involved in liturgical planning, the biblical readings make a good case for a rich fare of worship, evoking the Holy God. In this context, the Entrance Antiphon and its acknowledgment of God's utter transcendence before whom we bow becomes most appropriate. Isaiah shows a similar posture before the sanctuary of the Lord of Hosts. "Holy, Holy, Holy": we share the *Sanctus* with the awe of the prophet.

We know we shrink as Peter did before Jesus' wonders. Who among us could imagine the hope provided by Christ's holiness and the call to be holy as God is holy? Think of how many times we have refused grace—missed opportunities to see Christ fish in deep waters. (Illustrations: personal example invites the preacher's own acknowledgment of failure; some other specific moments in the local community.)

Yes: we are still invited to eat with the Lord and are called into mission by the God who sees us as a family (Collect). Can we imagine saying with the prophet Isaiah, "Here I am, send me!?" For the Eucharist was provided by Christ to sustain sinners, you and me, in our fragile lives (Prayer over the Offerings). (Image: Isaiah's embers from the altar have become the Bread of Life in the Christian vocation, sanctifying us into holiness.) We are called "to bear fruit," having seen the Lord, as the Prayer after Communion reminds us. And we are allied with Peter—sent forth to fish in the sea of life for the church and the sake of the world.

Sixth Sunday in Ordinary Time

Readings from the Ambo

Jer 17:5-8; Ps 1:1-2, 3, 4, 6; 1 Cor 15:12, 16-20; Luke 6:17, 20-26

I suspect that one of the fears that hinders Christian preachers from delivering the Good News is confronting a passage like this one from the prophet Jeremiah: "Cursed is the one who trusts in human beings, / who seeks his strength in flesh, / whose heart turns away from the LORD" (**First Reading**). The knee-jerk response to seeing a tough representation of God in the Hebrew Scriptures might be to ignore it altogether. That may be why so few homilies focus on the Old Testament; these are tough moments (Job, Jeremiah, Joshua); they articulate violence and anger at God and our fellow humans that we wish were not there. So we wind up with some deluded version of self-help advice from Jesus week after week instead of dealing with the hard questions posed by the Scriptures. There is no substitute for spending time with the word of God; we know from a historical-critical analysis of Hebrew Scriptures, particularly this one in Jeremiah, that underneath the prophet's anger lurks a redeemed message of consolation.

Chapter 17 in the book of Jeremiah is a retrospective turn to Israel's preexilic invasion and exile. Our passage forcefully begins with a curse because of the imminent threat that faces the chosen people. From a cultural-political point of view, for Jeremiah the trust in human beings and seeking strength in those other than God are the princes and the people who allied themselves with factions that were pro-Egyptian, ignoring the prophet's warning to the contrary. The result of such an axis of power was disaster. But the good news is the reward promised the righteous and the steadfast and, ultimately, the God who does not abandon his people. Indeed, the result

171

of steadfastness in the time of trial will be God-given strength in the desert. This "blessing" outweighs what looks like a complete abandonment of the prophet's vocation and trust in one's fellow human beings. Those who hope in the Lord still bear fruit, "like a tree planted beside the waters / that stretches out its roots to the stream." The **Responsorial Psalm** is textually linked to this passage in Jeremiah for reasons that should be obvious to those who are familiar with the psalm that begins the Psalter with the famous Latin line, *"Beatus vir,"* Happy the man. The psalm, at least on one level, has become a hymn for the postexilic community, celebrating hope in God and the righteousness of those who remain constant to the covenant of righteousness and the law. Psalm 1 and, indeed, Jeremiah's own return to the landscape of hope, become poems rejoicing in the hope that God alone can offer the Judeo-Christian community.

The Lukan version of the Beatitudes is also Good News to those who appear to be cursed—the hungry, the poor, the grieving, the despised. Jesus provides them with the hope that flourishes in troubled times and in difficult circumstances, even in a "year of drought." These sayings, well-known to be parallel with Matthew's version of the Beatitudes in chapter 5 of this **Gospel**, reverse the fortunes of those who consider themselves cursed. The unique twist, however, is that those who reckon themselves blessed or fortunate in the eyes of the world or rewarded are really the cursed ones—these will experience woes and devastation. Again, I think it is crucial that preachers mine the whole text in this Lukan passage simply because the blessings are only outstanding when we see the reversal of fortunes as Jesus depicts them. The overall thrust of this passage for the hearer, "from all Judea and Jerusalem and the coastal region of Tyre and Sidon," is that whether Gentile or Jew the business of blessings is God's to name and not ours. The world of grace bursts with the Good News that will confound those who think of themselves as blessed because, as Psalm 1 puts it, "the Lord watches over the way of the just, / but the way of the wicked vanishes."

In the **Second Reading** Paul tells the Corinthians in no uncertain terms that the greatest curse of all—death—has been reversed by the blessing of Christ's resurrection. Paul has demonstrated that he will venture down a logical turn of implications, if there is "no resurrection of the dead." He takes us to the bitter end, where we will be considered "the most pitiable people of all." But in his own reversal, Paul shows himself to be a person of hope in God's righteousness.

It is not just our fruit that produces fruit in the desert, but Christ himself: the firstfruits of those who have fallen asleep.

Connecting the Bible and the Liturgy

The **Collect** this Sunday sets the tone for the *"Beatus vir,"* the righteous one, who "delights in the law of the Lord / and meditates on his law day and night." We might say that those gathered for worship are contemplating the law of love, of perfect charity and the hope given to us by Christ himself, the *Beatus vir*, the righteous Son who has borne fruit and keeps faith forever, the firstfruits of those who have fallen asleep. Moreover, love itself has come to make his dwelling with those who bid him welcome at the Eucharist. So interpreted, the Collect becomes a plea from the assembly to be made into a righteous dwelling place: "O God, who teach us that you abide / in hearts that are just and true, / grant that we may be so fashioned by your grace / as to become a dwelling pleasing to you."

At the same time, our house needs to be swept clean from the scourge of sin, or what Jeremiah referred to as "a barren bush in the desert," which "stands in a lava waste, / a salt and empty earth." In a word, the people of God require a sanctification from all that is not of God, all that is not "true and just." The Eucharist itself promises this very sanctifying action as we make our offering in accord with God's will, the unifying action of Christ himself, who was righteous and blessed by God as Son, though thought to be cursed on the cross. As the **Prayer over the Offerings** says, "May this oblation, O Lord, we pray, / cleanse and renew us / and may it become for those who do your will / the source of eternal reward." This prayer points the congregation in the direction of the Beatitudes—the blessings that can be named at the liturgy through the gift of Christ's sanctification. The crucified and shamed Lord takes us up into the cross of blessing, freeing us from sin and death. We recognize that it is God who has justified us by raising Christ from the dead, reversing death's power over us. The preaching of that resurrection brings hope to those who are poor, hungry, and grieving. If left to our own devices we may find ourselves in a world of woes, satisfied for "now" but ultimately like "chaff which the wind drives away."

The Liturgy of the Eucharist, then, is formative and sanctifying as always in preaching Christ risen from the dead, the firstfruits of those who have fallen asleep. He is the cross planted near the running water of baptism "that yields its fruit in due season, / and whose leaves never fade." In the end, the grace of the liturgy gathers a people out of the exile of woes and into God's circle of promise for new life in Christ. And so the refrain for the Responsorial Psalm reminds us, "Blessed are they who hope in the Lord."

Strategy for Preaching

Chapter 15 in Paul's First Letter to the Corinthians is entirely absorbed in a clarification of the resurrection from the dead, the kernel of which forms the Second Reading, as we have seen. Paul's own preaching emerged from his experience of the risen Lord, so the question "how can some among you say there is no resurrection of the dead?" cuts to the core of the life of his experience of God in Christ. Put more generally and in the context of other readings this weekend, God has blessed us in the new life of grace, transforming the woe and curse of death into new life in Christ Jesus. To understand this core homiletic idea is to live the life of the Beatitudes as Luke represents them, reversals of worldly expectation into the hope coming from God's justice and righteousness.

A good strategy for beginning the homily is to lean into the potential darkness and doubt that we may want to avoid. But realistically speaking, such thick clouds often face those gathered for worship and they await a word of hope from the preacher. Paul must have sensed the Corinthians' ambivalence in regard to God bestowing new life as well and so deployed a deductive logic to dispel those doubts. What are the barren landscapes, with their barren bushes and salty wastes that have formed on our horizon? Name those demons. I will bet fear of death is near the top of the list.

But the Eucharist proclaims Christ as the firstfruits of those who have fallen asleep (Second Reading). The life of grace makes us long for the good, the work of charity to have "hearts that are just and true," as the Collect tells us. The place of worship gathers the hearers near the river of God, where Christ's cross bears fruit in due season, beside flowing waters. What was formerly a desert is now living water for the righteous who remain steadfast (First Reading; Responsorial Psalm).

There are probably a thousand and one reasons to doubt and lose hope. It is when we are surrounded by the hot lava and suffering of exile (image drawn from the First Reading) in sin that we face our bareness. (Illustrate with specific naming of difficult contemporary situations.) The Corinthians certainly had their own reasons for doubting—all of them realistic and, indeed, justified. And yet, perhaps this is less a question of justified reasoning than the One who justifies us by his own righteousness. For this is less a question of faith than it is of hope. And it is hope that drives the Beatitudes, which anticipate a complete reversal of fortunes for those who are poor, hungry, and longing for justice (Gospel). The resurrection was already being proclaimed by Christ to Jews and Gentiles alike even before it happened! We are sanctified by those fruits at this Eucharist (Prayer over the Offerings). This Eucharist has set the table of hope for all creation so that we may love more fully. That is the new life of the resurrection even now, which tells us what awaits us in the future.

Seventh Sunday in Ordinary Time

Readings from the Ambo

*1 Sam 26:2, 7-9, 12-13, 22-23; Ps 103:1-2, 3-4, 8, 10, 12-13;
1 Cor 15:45-49; Luke 6:27-38*

Today's readings marshal a preacher's dream insofar as these texts fit together to form an illustrative and theological unity.

The **Gospel** taken from chapter 6 in Luke continues the so-called "Sermon on the Plain" (Luke 6:17-49), which began last week with the Beatitudes. Having introduced the blessings and the woes, Jesus initiates not just a series of new ideas, but a completely new horizon for thinking as God does. Redemption comes because God has undone the mighty and lifted up the lowly. This attitude is the perspective of Mary's *Magnificat*, which, in some sense, is the lens through which Luke-Acts is conceived. The passage for today further glosses the new perspective that calls those blessed who may be despised. It is not a time for gloating over those mighty ones who will finally get what is due to them, but a moment to seize for the sake of loving. It is the one who is injured who will now do the blessing and must refuse to curse: "To you who hear I say, love your enemies, do good to those who hate you, bless those who curse you, pray for those who mistreat you."

We cannot grasp the theological importance of Jesus' use of the word bless because the earlier text on the Beatitudes uses this expression rather differently than what we see in today's readings. Recall that in a series of several astounding sentences, last week's Gospel referred to the downtrodden and the poor as *makarios*—that is, *beatus* or happy or blessed. Or, we might say, more colloquially, lucky. God has done the blessing here. But when Jesus says "bless those who curse you" (*kataromenous*) in the subsequent verses (6:27 ff.), he is saying in the imperative *eulogeite*—celebrate with blessings and praise—those who curse you. That makes us the agent of charity and bestows on the human subject the power to bless.

The illustration of such a blessing comes to this crucial theological precept and virtue in the **First Reading**, in which David refuses to murder the Lord's anointed. This is actually the second time in 1 Samuel that David has spared Saul's life (cf. chap. 24) and does so outside the norms of warfare and the clannish goading of Abishai. Indeed, to those who would see Providence working to their advantage, it would appear that even God favors the slaying of Saul, since Abishai tells David that "God has delivered your enemy into your grasp this day." Nevertheless, for David, the higher norm is doing good, even praising the Lord's anointed.

And for Paul in the **Second Reading**, all of us are the Lord's anointed since we bear the image of Christ. That requires a transformation from an earthly way of thinking to a heavenly perspective—a thinking with the mind of the Beatitudes. "Just as we have borne the image of the earthly one," Paul tells the Corinthians about the first man, Adam, "we shall also bear the image of the heavenly one." That is the image of Christ that all Christians own by virtue of their baptism. At the same time, since Christ died for the "many," those who bear his image are unknown to us. So the law of charity is universalized to all humankind, not just those who are good to us, but even those who cause us pain.

Connecting the Bible and the Liturgy

The **Collect** gathers the Christian community to ponder this second Adam, as it were, the spiritual man, Jesus Christ, when it says, "Grant, we pray, almighty God, / that, always pondering spiritual things, / we may carry out in both word and deed / that which is pleasing to you." I take it that *"quae tibi sunt placita"* means pleasing in the sense of being in union with God in Christ and living the life of the Beatitudes—perhaps a reversal of our usual way of thinking. So, pleasing God does not mean pleasing ourselves, but carrying the image of the spiritual man with us and recognizing the same imprint in our brothers and sisters.

There is a very poignant moment in the *Confiteor*, an option collectively recited during the **Introductory Rites**, of course, which acknowledges the honor we owe one another as images of the spiritual man, the second Adam. *"Confiteor Deo omnipotenti et vobis fratres."* When we "confess to almighty God / and to you, my brothers and sisters," we have been invited to bless one another and admit our own guilt, "that I have greatly sinned, / in my thoughts and in my words, / in what I have done and in what I have failed to do." This admission of wrongdoing before the whole assembly acknowledges the failure to *eulogeite* another, but, in a sense, cursed (*kataromenous*) them by thoughts, word, and deed. And in so doing, we have offended almighty God as well, who blesses those we have marginalized by our sins. There is a little Abishai in all of us, begging our David to slay the anointed before us. Jesus wants us to resist him.

The words of institution in the Eucharist urges us on to the law of love in the language of the kingdom, as the words of institution remind us. Christ took, blessed, broke, and gave the bread to his disciples after he had given thanks. And then gave the cup to his disciples, saying, "Take this, all of you, and drink from it, / for this is the chalice of my Blood, / the Blood of the new and eternal covenant, / which will be poured out for you and for many [*pro multis*] / for the forgiveness of sins." In such words of blessing, we encounter the supreme act of God's reversal of fortune: a covenant of love that redeems humanity. We witness to each other the image of the heavenly man in lives of love poured out for one another.

Strategy for Preaching

The perspective of the Beatitudes that embodies Jesus' Sermon on the Plain might be characterized as leaning into the surprising mercy of God's future. In this regard, the radical charity Jesus proposes in 6:27ff. bears witness to this future reality now. In this way, the world Jesus promises is not a dreamland, but the present world that gestures toward the future to come in which we bless and do not curse one another. So the core homiletic idea for today might be this: Jesus commands us to love one another now, and that charity remains his own image brought to the world.

An intriguing point of departure might be to explore the details of David's relationship with Saul (First Reading) and his refusal to strike down the Lord's anointed and its connection with how we live our lives to either please God or please ourselves. Blessing another is not what our society encourages. As the phrase goes in contemporary parlance, "Don't get mad, get even." David had an opportunity twice to get even, but honoring the Lord's anointed was more important than the satisfaction of revenge, even to one who sought his life.

We honor each other as anointed of the Lord as we come to worship. For the beginning we confess our sins not only to God but to one another (*Confiteor*). Our gathering as a baptized assembly is the acknowledgment that the first Adam has been replaced by the second Adam, the earthly for the heavenly (Second Reading). We have come together as one Body in Christ.

That is the now of the Eucharist: the law of love has come in our midst and changed our perspective from what our DNA says—thinking earthly—to thinking heavenly. (At this point, the congregation of listeners may be asking, "What does this look like?" So, illustrate the theological: What does it look like to see the law of love change our perspective or to live the Beatitudes?)

The Collect invites us to ponder these heavenly blessings right here among one another by naming grace in our midst. (Image: diversity in unity, such as a family reunion in which one of the family members brings back a spouse who is from another race or religion.) We surrender our swords, which is to say, our power interests, for the sake of Christ. Someone once described humility as having the power over someone else to get even but refusing to do so or use these "weapons," whatever they may be. Sounds a lot like David and Saul in 1 Samuel. This is what it means to encounter the Lord's anointed—as we do at this liturgy—which calls us to love now.

Eighth Sunday in Ordinary Time

Readings from the Ambo

Sir 27:4-7; Ps 92:2-3, 13-14, 15-16; 1 Cor 15:54-58; Luke 6:39-45

The book of Sirach may not count as one of the most thrilling texts in the Bible, but its wisdom to ancient and contemporary culture remains immeasurable. Human nature is what it is, to be sure, inflected by historical circumstances. Ben Sira, in yoking together wisdom for the dispersed Jewish community of his day—then undergoing the process of Hellenization—was tapping into deeply religious traits; his recollection would undergird not only the service of the law and Jewish tradition, but future generations of Jews (and little did he know, Gentiles) would look to the wisdom of Sirach for direction in the time of our own dispersion.

The larger portion of the book of Sirach, from which our very small section was taken for the **First Reading** today, deals with the wisdom of virtuous living. Revenge and its antidote, hospitality, slander and its remedy, kindness in speech, become thoughtful considerations to one seeking to reestablish a tradition of the law of Moses. But Ben Sira goes deeper to suggest what certain traits reveal about a person's overall character and integrity. In this regard, the triple metaphor the author deploys discloses how speech becomes a kind of test to uncover faults. We end with, "As the test of what the potter molds is in the furnace, / so in tribulation is the test of the just." Ben Sira means to tell us that it is speech that becomes the barometer to "the bent of one's mind."

In a similar way, Jesus begins to round out his Sermon on the Plain in Luke's **Gospel** with a series of parallels that also are meant to discover the truth of what is underneath. "For every tree [same image from Sirach] is known by its own fruit. . . . A good person out of the store of goodness in his heart produces good, but an evil person out of a store of evil produces evil; for from the fullness of the heart the mouth speaks." Such language supports Jesus' teaching on removing the wooden beam in one's own eye before trying to take out the splinter in someone else's eye. In a word, Ben Sira and Jesus are both suggesting that the core of human experience is authentic living while false behavior and hypocrisy will eventually show itself even in a flood of words.

Wisdom tells us to cling to what will last; words disappear and appearances betray. Paul's theology fits well here in the **Second Reading** when he tells the Corinthians to be "firm, steadfast, always fully devoted to the work of the Lord, knowing that in the Lord your labor is not in vain." Why? Because what endures is what matters. God has given us the victory in Christ to clothe our mortal bodies with incorruptibility. It is this immortality that will last, like the character of one tried in the fire or the fruit from a good tree. As Psalm 92 tells us, "They that are planted in the house of the LORD / shall flourish in the courts of our God."

Connecting the Bible and the Liturgy

If the biblical readings focus our attention on what language discloses, how it reveals the core of the human subject and directs our attention to what truly matters—the incorruptibility of God's gift—we might see a very interesting relationship unfolding between today's readings and the liturgy. What does the language of the Eucharist tell us about the heart of the church? Fascinating. Or again, we may probe: What does the language of the preacher tell us about our interior life?

In contemplating the language of the church's liturgy, we have meditation and fruits for a lifetime. In the final analysis, though, we are the people of God planted as so many trees in the soil of the world. And it is the church's liturgy that guides our path along the ways of justice and truth as we bear the fruit of Christ's victory over death to all. As the **Collect** says today, "Grant us, O Lord, we pray, / that the course of our world / may be directed by your peaceful rule / and that your Church may rejoice, / untroubled in her devotion." The heart of the church beats for the love of God's people, speaking, through Christ, a word of praise and thanksgiving back to the Father.

There will be an enormous range to consider in the language of the liturgy that speaks from the fullness of the gift of the Spirit given to us. I will briefly suggest three pivotal points in the Eucharist that disclose the heart of the church, three areas that we may point to as manifesting the fruit of our liturgical speech: the epiclesis, the words of institution, and the Our Father. Doubtless, many will offer other possibilities; I suggest these only as ways to uncover an understanding of the truth manifested in what we speak at the church's liturgy.

The epiclesis, of course, reaches down to the church's deep center, asking the Spirit to come pouring out upon the gifts we have presented in the most humble way imaginable. *"Supplices ergo te Domine, deprecamur,"* "by the same Spirit graciously make holy / these gifts we have brought to you for consecration, / that they may become the Body and Blood / of your Son our Lord Jesus Christ, / at whose command we celebrate these mysteries" (**Eucharistic Prayer III**). The language of petition is the ground zero of human expression: we have no words but petition to ask for the gift of the Spirit from the Father and ask in our deepest need that we might be worthy to receive the Body and Blood of Christ to feed his people.

Secondly, the words of institution suggest an ecclesial language in union with the Savior who offered himself once and for all as the perfect gift for humanity. *"Accipite et manducate ex hoc omnes . . . accipiter et bibite ex eo omnes"* and the words that follow these expressions of consecration inside the anaphora reveal a church at one with him who died for us, repeat that offering, and say again and again as a memorial: *"Hoc facite in meam commemorationem."* In this regard, the church's language is essentially a memorial of the God who loves us; we express in Word and sacrament God's deeds until he comes again.

Lastly, the Our Father reveals the church at communal prayer with an uplifted heart, giving thanks to the Father. Indeed, the Our Father comes as Jesus' response to his disciples on how to pray; its language is most essential to address the Father in our need. The multiplication of words at prayer reveals something about our interior disposition, but the Our Father does as well. The authentic prayer of one addressing God discloses the faith community asking that the will of God be done, that we receive our daily bread, that we are reconciled to God and one another, and that we are not led into temptations. The Our Father is the church at prayer—it is Christ praying in us in the Eucharist. And so, what other language do we need to address God in our need?

Strategy for Preaching

Contemporary American culture has seen, and will continue to experience, a great deal of tension around the First Amendment. Freedom of speech was legislated in the Bill of Rights to reinforce a constitutional guarantee. Groups on the left and the right have their perspectives on how to shape this Right. How the use of speech plays itself out will be something for the preacher to observe, especially as social networks grow on the Internet, religious groups become protective of their own freedoms and rights, and the changing world introduces more variables into the equation. As we are flooded with more and more words—some of which thrive simply on shock value—what does this do to the sacred text? Is our sacred Scripture and liturgical language just part of the flood of words? From the perspective of Ben Sira in the First Reading, it would seem that the human family has been entrusted by God to assess what we hear and make a judgment about its interior worth. Jesus certainly recognizes that what will come forth on the lips is indicative of what is in the heart.

One way of structuring the homily for today might be to use the liturgy as a way to explore these biblical values. The core homiletic idea for today might be, if the Body of Christ were to speak the language of prayer to the Father, what would that look like? Here, I am imagining an invitation to think with the mind of the church, as the saying goes, while maintaining freedom of expression and speech, and religious freedom.

Structuring the homily along the lines I have suggested in the previous section might be useful, mindful, of course, that the preacher must beware that his own language will be an indicator of who he is and what he is about. When we are at our best, when Christ lives in us as the people of God, we express the language of petition, memorial, and unity.

Here is something of an outline to start thinking about what this preaching might look like:

I. We can tell a lot about who people are when they are at their most vulnerable and needy (hospitals, funerals, even children serve as examples).

   A. *Epiklesis*: the church petitions the Father to send forth the Spirit, the Spirit we need to re-create us in Christ and who cries, "Abba, Father."

   B. Life in the Spirit reveals who we are by what we ask for (First Reading).

II. Our language is also a memorial. This is one of the primary functions of language: to reenact, to relive an original moment (stories are obvious examples and so are the traditions handed down in the family).

   A. Words of institution repeat Christ's words at the Last Supper; we receive life through the church's memory of the Savior on the night before he died for us.

III. We also reveal the Body of Christ as people of God in the Our Father. We show our commitment to be reconciled with one another, to forgive us our trespasses as we forgive, to be delivered from temptations.

   A. The Gospel confronts the hypocrisy we all share, the judgments we exercise against our brother and sister in the Lord.

   B. Jesus encourages us to be dependent on the Body of Christ, asking the Father for our daily bread.

   C. The church and our identity is revealed in the liturgical language of the Holy; we partake of eternal gifts so that we might be clothed in immortality (Second Reading).

Ninth Sunday in Ordinary Time

Readings from the Ambo

1 Kgs 8:41-43; Ps 117:1, 2; Gal 1:1-2, 6-10; Luke 7:1-10

It may seem at first blush that the three readings have very little in common in today's ensemble from the Sunday Lectionary. And yet Solomon, Paul, and Jesus encounter the word of God in different ways, each event revealing a great deal about who they are in relationship with the God and the people they serve.

Solomon's prayer in the **First Reading** is a portion of the larger oration from the monarch (8:12-61), well known to be authored by the Deuteronomic historian who was evidently editing several crucial strands of Israelite tradition in the present context. The reading today focuses on the sixth of nine petitions; this one concerns asking God to grant prayers to the *go'im* or Gentiles who pray in the temple. We get a snapshot here of a rather eclectic and, dare we say, global vision of Israel's monarchy, which images its wise king as the host of a temple for all people. This particular attitude may also say something about what Solomon's temple might include: a kind of central point of worship for all the nations. Even the short psalm (117) given as part of the **Responsorial Psalm** suggests such universal worship when it says, "Praise the Lord, all you nations; / glorify him, all you peoples!"

By contrast, Paul's message to the Galatians wishes not to centralize but to particularize those who gather for worship. "[I]f anyone preaches to you a gospel other than what you have received, let that one be accursed!" (**Second Reading**). The accusation the apostle makes to the community in Galatians comes as something of an astonishment in a Pauline greeting, usually characterized for its thanksgiving. But abandoning the word of God by listening to those

185

who "wish to pervert the gospel of Christ" certainly discloses the anger Paul felt at those who were undermining his evangelical efforts. And yet, when seen in the light of the First Reading, we can begin to understand the ancient and strange dialectic between pluralism (all nations gathering in the temple) and orthodoxy (there is only the one gospel "that we preached to you").

The Gentile centurion seems to make the case for a more inclusive **Gospel**, open to Gentiles. Despite his struggle with the Galatians, Paul would become a proponent to those outside Judaism, but still preach the same Gospel: it is the word that must gather those who would become one Body, the true word spoken by the Word himself. It is for this word that the centurion longs, "for I am not worthy to have you enter under my roof. Therefore, I did not consider myself worthy to come to you; but say the word and let my servant be healed." So Jesus pronounces the centurion as even greater than any Jew, for "not even in Israel have I found such faith." Jesus and Gentile can gather together in the one Gospel that has sent forth the word from the Word himself. Christ gathers all people who would hear the one Gospel to himself, a living temple of God: unity in the midst of diversity.

Connecting the Bible and the Liturgy

Perhaps the most obvious connection associated with the Bible and the liturgy this Sunday occurs in the congregation's response to the elevation of the consecrated elements at the *Ecce Agnus Dei*: "Lord, I am not worthy / that you should enter under my roof, / but only say the word / and my soul shall be healed." This liturgical prayer, with a significant alteration, mirrors the centurion's affirmation of Christ to heal his servant. In the same way, the baptized assembly prays to be sanctified by the gifts of Christ's Body and Blood. Saying the word—a gesture that comes from the Word himself—heals even outside the confines of boundaries, separating people one from the other. Jesus does not have to be present to heal: he has sent for his word to touch the servant. In this way, the Lord crosses traditional borders in ethnicity and religious practices, since the Gentile Roman centurion, an adversary of Israel, has given faith to a Jew.

The power of the word to gather and heal and galvanize is what Paul emphasizes to the Galatians and does not wish them to lose:

one Gospel that may not be perverted. The word has been turned loose and seems to have a life all its own, but it must be safeguarded in faith. As the Responsorial Psalm says, "Go out to all the world and tell the good news." And again at the **Dismissal**: "Go and announce the Gospel of the Lord." The congregation is charged with the healing power of the Good News to bring sanctification.

The **Prayer after Communion** reminds us to bring the word to all as well. In this regard, the mission of the people of God is to gather all nations into the great tent of God's mercy and compassion. "Govern by your Spirit, we pray, O Lord, / those you feed with the Body and Blood of your Son, / that, professing you not just in word or in speech, / but also in works and in truth, / we may merit to enter the Kingdom of Heaven." Our actions follow our words, if they be authentic and from the heart. Such tools of good works gather others into God's great circle of love.

Strategy for Preaching

What about the power of the word to be living and active in our lives and in the lives of those we serve in ministry? This is a good question for preachers, generally speaking, but certainly true today in a special way as the centurion places his complete trust in Christ to just "say the word." With all Paul's frustration with the Galatians, it is his own belief in the power of the living word, the Gospel of Christ, that causes him to be so forceful to those who seem to be slipping into "another gospel." This does not mean that we live without diversity; we just let the one Gospel gather all into one. The centurion's faith made him greater than an Israelite, according to Jesus. And Solomon's temple was the home for all nations to hear and make known the activity of the word. So the core homiletic idea for today might be that God has sent forth his word to gather, heal, and liberate his people and we respond in faith and mission.

Last week's readings are somewhat tentatively related to the present texts this Sunday insofar as the way language becomes an instance for a divine sacramental encounter for the human subject. So if we saw how we used language as a window into the self last week, this Sunday we might ask what the word has been doing in us. By way of introduction the homily may recall for the congregation the first moments of learning how to read ("See Tom go; run, Tom, run!") or being read to ("Once upon a time . . ."). These instances of childhood discovery are major moments of transformation with words; they show the power words have over us to shape who we are; they seem to have a power all their own.

The centurion's encounter with the living Word was life changing for him and his servant. Faith was a word that brought about a healing under his very roof; his faith in Christ allowed the Word to go forth and heal. We ask for the same healing as the divine elements are elevated during the *Ecce Agnus Dei*: "only say the word / and my soul shall be healed."

But corrupt words—gossip, slander, lies—also travel fast. Rather than heal, they tear down. (Story about how gossip or lies have injured a person's reputation or a modern parable using the same.) It is possible to pervert the word of God, as Paul tells the Galatians, so that the one Gospel is no longer proclaimed. When we gossip or lie, we are preaching another gospel.

How we hear the word and how we speak its truth have a direct effect on who we are and what we do. We will either be gathered into the temple of the Lord, that is, Christ himself, or we will scatter. The Dismissal says, "Go and announce the Gospel of the Lord." If we have encountered the Word deeply in this Eucharist—our soul healed—then this proclamation of the one Gospel of Christ will be compelled by the Spirit. Jesus, like Solomon before him, wants to gather all God's children into a temple of faith, ready to give thanks and offer our petitions for our needs. We ask for a word to be healed. This is the Word that gathers us. This is why we have come—so our souls will be healed.

Tenth Sunday in Ordinary Time

Readings from the Ambo

*1 Kgs 17:17-24; Ps 30:2, 4, 5-6, 11, 12, 13;
Gal 1:11-19; Luke 7:11-17*

The meaning of the prophet Elijah's name is a clue to his fate: "My God is the Lord." He is a man utterly focused on God's will and the destiny of the northern kingdom. His involvement with Ahab and Jezebel is perhaps his most famous relationship, but Elijah is an other-worldly figure, a bigger than life prophet who is even able, as we see in today's **First Reading**, to raise the dead.

Elijah is in fairly dangerous territory when the prophet is sent by God to Zarephath of Sidon to the house of a widow. This area would be Phoenician territory, dominated by the worship of Baal. In the midst of this area, Elijah stays with a widow who feeds him and whose son suddenly dies. At this point, we can sense the close alliance 1 Kings 17:17-24 has with Luke 7:11-17 (together with 2 Kings 4:8-37, when Elisha, Elijah's protégé, raises the Shunammite's son). The two widows of 1 Kings and Luke's **Gospel** have lost their sons, placing the women in a very precarious and difficult position. We know that from antiquity Israel has been advised to care for the widow and the orphan, but that did not change the reality of a social condition that would have named such widows as cursed. This is why the widow in 1 Kings reacts so violently to Elijah when she says to him, "Why have you done this to me, O man of God? Have you come to me to call attention to my guilt and to kill my son?" She believes that her guilt has been discovered by the prophet (the passage does not say for what). Therefore she is now cursed. Although Jesus has no such conversation with the widow of Nain, we can also surmise that the loss of a son for a widow in first-century Palestine also meant shame and curse.

We might say that bringing new life to the sons of both widows meant not only restoring someone from the dead, but revealing a God who is about blessings and not curses. In both instances in our readings today, the sons are returned to the mothers, indicating a restoration of family and community. For the widow at Zarephath, the implication is that God does powerful works outside of Israel's domain, as Jesus would be quick to point out in Luke 4:25, to the consternation of his hearers at the beginning of his public ministry. For the widow at Nain, the restoration was indicative of the wonders that generated proclamation. New life brings the Word into being. "This report about him spread through the whole of Judea and in all the surrounding region."

As Paul looks back on his conversion, he is able to see the grace that the revelation of Jesus Christ gave him in lifting the shame and guilt of the past as well, "how I persecuted the church of God beyond measure and tried to destroy it . . ." (**Second Reading**). But in Paul's mind and in the lives of those he serves, he has been given new life because God "was pleased to reveal his Son to me, so that I might proclaim him to the Gentiles." Saul is dead; the new man, Paul the apostle, has risen. Much like the God who sent Elijah outside of Israelite territory, Paul has been missioned into the furthest ends of God's province, where there are no boundaries, no fences, no shame—just eternal life in Christ.

Connecting the Bible and the Liturgy

It would not take newcomers to the faith very long to figure out that the readings for this Sunday proclaim the new life already present among us and in a community of faith, living in the light of the risen Christ. The shame of sin, guilt, and death have been exiled, blotted out by Christ's redeeming work. The stain of the past, as Paul was astute to recognize, has been brought into the new hope of God's future. The Eucharist is the hope that brings new life. In chapter 17 of 1 Kings, Elijah revives the widow's son, having just before fed the famished household. The power of God has been unleashed on the prophet so that the jar of meal and the jug of oil "shall not go empty, nor . . . run dry"; there will be rain in the drought.

The invitation to the congregation to proclaim the **Mystery of Faith** has three different options, according to the *Roman Missal*,

but all of them announce the new life made possible by the grace of
the eucharistic Lord. All three profess liberation from sin and earth
by the proclamation of the one bread and the one cup. The third of
these has a special relationship with the biblical readings for today.
"Save us, Savior of the world, / for by your Cross and Resurrection /
you have set us free." This proclamation of the *Mysterium Fidei*
announces freedom not only from death, but also for those who are
shamed and cursed. We are brought into the eucharistic assembly
by the Christ who has gathered us at his table, restoring us from
alienation to community, true community. The first and second
options for our responses to the *Mysterium Fidei* for the assembly
will express the seemingly impossible reality that the baptized assembly will proclaim—Christ's death and resurrection and our hope
in God—*donec venias*, "until you come again." This is our response
in faith to the one who has freed us and will feed us. We have seen
wonders at this Eucharist, even as the widow of Zarephath sees and
believes: "Now indeed I know that you are a man of God. / The word
of the LORD comes truly from your mouth." The promise of new life
and restoration to the human family has brought hope where there
was despair and a future where there was despair and a dark past.

Strategy for Preaching

There is not an adult member of the baptized assembly, I would
bet, who has not wondered about—and sometimes confronted very
profoundly—the mystery of death and its consequences. In a sense,
the widows in the Hebrew Scriptures and the Gospel today were, for
all intents and purposes, as "dead" as their sons, since their life in
community was virtually destroyed by their childs' death by their
shame. Preachers are almost always pastoring someone and they will
invariably find those who have taken on shame, anger, and guilt
when someone close to them dies. I heard one woman at a hospital
say after her daughter died, "God is punishing me for something I
did." That attitude is not as uncommon as we might imagine; it is
sometimes voiced, sometimes not. But such thinking leads to bitterness and a loss of community. That is why Jesus and Elijah before
him restore community and human dignity by disclosing a God who
loves and blesses in the midst of darkness and death. To recognize
God's power over sin and death is to proclaim the mystery of faith.

So the core homiletic idea for this Sunday might be that in proclaiming the death and resurrection of the Lord in the Eucharist, we acknowledge God's power to save.

Any of the Memorial Acclamations of the Roman Rite, which were introduced in 1969 and revised in English in 2011, would be useful as a three-part structure. Let me use one of them by way of example, other than the one in the previous section: "We proclaim your Death, O Lord, / and profess your Resurrection / until you come again."

The introduction might focus on the reality of death and move toward the consequences—alienation, loneliness, meaninglessness. It would be useful, it seems to me, to bring in a cultural analysis of the history of Jewish widowhood at the time of Elijah and Jesus.

We proclaim Christ's death because God wants us to know that he has power over sin and death. God has no boundaries to his mercy (First Reading) in a territory that we would not expect. Jesus interrupts a funeral liturgy to bring restoration to another widow in the Gospel of Luke. (Image: restoration to family; could be a historical example of a kidnapped victim returned to parents and loved ones or perhaps a child lost in an amusement park and then found. Preachers should be attentive to the concrete details needed to enflesh the mystery of God's restoration.)

At a very important part in the Eucharist, we respond to the mystery of faith when we proclaim the death of the Lord and profess his resurrection. And God not only trumps the power of death, but its consequences as well. When we say that we acknowledge the new life that is possible in Christ Jesus we are, as brothers and sisters, returned to community right here at this Eucharist. Paul knew the power of proclaiming the risen Lord when he told the Galatians that God called him to preach to the Gentiles, despite his past persecution of the church. The past is just that: past. The past is erased by the glory of the resurrection. (Story of someone who perhaps faced an addiction but now has found new life.)

So we wait until he comes again. That will be the moment when Christ will draw all things to himself. The Eucharist, then, is a memorial of that saving meal he handed on to us on the night before he died because it proclaims Christ as victor. This bread and this cup are the language of the church, speaking back a word of praise and thanksgiving to the God who has loved us. That is the mystery of faith we profess.

Eleventh Sunday in Ordinary Time

Readings from the Ambo

2 Sam 12:7-10, 13; Ps 32:1-2, 5, 7, 11;
Gal 2:16, 19-21; Luke 7:36—8:3

Taken together, today's readings bring theological speculation into praxis: Paul famously tells the Galatians that "a person is not justified by works of the law but through faith in Jesus Christ" (**Second Reading**). Part of the background to this crucial claim is Paul's confrontation with Peter in Antioch, asking him how he could compel Gentiles to live like Jews, when Peter himself was living like a Gentile. So Paul proclaims that Jewish law will neither save nor justify, but only faith in Christ Jesus. This speculation, then, releases Gentiles from Jewish observance. But the implication is clear enough: both Gentiles *and* Jews are only justified by Christ, "that I might live for God. I have been crucified with Christ; yet I live, no longer I, but Christ lives in me; . . . for if justification comes through the law, then Christ died for nothing."

Two paradigms emerge in the context of Paul's discussion of justification; both concern the mercy and forgiveness of God. A case in point surfaces in the **First Reading**. Under Jewish law, David deserves to be stoned for committing adultery and strategically orchestrating the death of Uriah, the husband of his lover, Bathsheba. The prophetic intervention of Nathan confronts Israel's most illustrious king that he has "spurned the LORD and done evil in his sight." At the same time, however, comes the forgiveness of his grave sin, which David acknowledges. "The LORD on his part has forgiven your sin: you shall not die." There is still a penalty to pay, however, for "the sword shall never depart" from David's house and his descendants will face a long legacy of death and rebellion, a portion of which Israel's great king will himself witness as his dynasty unfolds.

In something of a contrast to David's sin portrayed in the First Reading, the gift of forgiveness Jesus offers to the woman who anoints his feet in Luke 7:36ff. is completely gratis, with no questions asked (**Gospel**). I think that a meditative moment in this very human encounter discloses precisely what is at stake between justification by the law and faith in Christ. Simon the Pharisee may be an observer of the law, as far as it goes, but his observance only takes him so far; it is limited and sterile, judging from his sense of hospitality. In a marvelous reversal, however, it is the woman Simon disdains by virtue of his self-justification of the law who becomes the true host in the household; she is the new host because of her love of Christ and the Lord's unconditional acceptance of her and her past. Her love, which is manifestation of her faith, has made her justified and righteous in the eyes of the Lord, something from which the Pharisee has been blinded. Simon can say very little in his defense, and, like the law itself, has no voice in the house of love, made fragrant not by speech but by the fragrant perfume of a justified sinner.

Connecting the Bible and the Liturgy

The *Roman Missal* advises that the Eucharistic Prayers for Reconciliation be used for a variety of occasions that support charity, forgiveness, harmony, and peace. Since the readings for today focus in a special way on God's mercy and forgiveness and the various responses to this divine action, at least adverting in some way to these Prayers (if not using them specifically on a Sunday in Ordinary Time) would seem appropriate.

When Jesus engages the woman in the house of Simon the Pharisee, it is the occasion of a great unfolding of God's mercy; the sheer literary force of the passage pulls no punches. As the **Eucharistic Prayer for Reconciliation I** says, "being rich in mercy, / you constantly offer pardon / and call on sinners / to trust in your forgiveness alone." Paul addresses the matter of how much sinners could be justified in his Letter to the Galatians, but the Preface echoes a similar reality of all of us being made righteous, even "though time and again we have broken your covenant, / you have bound the human family to yourself / through Jesus your Son, our Redeemer, /

with a new bond of love so tight / that it can never be undone." One senses here the Pauline version of "I have been crucified with Christ; yet I live, no longer I, but Christ lives in me." That bond of the cross is the "new bond of love," made not by us but by Christ's sacrifice.

The genius of this Preface keeps the reality of reconciliation not in the past but in the present, much like a sweet fragrance filling a whole household. This is God's offer to David, after all, at once confronted with his sin, but now facing mercy not under the law, but before God himself. "Even now you set before your people / a time of grace and reconciliation, / and, as they turn back to you in spirit, / you grant them hope in Christ Jesus / and a desire to be of service to all, / while they entrust themselves / more fully to the Holy Spirit." This is the language of opportunity made manifest in the Eucharist, which is the now of God's great mercy, a *kairos* moment in the life of the community of faith gathered for worship. Indeed, the implication for the baptized assembly is that we may have transgressed greatly, like David, but God's offer is irrevocable. As Paul says, "I do not nullify the grace of God; for if justification comes through the law, then Christ died for nothing." Additionally, we might also see Simon the Pharisee in the background in this regard. We never hear his response, but that also suggests that he is poised at the edge of opportunity, much like the congregation at a dinner with the Lord.

Strategy for Preaching

I do not think it is possible to preach too much about reconciliation; by this I mean we cannot say enough about justification by faith and not by works alone, as Paul would have it. Too many of us think that we have to earn the love of God or, still more problematically, that it is all up to us to win our salvation. That God could possibly forgive gratis seems to suggest something for nothing, but that is precisely the point—or else Christ died for nothing. He died for something—or better put, *someone*—that is, you and me. The homily presents an avenue for the congregation to walk the way of forgiveness, even outside of Lent or Masses celebrating the sacrament of reconciliation. So the core homiletic idea for today might be that God's rich mercy brought us forgiveness through Christ, which even now awaits us in love.

We should be able to structure the homiletic text with the coordinates supplied by the Preface for Reconciliation I, as I have discussed that text in the previous section. The introduction might be entirely biblical in nature, an elaboration on the story of David and his life, including the famous episode in the First Reading (for which, unfortunately, he is almost always exclusively recognized).

The body of the homily could begin with a question directed at the congregation in order to get at the first part of the Preface, which promotes this structure:

I. God is rich in mercy. What would we do with David? By our standards today, he deserves prison or worse; by Jewish law, he deserves to be stoned to death for an act of adultery and plotting the death of his lover's husband. But God has a different idea. Why? God is rich in mercy and constantly offers sinners pardon. How much more mercy could God have given King David?

    A. Contemporary application: witness of those who come to the sacrament of reconciliation or find healing from God, even after many years away from the church (specific instances, obviously not drawn from real life).

    B. Psalm 32.

II. Why? Because God never turns away, even if we expect him to do so. Most of us treat God as Simon the Pharisee imagines the Lord—a harsh judge, ready to condemn a woman with a difficult and sinful past. Do we want to test God to see if we can justify ourselves when it comes with pointing fingers at other people?

    A. Paul's theology elaborated; we are justified through faith in Christ, not by the law or its works.

    B. This does not mean we stop doing good works. The woman herself is performing an act of charity to Christ. It means that our salvation is not up to us.

    C. Image: God's merciful love perfume filling a house, picturing the woman pouring ointment on the feet of Jesus. She was forgiven because of her great love, her faith in Christ.

III. So the Eucharist is an opportunity for us all because even now we have come with our alabaster jars of perfume ready to pour its contents on the Body of Christ, as he gives his life for us in love.

    A. To be crucified with Christ (Second Reading).

    B. United in the Eucharist with Christ's redemption and forgiveness.

    C. David's house will be full of violence and sadness, but I imagine he will always remain mindful of God's mercy toward him and the missed opportunity of gratitude for the gifts God has given him. But here we unlock the door of the eucharistic meal and come to pour out our hearts on the wounds of the feet of the one who died for us.

Twelfth Sunday in Ordinary Time

Readings from the Ambo

Zech 12:10-11; 13:1; Ps 63:2, 3-4, 5-6, 8-9;
Gal 3:26-29; Luke 9:18-24

The **Gospel** text for today sets the scene for the disciples' revelation of who Jesus really is and how the Messiah has come. It is a bit difficult to comprehend the relationship Jesus has with the disciples, or further, even imagine what the scene looks like today because of the puzzling translation of the opening line: "Once when Jesus was praying in solitude, and the disciples were with him . . ." We might ask how someone can pray in solitude with others, but the awkwardness of the linguistic structure here points a way to a theological reality. Indeed, the strange language notwithstanding, the text immediately alerts us to the jarring disjunction between the Lord and the disciples, which will become clearer as the Christ defines his mission as the one who "must suffer greatly and be rejected by the elders, the chief priests, and the scribes, and be killed and on the third day be raised." In a way, this is the Christ in solitude, which the disciples fail to understand, although now through the voice of Peter comes to be named, finally, as the Christ of God. His followers will, unfortunately, be unable to unearth the unique solitary nature of Christ's messianic identity, even though Jesus gives them yet another clue to his identity. The invitation involves desire and not just naming, as Peter has done. The Lord wants his disciples to follow in his footsteps all the way up to the cross.

We see some trace of that cross already in the **First Reading**. Zechariah says that the house of David and the inhabitants of Jerusalem will be the beneficiaries of "a spirit of grace and petition; and they shall look on him whom they have pierced . . ." This reference to the pierced one coming from a fifth-century-BCE oracle (we know now to be Second Zechariah) has no clear identity, but I think we can take the one who suffers and those who mourn for him as part of the purification of the house of David, "a fountain to purify from sin and uncleanness." In this sense, Jesus is well within his own Jewish tradition by interpreting his own role—the solitary one who will be pierced for the sake of the people—and as the one who will suffer but be vindicated. Ironically, it is Jesus who traces his lineage to the house of David and who must sanctify the sin and violence of his own dynasty, which is to say, humanity is to be freed by his messianic presence.

If Jesus tries to help the disciples understand his role as the pierced one by telling them that they must take up their own cross, Paul helps the Christian community live out this reality sacramentally. "For all of you who were baptized into Christ have clothed yourselves with Christ" (**Second Reading**). In a word, we share the identity of the crucified one by virtue of our baptism, making us disciples. So we "come after him" by a desire to live our lives according to the indelible mark of grace that has been traced on us in those saving waters. That baptismal death will invariably take us up into the life, death, and resurrection of the one who bore the cross of shame and iniquity.

Connecting the Bible and the Liturgy

If the Gospel challenges Jesus' disciples to discover the Lord's identity (they will never get its true reality until Pentecost, the second half of Luke-Acts) and live out that vocation through self-denial, the **Collect** for today immediately focuses our attention on the identity of Christ, which Peter himself articulated for all of us in the Gospel. "*Sancti nominis tui, Domine,*" begins the Opening Prayer, as if to underline the importance of claiming the name as Peter himself did. "Grant, O Lord, / that we may always revere and love your holy name, / for you never deprive of your guidance / those you set firm on the foundation of your love." The Collect is our summons to affirm the holy identity of the living God. It is as if the baptized assembly are together being asked, "Who do you say that I am?" Just as the naming of Jesus as the Christ brought Peter a response he did not expect, so, too, we begin to understand (barely) that affirming the holy name of

God means accepting the guidance we have been given. The "firm foundation" of God's love has been set in baptism, and the teaching of the Holy Spirit continues to whisper into the ears of those who have been plunged into those sacred waters.

This divine guidance will take the true disciples into the foundation of God's love, which means embracing the life of the Anointed One—yes, the one who was pierced for our sake. His self-emptying is our self-denial; his cross is our cross, made so by our baptism into his death. So the language of the **Prayer over the Offerings** takes the baptized assembly up into the mystery of Christ's saving act of the cross, of which we are not only witnesses but participants by this sacrificial offering: "Receive, O Lord, the sacrifice of conciliation and praise / and grant that, cleansed by its action, / we may make offering of a heart pleasing to you." Is this not what Jesus is asking his disciples: a complete following in his footsteps? The oration further recalls that those baptized into Christ have clothed themselves with Christ. The invitation to take up the cross of the Master and put away the things of compulsive selfishness are here when we "make [an] offering of a heart pleasing to you." Moreover, in our self-surrender to Christ's own sacrifice we are "cleansed by its action," an efficacious act that sanctifies our offering, which is a willing heart offered into the work of Christ's redemption.

In this saving action we know that in the losing of our life by offering it up through the cross of Christ, we have lost our life, but in so doing, we have found it—as the Body of Christ worshiping as the Christian assembly at the Eucharist. This Eucharist becomes the Christ who lives in us. The communion we share with the crucified and risen Lord is the sure sign of the salvation that is "[r]enewed and nourished / by the Sacred Body and Precious Blood of your Son." And so, "we ask of your mercy, O Lord, / that what we celebrate with constant devotion / may be our sure pledge of redemption" (**Prayer after Communion**). This "*devotione frequenti*" will be the engine behind the "heart pleasing to you" and, above all, the disciple who willingly takes up his or her cross and follow God's Anointed.

The naming of Jesus' identity is less a question of knowledge and more an awareness of divine love. We can only come to "constant devotion" through the practice of love, which increases in our relationship with the eucharistic Lord. The working and labor of the Holy Spirit allow us to partake of Christ's messianic identity as the baptized assembly come to a deeper awareness of how and why the Lord suffered and why we follow him.

Strategy for Preaching

More often than not, preachers tend to avail themselves of the window into discipleship presented by Jesus' challenge to Peter: "Who do you say that I am?" This tactic is a good strategy but its dynamics might be pushed; this is a call not only to name Christ but to name *ourselves* as true disciples baptized in his blood. To this end, the Presidential Prayers for this Sunday provide an altogether useful structure for the homily, as well as a thoughtful theology. So the core homiletic idea for today may be to consider that those of us who call ourselves Christian disciples find our identity not only in Jesus' name but also in his cross.

An introduction might ponder the importance of naming in human history and our culture, but also recognize that naming is only the beginning of the true self. Our names can be forged; our "identities" robbed on the Internet, but who are we really at the core of our being? Our true identity as Christians comes only when we gradually uncover our life as baptized children of God who follow Christ and his cross.

The Eucharist brings our identity in Christ into focus by calling us to gather around the name of the Lord, the holy name of God, a name Peter was asked to claim by Jesus in today's Gospel and which is again affirmed in the Collect for today. (Illustration: scenes from different global contexts of liturgy all called to worship at the Eucharist, but all acknowledging who Jesus is. We are asked, "Who do you say that I am?")

But that question for us, as it was for Peter, is only the beginning of our journey. We are brought to our true identity with a desire to pick up Christ's cross, to follow the pierced one. For we have clothed ourselves with Christ (Second Reading) who was crucified for our sake (First Reading). The liturgy reminds us that our offering of a heart pleasing to God is "the sacrifice of conciliation and praise" (Prayer over the Offerings) that asks us to live out of self-gift rather than self-absorption. That gift continues in self-denial and charity long after the Eucharist has concluded. Our mission will always be discipleship. (Examples: ancient and contemporary, none of which should be eccentric but everyday offerings of service in love and sacrifice.)

So we celebrate our true identity as those disciples living in communion with the risen Lord. We hope to leave behind a portion of our lives when we walk in the church door so that we may find them here at this altar. That mingling of our blood and Christ's is the ratification of our baptism. (Example: Archbishop Oscar Romero, who was murdered while celebrating the Eucharist, an unusual instance of discipleship played out graphically on the altar.) All of us have our own path of discipleship to tread, which probably will not involve actual martyrdom, but will invariably mean picking up our cross each day. And we do so nourished by the Body and Blood of the Lamb, as a "sure pledge of [our] redemption" (Prayer after Communion).

Thirteenth Sunday in Ordinary Time

Readings from the Ambo

1 Kgs 19:16b, 19-21; Ps 16:1-2, 5, 7-8, 9-10, 11;
Gal 5:1, 13-18; Luke 9:51-62

As is well known, Luke 9:51 begins a new section in that **Gospel**, often referred to as the travel narrative in Luke. The rather lackluster discipleship demonstrated at the end of the previous (Galilean) section, arguing over who is greatest or their failure to understand Jesus' mission, contrasts with Luke's description of Jesus who "resolutely determined to journey to Jerusalem." The Greek is even more powerful when it says, *"kai autos to prosopon esterisen"* or, literally, and "he set his face to go."

Jesus sets the gold standard for discipleship at the very beginning of this travel narrative. How the disciples will measure up to that calling remains something Luke is keenly interested in showing us. Indeed, the beginning of Jesus' journey sets the stage for questions concerning broader discipleship (Samaritans, for instance), the relationship of disciples with family ("Lord, let me go first and bury my father"), and attachments to the past. The journey represents a break with the familiar and a movement toward risk and the cross.

The sense of separation from familial constraints also faces Elisha in the **First Reading**, who sets familial departure as one of his conditions for following his new mentor, Elijah. Now we might recall that Elijah was given Elisha as part of his mission from God, so Elisha's clinging to the past becomes all the more touching. One gets the sense that the wild prophet Elijah has stumbled into a kind of domestic scene with his new disciple, whose farming responsibilities hold him to house and family. But unlike Jesus' disciples, Elisha makes a complete renunciation and sets his past ablaze—quite literally—by boiling his oxen and using their yoke as firewood. Later, in 2 Kings 2:12, when Elijah is taken up to heaven in a chariot of horses and fire, Elisha says, "My father! my father!" This is almost certainly a sign that his mentor has become his new father and led this disciple on a road to prophetic leadership, which he now accepts by bearing a share of his power and his mantle.

In the **Second Reading** Paul suggests our own apprenticeship as Christians is within the life of the Spirit, not an infrequent refrain on the part of the apostle. "[L]ive by the Spirit and you will certainly not gratify the desire of the flesh." Being guided by the Spirit means setting our face to resolutely follow the path of discipleship in Christ—setting the past on fire, leaving the life of sin behind, including all the attachments that may have accompanied such behavior. One would think that this prospect of liberation from what Paul says is "the yoke of slavery" (a coincidental image found in the First Reading, by the way) would be readily embraced; but not so, or Paul would not have written the present text in the first place. Rather, it was "[f]or freedom Christ set us free," surely one of the most consoling phrases in the Pauline corpus; we have been liberated in order to act in freedom, not to be under the constraints and the yoke of the law or, on the other extreme, to live in complete licentiousness. But rather we abide in the Spirit as our mentor and guide.

Connecting the Bible and the Liturgy

How will we choose to engage the eucharistic liturgy this day? This is a question the baptized assembly may ask themselves, provoked to discover the demanding relationship between the Master and the disciple, set forth in magnificent story by the author of the book of Kings and Luke's Gospel. Discipleship is really the issue of the day, traced in the footsteps of Elijah and Elisha, Jesus and those he meets on his journey to Jerusalem and the cross, and, indeed, Paul's advice to the Galatians to "live by the Spirit / and you will certainly not gratify the desire of the flesh." I think we should read the desire of the flesh here very broadly, and see it as an attachment to created things (our oxen and our yoke), as the capacious tradition of Catholic spirituality has taught concerning renunciation over the centuries. Therefore we find Elisha and the journeymen with Jesus caught not in the allurements of sexual appetite, but the flesh of the past, even family attachments—literally the desire to be with one's own flesh and blood—that is human obligation and duties. These are the things that hold us back from the journey, which is mobile and for which one must travel very lightly.

The **Collect** makes great use of the relationship that all the baptized in Christ have with God, by referring to the new partnership with the Spirit, which, like Elisha when he sees the heavenly journey of his mentor, names him "Father, Father!" "O God, who through the grace of adoption / chose us to be children of light . . ." We have been taken up as children of God by virtue of Christ's redeeming love. So discipleship comes not only as an act of will, but also through grace.

The Christian faithful face the necessary turning away from those things that enslave our areas of "unfreedom." Paul brings this home clearly: "For freedom Christ set us free; so stand firm and do not submit again to the yoke of slavery." In other words, true discipleship hinges on our ability to detach ourselves from everything that does not lead to God. So, the Collect continues, "grant, we pray, / that we may not be wrapped in the darkness of error / but always be seen to stand in the bright light of truth." We can read "error" here as an element that leads us away from discipleship, since it is knowledge of Christ that leads us to "the bright light of truth." Further, we can also see "error" as delusional thinking, which is to say, the "desires against the Spirit," those things that constrain us from following our life of discipleship. Walking in "the light of truth" means traveling with Jesus, firm in baptism and by which we are made children of adoption. We are guided by the Spirit and able to set our hands to a new plow, free from yoke and oxen, and anticipate the kingdom of God.

Strategy for Preaching

This journey that begins for Jesus so resolutely in Luke 9:51 represents an obvious invitation to bring to a boil a discipleship that may have grown tepid. The biblical texts for today all reference classical instances for a way of deepening spirituality: detachments, avoidance of sin and the things that lead to sin, accepting the grace and mercy of God in owning the grace of baptism. These three coordinates or touchstones are reinforced by the Collect today. Taken together, they inform a homily that could use as its core idea the following: Christian discipleship will take us along the road of detachment, staying away from sin and living out our baptism. There is really nothing new here, but that is perhaps the point. The preaching should reignite the fires of discipleship so that the journey becomes one of desire rather than listless obligation.

If the preacher feels comfortable with stretching out the metaphor of the journey with these three touchstones, as I have described them in the core idea, then let me suggest visualizing these rather abstract coordinates as little villages that the Christian pilgrim visits along the way on our journey to God.

Like Jesus, we must resolutely set our faces to the city of Jerusalem, that is, the cross, in embracing our discipleship. Beyond it lies the kingdom of God. We will need to pass through several cities on the way:

I. The City of Detachment.
  A. Difficult to run away from things—even good things that do not lead to God or the discipleship that remains part of God's will.
  B. Elijah and Elisha.
  C. Men Jesus met cannot detach themselves.
  D. Life of letting go of things, not power and calling fire down upon others (Gospel).
  E. Contemporary example of this as illustration.

II. The City of Avoidance of Sin.
  A. Turning away from areas of "unfreedom."
  B. "For freedom Christ set us free" (Second Reading).
  C. Burning the things that hold us back from God (First Reading).
  D. Walking in the light (Collect).
  E. Story of conversion.

III. The City of the Kingdom of God.
  A. Living here in fullness of the Spirit through our baptism anticipates this city.
  B. Collect: grace of adoption.

C. Living by the Spirit (Second Reading).

D. Walking with Christ as a new creation to the new Jerusalem.

E. What would you take with you on the journey to Jerusalem with Jesus? (Name some possibilities.)

Fourteenth Sunday in Ordinary Time

Readings from the Ambo

Isa 66:10-14c; Ps 66:1-3, 4-5, 6-7, 16, 20;
Gal 6:14-18; Luke 10:1-12, 17-20

If last week's **Gospel** concerned the struggle of discipleship with detachment from the things that did not focus on the one thing necessary to live in the kingdom, Jesus gives very specific advice in today's Good News about how his followers mission into freedom: "Go on your way; behold, I am sending you like lambs among wolves. Carry no money bag, no sack, no sandals; and greet no one along the way." When spiritual masters such as St. Francis of Assisi or Dorothy Day heard these lines, they must have further realized their own inner poverty and need not to carry any excess baggage on their respective journeys—either physical or spiritual.

In some sense, Jesus is recalling his own identity here as the one who has engaged in a kenosis for the sake of the kingdom or the reason that "foxes have dens and birds of the sky have nests, but the Son of Man has nowhere to rest his head" (Matt 8:20). In carrying nothing, then, we bear the imprint of Christ, as St. Francis himself would discover when he received the gift of the stigmata at the end of his earthly existence. In this way, the disciple bore "the marks of Jesus" on his body, boasting only in the cross of Christ. Paul sees the carrying of these wounds by disciples as foundational, the marks of the true follower of Jesus, "through which the world has been crucified to me, and I to the world" (**Second Reading**). That is why Paul tells the Galatians that he will "never boast except in the cross of our Lord Jesus Christ." In other words, Paul has truly engaged separation and detachment because the world as he knows it has been crucified (*estaurotai*). There is cause for boasting then and only then: in the liberating power of the cross.

Having suffered the cross of exile, the people of Israel hear a new day for Jerusalem from the prophet (Third) Isaiah. The maternal images the author deploys in this oracle for the **First Reading** suggest a new life and a new beginning for a people who may nurse with delight like young children at the "abundant breasts" of Jerusalem. The city, which was once barren and deserted, has now become a mother nurturing her children. In a certain sense, Isaiah has taken the hardship of exile and transformed it into a life-giving momentum by the power of God's word. It is the detachment from the homeland that has now yielded to a new Jerusalem, not like the one from of old, but under the care of the Lord who says tenderly to Israel, "as a mother comforts her child, / so will I comfort you; / in Jerusalem you shall find your comfort." The wounds of exile have been exposed so that "the LORD's power shall be known to his servants." Mother Zion will bring Israelites and the inhabitants of Jerusalem to great rejoicing—or what Paul may call *boasting* in the Lord.

Connecting the Bible and the Liturgy

The Gospel prescribes—in very direct and specific ways—how the true disciple is brought into mission. Paradoxically, instead of taking some equipment and food for the journey, Jesus' advice is to carry nothing. Nothing at all. Christian mission remains congruent with Christian discipleship; this means setting one's hand to the plow without looking back. The Master himself is without a place to lay his head and that life of the journeyman, ready for any encounter, becomes a blueprint for discipleship. We can only encounter those on our journey if we are freed from our own baggage; for some it may be money, for others it is a difficult past or addictive relationships. The pilgrim carries nothing in order to embrace the reality, the full personhood of those before him or her more fully.

The **Collect** brings to mind the self-emptying of Christ when it begins, "O God, who in the abasement of your Son / have raised up a fallen world . . ." There is, of course, a nice play on the Lord's "abasement" (the Latin is *humilitate*) who has "raised up" (*erexisti*) a "fallen world" (*iacentem mundum*). Now, the *Sacramentary* of 1974 used the word "obedience" instead of "abasement," which, I believe, does not grab the reversal available in the Latin original. Through self-humiliation or abasement, Christ has raised us up.

That is all the more reason to "boast in the cross of Christ" as Paul does, because the abasement has been transformed into redemption. As we leave our own baggage at the door of the church when we come to this liturgy, we, too, are empty and abased because of our sin. So we ask God to "fill your faithful with holy joy, / for on those you have rescued from slavery to sin / you bestow eternal gladness." The dynamic present in this second portion of the Opening Prayer is not unlike Third Isaiah's call to "[r]ejoice with Jerusalem and be glad because of her, / all you who love her." The Christian community has been brought out of the exile of sin and been given a new lease on life.

How? Through the nurturing Christ or what the fourteenth-century mystic Julian of Norwich referred to in her writings *Showings* as "Christ our mother." We are fed by the abundant breasts of the sacramental life of the church, which sustains God's people in a "fallen world," from which we have been "raised up." Such sacramental sustenance becomes clear in both the **Communion Antiphon** and the Prayer after Communion: "*Gustate et videte, quoniam suavis est Dominus.*" "Taste and see that the Lord is good." We are not just told that the Lord is good; God wants us to experience that goodness as we celebrate the food for the journey. "Blessed the [one] who seeks refuge in him." We take shelter in God like a fortified city. Similarly the **Prayer after Communion** focuses on the food that not only sustains but thanks the Lord for "having been replenished by such great gifts" (*Tantis, Domine, repleti muneribus*). "Grant, we pray, O Lord, / that, having been replenished by such great gifts, / we may gain the prize of salvation / and never cease to praise you." After such saving food, what need has the Christian community to carry anything with them on their journey? And the lighter we are, the more we will enjoy the food that lasts forever. All we need to carry are the imprints of the crucified Lord, for we are sustained by his love.

Strategy for Preaching

We have our own arrogant ways of boasting about ourselves, some subtle and some not so. There are some who never fail to mention the latest purchase for their fall clothing collection. Others cannot stop talking about their children's success stories on team sports or school. Facebook or Instagram or Twitter are yet more forums to share what we think is important about ourselves. In this day and age no statement seems to be more true than, "It is all about me."

The preacher might face the seemingly paradoxical image Paul presents to the Christian community of "boasting in the cross of our Lord Jesus Christ." We look to achievement and success during the week, but then come to worship a crucified God on Sunday. What is wrong with this picture? That compartmentalization will probably not show up on any social media in the near future.

Well, what is wrong with this picture is that it does not have our baptismal imprint on it, or the one whose wounds we bear because of the sacrament. Or rather, we have not allowed ourselves to be crucified with Christ to the world and allowed that reality to inform everything we do. Yes, even our boasting. How things would change if the crucified Lord became a constant companion with us on our journey. (What does this look like from a practical point of view for the congregation of hearers? Power struggles at work? Maintaining a difficult marriage?) Do we really want to go with Christ on the journey to Jerusalem and the cross or would we rather walk down the streets of Hollywood and wish we were among the stars? As Jesus' disciples travel with him, they think it is all about power. They want to bring down fire from heaven, as if that was the real reason Jesus came to live among humanity. They have yet to be convinced that it is about the cross we carry and not the twin swords of power and prestige. Imagine a different scenario where we left our baggage of power at the door and just encountered others as the Christ living in us. (Sketch some scenes for the assembly of going out to meet others not with tales of success and conquests, but humble service. What if we brought someone a casserole instead of a photo of our new car?)

Christ has done it before us, it is comforting to know. The Collect says that it was through Christ's abasement, his humility, his utter reduction to nothingness, that God raised us up. Lowliness has made us a resurrected people. His emptiness has made us full. Christ's cross given to us at baptism began this journey with us. (Recall the Rite of Christian Baptism in which the cross is traced on the forehead of the one to be baptized. Visualize this for the assembly by naming specific first names.)

That is why we rejoice as we carry the Gospel and nothing else. We hold up that Gospel book with joy just before the proclamation of the Good News as if to say, this is all the library books I will ever need. We are delivered from exile into a new Jerusalem, which has nurtured us into being (Communion Antiphon; Prayer after Communion). The Eucharist is both where we are now and where we are headed. The church replenishes us with this great gift day after day. This is not only food for a lifetime, but it is food for life. As we journey along the road with Christ with our saving meal, we come to know our reality in him in the breaking of the bread.

Fifteenth Sunday in Ordinary Time

Readings from the Ambo

Deut 30:10-14; Ps 69:14, 17, 30-31, 33-34, 36, 37;
Col 1:15-20; Luke 10:25-37

In some ways all the readings we have before us today in this Sunday's Lectionary deal with ways of interpreting the "law": the law of Moses, the law of love, and the law of Christ.

We know that one of the universal features concerning the book of Deuteronomy is that this unique narrative calls our attention to the law as it is contained in a book, passed down to future generations. In some ways, Deuteronomy is about communal memory itself. That a Code would move from one age to the next begs the question, How do we make sense of these commandments in our own idiom? Moses insists that these mandates and statutes are not remote: "It is not up in the sky, that you should say, 'Who will go up in the sky to get it for us and tell us of it, that we may carry it out?' . . . No, it is something very near to you, already in your mouths and in your hearts; you have only to carry it out" (**First Reading**). This is the word dwelling among God's people, not a series of abstract concepts and proposals, but something to be owned and loved as the word of God, which has come terribly near.

Maybe that word is just too close for comfort, at least for some. When Jesus is interrogated in today's **Gospel**, it is from the scholar of the law who asks the Lord what he must do to inherit eternal life. Jesus puts an interpretive question back to the man concerning the law and how he reads it; the scholar replies with the two Great Commandments. But it is unclear to him, or so it would appear, and because he also wished to justify himself, he asks, "who is my neighbor?" There is an irony here, since the scholar of the law seems so far removed from the human condition that he does not even know how to apply the law of his profession—despite the injunction present from Moses himself in the book of Deuteronomy: the word is very near you. As far as the scholar of the law is concerned, the neighbor might as well be up in the sky.

So Jesus brings the law home to the scholar with the law of love in the parable of the Good Samaritan, where the up close and personal illustration of mercy shown to a Samaritan forces the scholar to see who the real neighbor is in this scenario and what law governs the story. In the end, the new commandment could not be more personal or nearer and a new Moses for both Samaritan and Jew becomes more obvious: "Go and do likewise."

Paul's address at the beginning of the Letter to the Colossians also insists that God is not distant but very near indeed: "Christ Jesus is the image of the invisible God / . . . For in him all the fullness was pleased to dwell, / and through him to reconcile all things for him, / making peace by the blood of his cross / through him, whether those on earth or those in heaven" (**Second Reading**). God could not be nearer to Jesus, since he is "the image of the invisible God." Further, as the image of God, Jesus dwells not up in the sky but with God's people, closer than we can imagine—in sickness or in health, life and death, sadness or joy. As the living Word dwelling among us, Christ is beyond the book of the law, because "he is before all things, / and in him all things hold together." Christ is holding the law of charity together as he reinterprets the law and makes enemies neighbors.

Connecting the Bible and the Liturgy

Since the biblical readings seem to draw several instances of interpretation into a new light, with Jesus himself provoking a scholar of the law to read that book in a new way—different, perhaps, than any of his contemporaries might have done—the obligation to "Go and do likewise" is enjoined not only on the scholar of the law, but the worshiping Christian community as well. To this end, the liturgical prayers are given a new reading when seen in the light of today's Scripture.

"O God, who show the light of your truth / to those who go astray, / so that they may return to the right path . . ." The beginning of the **Collect** for today might appear to be praying for those who have lost their way in the faith or who are otherwise absent from the Christian assembly this day. That makes those of us who have come to worship feel pretty good, I would dare to suggest. After all, here we are in church and we did not go astray; we have been justified by our very attendance at the Eucharist. That sounds familiar. "But because he wished to justify himself, he said to Jesus, / 'And who is my neighbor?'" At the same time, though, I think we can presume that we have all lost our way and are on our way back through Christ. Indeed, there are several folks who have gotten waylaid in the Gospel and seek to return. First there is the injured man himself. When Augustine read this parable of the Good Samaritan, the man on his way from Jerusalem to Jericho is all of us, all humanity gone astray until Christ the Good Samaritan brought us to the inn of the church to be healed by the balm of the sacraments.

There are others who also lose their way in the parable—the priests and the Levite think they are following the right path by observing laws of ritual purity, but they are, in fact, violating the Great Commandment to love their neighbor as themselves. That love is the bottom line and Jesus the only path to follow in order to be justified. And so the Collect urges us on to integrate our faith with the here and now: to see Jesus as the icon of the invisible God, to understand the word as near and not far off on our side of the human divide between human beings and God. The Word is living and active in our midst. So the Collect continues: "give all who for the faith they profess / are accounted Christians / the grace to reject whatever is contrary to the name of Christ / and to strive after all that does it honor." By making our Christian life accountable to a new law—"whatever is contrary to the name of Christ"—we insure that the Word is not far off: "No, it is something very near to you, / already in your mouths and in your hearts; / you have only to carry it out."

Strategy for Preaching

These liturgical and biblical readings could not be any more demonstrative about the preaching dynamic: making the word near for the Christian hearer. The dark side to this is that the homily will need to be absolutely near the listening assembly today—or else the vehicle that would carry the word to the people of God would run right past these faithful, barely stopping to pause in their midst.

The Lectionary readings today are clearly pushing us to grasp the mystery of the incarnation more deeply, to understand the nearness of the living Word—the image of the invisible God—present to us in ways we may not be willing to acknowledge. The parable is surely one of the most iconic instances of Jesus' teaching in the New Testament, easily recognizable even by the secular community who have adopted nomenclature such as the "Good Samaritan Law," which protects people giving reasonable assistance to those who are injured or in peril. In some ways, the Good Samaritan Law has become a secular version of the higher law of love that Jesus asks his followers to observe as we (figuratively speaking) move along the highway from Jerusalem to Jericho.

But how can the preacher make the well-known parable an instance of the nearness of the living Word and not simply the occasion of retelling a familiar story? "Go and do likewise" is the call to conversion, not a request to retell a parable. The preaching for today, then, could be an opportunity to calling the congregation to expand their personal, cultural, and religious boundaries by reinterpreting their own law that governs the definition of their "neighbor." So an interesting core idea for the homily could be, God is very near to us, maybe nearer than we think, imagine, or want him to be.

A good point of departure here would be an introduction that briefly handles the need for all of us to make choices on the road to life and the freedom we are given to do so. That initial stage of the homily would then move to the body of the text, dealing with the reinterpretation or renegotiation of our personal, cultural, and religious boundaries.

The Collect asks that "those who go astray . . . may return to the right path"; that means us. The first one to pass up the injured man is a priest. His special status probably prevented him from showing any help to the injured. We have no reason to believe that the cleric actually even took a closer look at the injured man. Scholars think that when the priest and the Levite saw the man, they passed on the opposite side because he was unclean. We all have our untouchables, don't we? They are those who everyone else shuns. Street people, convicts, maybe those we have determined do not fit our moral profile of what we think they should be doing. We have placed them in a foreign country and said, "Stay out."

Then there is the Levite in us, the member of a special family. We have a little of him that makes us go astray as well. We cross on the opposite side of the road of charity when we idolize the "in-group," desire to be an insider to gossip, to know the real story. Just watch children in a school yard, or take a frightful look at the bullying on the Internet. (Illustration, perhaps from real life. I am thinking of a famous case in which a bus driver was harassed to tears by children on a bus because she was elderly and overweight.)

The parable of the Good Samaritan also confronts us with hope. Someone dared to cross the boundary and rescue the wounded. That was a risk. The Collect for today asks God to help us "reject whatever is contrary to the name of Christ." This means everyone is our neighbor and thinking in the name of Jesus about how we love or fail to do so. The neighbor might have once been thought of as an object to be pitied or scorned, but the Samaritan is the one who breaks through boundaries. He made the first move. So what would you do if a person you really could not stand rang your doorbell this evening and handed you some freshly baked cookies and brownies? Yes, it is that kind of Gospel.

Sixteenth Sunday in Ordinary Time

Readings from the Ambo

Gen 18:1-10a; Ps 15:2-3, 3-4, 5; Col 1:24-28; Luke 10:38-42

In their own ways, the **First Reading** and the Gospel for today accentuate the virtue of hospitality, although the passage concerning Abraham's encounter with his visitors is wrapped in an announcement of the birth of Isaac. This Yahwistic account of the great patriarch's future contrasts with the previous (Priestly) author in chapter 17; it is a more majestic revelation in which God appears directly to Abram when the old man is ninety-nine. Chapter 17 focuses on a new era that is about to unfold with Abraham as its Father. At the same time, our passage in chapter 18 is rather typical of the Yahwistic author, who disguises divine announcements in human encounters. Here we are in the ambiguous territory between God and human beings. "The LORD appeared to Abraham by the terebinth of Mamre" quickly shifts to the embodiment of the Deity with "three men standing nearby." The anthropomorphic undertones in the passage have encouraged a trinitarian reading, the most famous of which is the Rublev icon of the Holy Trinity, probably painted in the fifteenth century.

I think we should not miss that the announcement of future generations and newness is disclosed in the context of hospitality. Indeed, Abraham is the supreme host, "welcoming angels unaware," as the saying goes. And the announcement of Isaac's birth appears to be a kind of response to such welcome. Abraham will welcome what he thought would be impossible because God will not be outdone in generosity.

Jesus affirms Mary's action of simple affection of the guest, in this rather low-key domestic episode at the house of Mary and Martha.

For centuries, this passage became emblematic of the endorsement of the contemplative (Mary) over the active (Martha). But the short reading is as sensible as it is profound: there is no substitute for welcome. That virtue is a reflection of the trinitarian indwelling of God and a practical application of the love command, which emerges out of Luke's **Gospel** in the previous section (10:25-37) in the parable of the Good Samaritan. True hospitality crosses all boundaries, divine and human (Abraham and his visitors) as well as national and ethnic (an injured Jew is cared for by a Samaritan).

In the **Second Reading** Paul seems to suggest that we might cross yet another boundary between ourselves and Christ, or our life and the lives of those around us, when we offer our suffering for "what is lacking in the afflictions of Christ on behalf of his body, which is the church." Indeed, God is himself the most transcendent of hosts, offering a welcome of salvation "manifested to his holy ones, to whom God chose to make known the riches of the glory of this mystery among the Gentiles." Divine hospitality, which has taken up residence in our own tents, knows no boundaries and neither should we.

Connecting the Bible and the Liturgy

In our modern democratic culture in the West, we are apt to pass by a word like "servant" in something of an anomaly, depending on what class we are from. How many people do we know have servants? These folks are usually referred to as "the help." And yet, in Gospel language we are all servants of the God who became a servant for our sake. We are sent into mission as servants. Indeed, concerning the work of hospitality we see portrayed in the readings today, "servant" (*famulus*) appears in both the **Collect** and the Prayer over the Offerings, another reminder that at the Eucharist we bring our humble and contrite hearts to the tables of Word and sacrament.

"Show favor, O Lord, to your servants / and mercifully increase the gifts of your grace, / that, made fervent in hope, faith and charity, / they may be ever watchful in keeping your commands." Like Abraham and Mary, we are at the service of the Lord, offering hospitality to the Divine Guest who has himself invited us to be his guests at the eucharistic banquet. And with that welcome comes the regeneration of gift, the theological virtues of faith, hope, and love, which will see us through the future to obey the Lord's commands. It is the very act of hospitality that provides the grace to be "ever watchful in keeping your commands." Like good hosts, we keep vigil for the sake of the guest, waiting for him to enter our dwelling.

In the light of radical welcome, it becomes remarkably clear how Jesus could tell us that "[t]here is need of only one thing. Mary has chosen the better part and it will not be taken from her." The docility Mary exhibits before the Lord in her own house becomes the gateway to all grace because such a state is radically open to receive the gift and not be "anxious and worried about many things." By surrendering her place to sit at the feet of the guest, Mary is offering service at the table of welcome and hospitality, a real and certain parallel to the faithful who have come as servants at the Eucharist, offering our own gifts: "O God, who in the one perfect sacrifice / brought to completion varied offerings of the law, / accept, we pray, this sacrifice from your faithful servants / and make it holy, as you blessed the gifts of Abel, / so that what each has offered to the honor of your majesty / may benefit the salvation of all" (**Prayer over the Offerings**). Indeed, as members of the worshiping community, we are akin to Abel, who brought more than a material offering but his own self, a prefiguring of our Lord's own self-gift, into which we have been taken up so that what we bring together with our Host "may benefit the salvation of all." The offering we make, then, becomes an Abraham-filled hospitality of loving friendship for the church and the whole world.

Strategy for Preaching

A very purposeful introduction (is there any other kind?) would grab the theological issues at stake in Paul's Letter to the Colossians. Paul's famous statement to the Colossians that "in my flesh I am filling up what is lacking in the afflictions of Christ on behalf of his body, which is the church" represents a theological conundrum that scholars have tried to unravel for centuries: How could there be anything lacking in the *pathema* (suffering; here translated as "afflictions") of Christ? And secondly, how can anyone, Paul included, hope to complete (*antanaplero*, he says) that supreme sacrificial offering? A substantial support for expanding this introduction might be gained from accessing the *New Catholic Encyclopedia* on the

"Doctrine of the Atonement"; the *Catechism of the Catholic Church*, especially section 618 on "Our participation in Christ's sacrifice," under "III. Christ Offered Himself to His Father for Our Sins"; and various resources available on the Internet. This introduction does not have to be abstract, but can be an opportunity to link a pivotal theological and creedal teaching to the virtue of hospitality, which can form the body of the homiletic text.

When we examine this passage, we can say that Paul really does not mean that a human being completes Christ's work of atonement as much as participates in the sacrifice Christ offered once and for all in his Body, the church. Paul offers his own body in hospitality service to the one Body. Our hospitality welcomes the afflicted and suffering Lord and sits patiently with him as we offer our lives of silent witness. In so doing, we become taken into the manifold work of praise and thanksgiving, through loving service, enabling us to carry on Christ's mission on earth, which is to love. Like Mary, we choose the better part by participating in the life of contemplative listening. So the core homiletic idea for today might be that in our lives of welcoming the Body of Christ, we receive him and the gifts he brings.

Let me tease this core idea out a bit. Paul's address to the Colossians would be an appropriate and magnificent starting point for a homily that needs a theological gloss for the Christian faithful. A brief consideration of Christ's redeeming sacrifice and our participation in that offering, as Paul understands it, is in order. Indeed, the passage itself in Paul begs for a theological understanding because "[i]t is he whom we proclaim, admonishing everyone and teaching everyone with all wisdom, that we may present everyone perfect in Christ."

The Christian faithful are welcomed into the Body by Christ's atonement, into which we participate by our very lives and at the Eucharist. The homily might then move into an understanding of how hospitality weaves in and out of the biblical and liturgical readings for today. Abraham welcomed the visitors at his door as the Lord and received a promise of an heir. God bestows fertility and generativity as a gift, a blessing from the Giver of all good gifts. Servants receive such gifts in God's house (cf. Collect: the emphasis is on our role as servant, which increases the gifts of faith, hope, and love). Similarly, Jesus affirms Mary's resting at the Lord's feet, a passive posture that participates in Christ's own life of dialogue, teaching, and, in Paul's mind, afflictions. This gesture of welcoming hospitality hints at the church at prayer, the Body offering itself as the gift to the Father who bestows gifts on his Beloved. In so doing, we see what will "benefit the salvation of all."

There are many weighty matters to consider in this homily that might move toward a very practical conclusion. How does "my sacrifice and yours" become "acceptable to God, the almighty Father"? The answer: through Christ, but our hospitality as the Body participates in that gift of the Lord's own self. We have to do nothing but offer who we are for the sake of the church and the world; that is our table service.

Seventeenth Sunday in Ordinary Time

Readings from the Ambo

Gen 18:20-32; Ps 138:1-2, 2-3, 6-7, 7-8; Col 2:12-14; Luke 11:1-13

The refrain that underlines all the biblical readings today is used in the **Responsorial Psalm**: "Lord, on the day I called for help, you answered me." Not surprisingly, the Yahwistic account in the Abraham cycle continues to deliver an anthropomorphic reflection of God. In this instance in the **First Reading**, God's mercy eclipses his justice through the bold intercession of the patriarch, who has absorbed some sense of responsibility and care for the innocent of Sodom. The conversation might be a model of prayer, mirroring the human heart eager for good works and a merciful God who listens.

The idea of bargaining with God may strike even common-sense Christians as somewhat preposterous, but this dynamic is a biblical tenant that stresses relationship above all with God—not robotic submission. Here the Yahwistic author brings the anthropomorphic coloring of God to the fore, as it disarms us with its charms and direct encounters with God. The scene of Abraham bargaining with the Lord is marvelous in its ability to stretch out a scene that might have occurred in a marketplace concerning some bartered goods. God shows a willingness to compromise and to hear a plea from the one with whom he has made a covenant. We should not let the echo of the courtroom go unnoticed, nor the profound issue at stake in this conversation between the patriarch and the Deity: Should the innocent be punished with the guilty? And secondly, we have the power to engage God not as an abstract entity who has predetermined our fate, but as a kind of dialogue partner on our journey. One question we do not see answered at the end of Abraham's bargaining session with God is how much this dialogue changed the patriarch himself in his own understanding of a God of mercy, which the conversation hints is endless.

In some sense, Jesus' **Gospel** teaching on prayer is of the same mind as the Yahwistic author portrayed in the First Reading, insofar as he is encouraging his disciples to see the relationship underneath their encounter with God: "ask and you will receive; seek and you will find; knock and the door will be opened to you." Jesus' illustration of this kind of prayer is a story of a persistent friend or an analogy of one who keeps knocking at the door, someone, perhaps, like Abraham. This teaching on prayer is at its core a doctrine of desire, a heartfelt pattern that will guide Christian spirituality throughout the ages. Holy zeal, a sanctified will, a righteous heart: these virtues call out the Abraham in all of us. At the same time, we are also mindful of God's merciful compassion and that we only see the need to cling to the one true God for "our daily bread." God sees the whole universe in a timeless grasp (although the Yahwistic author portrays God quite differently) and so Jesus adds, "thy will be done." That docility should not prevent us from using the moxie needed to ask for the gift of the Holy Spirit. We will all the more readily be given that gift of the Spirit, since, as Paul tells the Colossians, we "were buried with him in baptism." Baptism is our covenant, through Christ, which engages and fortifies our relationship with God and one another, enabling us to cry out "Our Father." If the example of Abraham in the First Reading becomes a paradigm for prayer for us, the Christian community will not fail to remember that the God who keeps covenant with us forever listens to our prayers in the endless ocean of his great mercy.

Connecting the Bible and the Liturgy

The Liturgy of the Eucharist speaks for itself when it comes to the prayers of petition, thanksgiving, and praise through Christ when the baptized assembly is gathered. Where would we be without the "source and summit" of our prayer? Without voice, I dare say, and indeed, without hands to knock on the door so that it shall be opened. The Eucharist joins the faithful together to beg, "Give us this day our daily bread."

Like Abraham, though, we are able to draw out our "bargaining" with God after we say the **Our Father** at the Eucharist through the embolism or an elaboration of the Our Father. "Deliver us, Lord, we pray, from every evil, / graciously grant peace in our days," says the prayer through the presider, as the embolism continues the "Our" embedded in the "Our Father": "*Libera nos, quaesumus, Domine, ab omnibus malis, da propitius pacem in diebus nostris.*" The first word is a shout to God for freedom. This indeed is a cry for mercy for all of humanity for peace—not in some future time, but in our days. Like Abraham, we ask for the immediacy of God's action in our lives and in the world.

We know that such divine action can only be accomplished "by the help of your mercy, / we may be always free from sin / and safe from all distress." Paul has told us as much in the **Second Reading**, when he tells the Colossians that "even when you were dead in transgressions and the uncircumcision of your flesh, he brought you to life along with him, having forgiven us all our transgressions." In a sense, the Christian community cannot fail to identify with Paul's hearers, since we recognize the reality of our forgiveness, but also ask for preservation from sin: "*et a peccato simus semper liberi et ab omni perturbatione securi.*" The deliverance from "distress" (translated from *perturbatione*) is a change from the *Sacramentary*, which was "anxiety." That shift is probably all for the best, since anxiety these days is often associated with clinical disorders rather than the fear that underlies human distress and tribulations.

Finally, the "thy kingdom come" is once again uttered and brought into high relief with the promise that "we await the blessed hope / and the coming of our Savior, Jesus Christ," while the congregation acclaims, "For the kingdom, / the power and the glory are yours / now and for ever." While the baptized have joined in a zealous petition for peace, forgiveness, and protection from evil, we are open to God's future reign. "Thy will be done" remains Christ's final gift to us, as Paul reminds the church, because Jesus' acceptance of the Father's will was responsible for "obliterating the bond against us, with its legal claims, / which was opposed to us, / he also removed it from our midst, nailing it to the cross." And so, too, the baptized: "*exspectantes beatam spem et adventum salvatoris nostri Iesu Christi.*"

Strategy for Preaching

As I suggested in the previous section, the embolism at the Eucharist, said or sung after the Our Father, is a kind of elaboration or descant on Jesus' teaching on prayer in the Gospel and the liturgy itself. For example, we ask for deliverance from evil in the Our Father and the embolism that follows begs for deliverance from every evil and asks for peace in our day. As I understand it, these elaborations are both communal and personal: all members of the worshiping community will have hearts that desire to be freed from something they alone know. Moreover, this prayerful elaboration mirrors Abraham's own bargaining with God in Genesis 18. So the core homiletic idea for today might be that we ask boldly in prayer to be delivered from all evil through the God of all mercy, as we await the coming kingdom. To this end, the homiletic text could be structured in three parts, using the embolism following the Lord's Prayer.

An informed introduction would say something briefly about the nature of prayer, particularly from a relational perspective. Abraham is boldly accessing his friendship with God in his petition for the lives of the innocent.

I. Jesus' teaching on prayer enjoins his disciples to boldly and urgently knock on the door of God's heart for the things that matter.

   A. Gospel illustration of the man knocking at night.

   B. Example of urgency or desperate request from a contemporary situation.

   C. Our hearts expand at the liturgy: "Deliver us, Lord, we pray, from every evil . . ."

   D. Abraham: boldly relational. Other biblical examples.

II. But we rely on God's mercy and compassion as we surrender to his will.

   A. God wants us to be free from sin and all distress (embolism prayer expanding on the Our Father).

   B. We ask for the gift of the Spirit to guide us in our discernment.

   C. Buried with Christ in baptism, we are freed from original sin, "the bond against us" through Christ's cross (Second Reading).

III. So we await Christ's coming as a fulfillment of our petition in freedom.

   A. "[A]s we await the blessed hope / and the coming of our Savior, Jesus Christ."

B. Jesus brings us into the kingdom now as we knock on the door of God's heart.

C. We are raised up with Christ (a concrete image would be useful here) passing through the gate of death to new life.

Eighteenth Sunday in Ordinary Time

Readings from the Ambo

Eccl 1:2; 2:21-23; Ps 90:3-4, 5-6, 12-13, 14, 17;
Col 3:1-5, 9-11; Luke 12:13-21

The problem with Pauline authorship concerning the Letter to the Colossians notwithstanding (most scholars believe the letter to be controverted), this so-called "prison letter" of Paul deals with some fascinating issues, some of which are contained in our passage today. The difficulty Paul had with the Colossians was their worship of strange gods, the planets, for instance, a kind of branch of what we might call astrology. Interestingly enough, however, Paul uses this fascination with the heavens to his advantage from the very start when he cunningly shapes Christ's cosmic role in creation as the image of the invisible God (1:15–2:23).

So it is probably not coincidental that in the **Second Reading** Paul focuses on the Christ who dwells above and to whom we have access not by astrological manipulations or configurations but by baptism: "If you were raised with Christ, seek what is above, where Christ is seated at the right hand of God." When he tells them, "Think of what is above, not of what is on earth," he is not advising them of anything they do not already know—they have searched the heavens—but he is now telling them that the Christ who is above (unlike the planets) has a moral claim on them. Based on their relationship with Christ, they are to refrain from all that is earthly, such as "immorality, impurity, passion, evil desire, and the greed that is idolatry." They have stripped off the old self, as a garment. So in a very real sense, Paul is getting the Colossians to live out of their own vista, a heavenly one, but to observe that the Christian cosmos is composed of moral principles that come with a relationship with Christ, not cosmic identity.

Jesus warns us in Luke's **Gospel** today that this kind of idolatry has eschatological implications and consequences. Indeed, the parable of the Wealthy Fool is indicative of this section of Luke, beginning with chapter 12, verse 1, with the exposure to light to what was hidden in the dark, the killing of the body rather than the soul, and the advent of the truth before the Son of Man. This is the "vanity of vanities" of Qoheleth, as expressed in the **First Reading** where our earthly concerns will amount to very little in the big picture. Jesus underlines the futility of racking up things that will make us feel better and more secure, or storing up treasure for ourselves; that is tantamount to what Paul equates with "the parts of you that are earthly." Therefore, in Jesus' parable the question of possessions really gets at the root of the anonymous question posed to him and its theological underpinnings: "the things you have prepared, to whom will they belong?" The issue is attachment, building our own kingdom, and idolatry that deprives rather than shares with others; these are "not rich in what matters to God." Vanity of vanities.

Connecting the Bible and the Liturgy

Each and every day of the year and several times a day in the church year we begin the Liturgy of the Hours with a verse from Psalm 70: *"Deus in adjutorium meum intende domine ad adjuvandum me festina."* The invocation is also part of the **Entrance Antiphon** today, which, fittingly enough, sets the tone for the biblical readings for this Sunday.

A common thread that runs through the selections from today's Lectionary is the transitory nature of our lives and the crucial importance of "seek[ing] what is above, where Christ is seated at the right hand of God," or becoming "rich in what matters to God." Acknowledging that we need God's assistance, as the Entrance Antiphon affirms, is the first step to giving away our treasures on earth, or our "vanity of vanities." These possessions from which we are divesting ourselves might be the will to power and control, or the "immorality" of which Paul speaks, recognizing that we have "taken off the old self with its practices / and have put on the new self, / which is being renewed, for knowledge, / in the image of its creator."

With the assembly of the Christian community for Eucharist, there is an invitation to redefine our corporate and personal identity as the living Body of Christ, rather than as consumers in the modern culture. We stand ready to receive word and sacrament as children of God. So the **Collect** prays for this very reconstruction of a new self in the image of Christ, our true selves given to us in baptism, "for those who glory in you as their Creator and guide, / you may restore what you have created / and keep safe what you have restored." There is a nice play here in English that preserves the Latin original: "*et creata restaures, et restaurata conserves.*" That the one who created us will be the one to restore and keep can only keep us ever mindful of the love of God. Moreover, the Opening Prayer suggests that in this very act of restoration we are growing "rich" in the sight of the God who restores what he has created.

The **Prayer after Communion** makes an explicit connection with the riches in the things of God, when it says, "Accompany with constant protection, O Lord, / those you renew with these heavenly gifts / and, in your never-failing care for them, / make them worthy of eternal redemption." The communion we share of the one bread and one cup are heavenly gifts that make us rich in the sight of God. We are rich at this Eucharist in the Father's sight because he loves us as his Son with love. All is not vanity of vanities at the Eucharist —we could not be further from that condition, since Christ has made us lovely and rich in God's eyes. Rather, as Paul tells the Colossians, we are renewed in the image of the Creator, and it is then that we can say that "Christ is all in all."

Strategy for Preaching

We are taught from a very early age to build our barns big, red, and beautiful—large enough to hold as many treasures as we can hold until we die. And the more barns, the better! Just think of the storage companies now multiplying in towns near you. We are out of rooms, so we get more rooms. Sound familiar? We might meet the Rich Fool on our way to purchase another storage facility.

There is more here. All our biblical readings have some sage advice about hoarding, not only material goods, but anything that weighs us down. The barns are our kingdoms, which really begin to blind us to the real kingdom of God at hand. Our barns are the constructs of our own egos, which Qoheleth in the book of Ecclesiastes swiftly deflates: "For what profit comes to man from all the toil and anxiety of heart / with which he has labored under the sun? / All his days sorrow and grief are his occupation; / even at night his mind is not at rest. / This also is vanity." Qoheleth must have been an ancient psychiatrist. This vanity or, as Jesus would construct it, building barns is really about how we construct our identity, or how we define ourselves. So when God calls for us to take us home, do we want him to find a barn full of stuff or a soul longing for his presence? "Those who store up treasure for themselves" can be read in lots of different ways: treasure so that I am important; treasure so that I seem smart; treasure so that I can be admired by everyone in my neighborhood who has a smaller barn. Ego craves praise and admiration more than we may realize. Before we know it, we have selves that are choked with needs we have accumulated. Or better put: wants that we have stored up. They say that Napoleon Bonaparte was continually amazed at what his soldiers would sacrifice in order to claim a medal or a little piece of colored ribbon. Some of us will do anything for an honor or even a pat on the head.

Yet Paul asks us to take off the old garment and put on the new one. The only piece of clothing we need to ever worry about is our baptismal garment. An exaggeration, perhaps, but let's take our commitment seriously. What makes us more lovely than that white garment standing before God in our poverty of spirit asking for his help alone (cf. Entrance Antiphon)? We come to the liturgy to be refashioned and restored (Collect). The Eucharist is like the Garden of Eden in which we are created anew. (Image: children creating art in the classroom with various projects.)

And so we gather our treasure here—the heavenly gifts (Prayer after Communion)—which can be the source of making us rich in the things of God. We are made whole here and protected as Christ becomes all in all (Second Reading).

Nineteenth Sunday in Ordinary Time

Readings from the Ambo

Wis 18:6-9; Ps 33:1, 12, 18-19, 20-22;
Heb 11:1-2, 8-19; Luke 12:32-48

In the **First Reading**, we seem to have caught the author of the book of Wisdom in the midst of a profound moment of recollection concerning the sacred tradition of the Passover and its mysterious links to faith and holy memory. "For in secret the holy children of the good were offering sacrifice / and putting into effect with one accord the divine institution." It is as if we have wandered into the prayer of some elder who, in the intimate space of his heart, has disclosed a monologue of thanksgiving for God, together with his action and the response of the chosen people. In a short paragraph, the author shows us a telescoped history of God and his people and the legacy that cannot be forgotten—for all the ages to come.

The Letter to the Hebrews, a portion of which is excerpted today for the **Second Reading**, is also a kind of recollection of a wisdom figure, solidifying a sacred tradition and making that history present for us here and now in the faith community. As the author reads the history of the chosen people, it is a tradition of faith in which, according to the book of Wisdom, God's people "awaited the salvation of the just / and the destruction of their foes." So the author of the (anonymous) Letter to the Hebrews says, these ancestral witnesses are models of faith, "the realization of what is hoped for and evidence of things not seen. Because of it the ancients were well attested." Once again we see that sacred memory plays a crucial role in the faith experience; it comes alive because of the faithful witnesses of the past who, because of the persistent communal memory, do not even seem to have passed away forgotten into another world—still less have they been blotted out—but are alive in faith.

Abraham, then, is a model for the Christian people because of his obedient faith, from which "he received power to generate." Abraham makes the tradition of Israel alive in the Christian community by his faith, a pivotal theological point Paul would also make in Romans 4 when he argues that Abraham was justified by faith. Recalling such witnesses is not thinking about some distant, incoherent past, but a loving memory of witnesses who hoped and believed in the same God who, like the Christian community, "desire a better homeland, a heavenly one."

In the **Gospel** for today, Jesus more than gestures at the connection between faith and the Promised Land, a kind of longing for a new Passover to a Promised Land. He tells his disciples, "Do not be afraid any longer, little flock, for your Father is pleased to give you the kingdom." At the same time, the urgency of the coming kingdom will demand that our lamps be lit. There is a very interesting and provocative image Jesus uses and then reverses here. He compares the arrival of the Master to a return from a wedding for which the servants must be prepared. Fair enough. But when he gets there, the master "will gird himself, have them recline at table, and proceed to wait on them." The humble action of the Master underlines the importance of service, an activity with which the good steward will be occupied until the Master returns.

Connecting the Bible and the Liturgy

Covenant. Need we say more? The **Entrance Antiphon** could not be more appropriate in setting the scene for the liturgy today when it says, "Look to your covenant, O Lord, / and forget not the life of your poor ones for ever." This is Psalm 74 calling out to the Lord to remember the past, even as we are gathered to keep memory of the Lord. We are made mindful of the history of the promise made to Abraham, the oath he swore to Isaac (Ps 105:9).

One way of summarizing the activity of the faithful community Jesus left is like this: the church remembers God remembering his people. As we hear today in the **Prayer over the Offerings**, "accept the offerings of your Church, / for in your mercy you have given them to be offered." We are recalling the works of the past, particularly Christ's work on the night before he died for us, even as the Scriptures recall the past in order to ignite the faith of the present. The author of the book of Wisdom clearly writes out of a horizon of the past "fathers of the faith," with "sure knowledge of the oaths in which they put their faith, / [that] they might have courage." The **Responsorial Psalm** ratifies that experience of the blessed nation "whose God is the LORD, / the people he has chosen for his own inheritance." The author of the Letter to the Hebrews draws our attention in particular to one of these patriarchs, the greatest of them all because "he went out, not knowing where he was to go." Abraham was the first to leave his household gods behind without the wisdom tradition that would guide the future generations. It was this faith that gave Abraham the "power to generate." Finally, Jesus' promise of the return of the Master will once again put God's stamp on a promise he made long ago and will come in a way we least expect him: he will have his vigilant servants "recline at table, and proceed to wait on them."

In **Eucharistic Prayer IV**, we will note a kind of recapitulation of salvation history, a remembrance of the plan of salvation in Christ, with an emphasis on God's renewal: "Time and time again you offered them covenants / and through the prophets / taught them to look forward to salvation." The Letter to the Hebrews is in the background here as Abraham is showcased as the one who responded to this covenant through "the generation to come." Moreover, Eucharistic Prayer IV further highlights Christ's role as the one who renewed this covenant, the Passover once celebrated from of old and now "the celebration of this great mystery, / which he himself left us / as an eternal covenant." That eternal promise, that everlasting covenant or *foedus aeternum*, is definitive, not only because it is a divine covenant but because that covenant was entrusted to us through memory. It is a new covenant because Christ's blood has sealed the memory of that divine promise. Indeed, the words of institution that follow shortly ratify that divine testimony as Jesus says to his disciples, "this is the chalice of my Blood, / the Blood of the new and eternal covenant, / which will be poured out for you and for many / for the forgiveness of sins. / Do this in memory of me." So we keep the covenant entrusted to us until the end. "Blessed are those servants whom the Master finds vigilant on his arrival."

Strategy for Preaching

We do not really live in a culture of covenant and promise, the legacy of a post-Christian civilization. The society that prizes disposable objects extends the (dis)value to relationships. There is no practical reason for a covenant unless it is going to benefit me, so why do it? A social contract of the kind that informs our own is more in keeping with a pragmatism that lives in the immediacy of the moment; that kind of "covenant" specializes in safeguarding mutual interests and services. That the Master would gird himself and wait on his servants could only strike a contemporary as preposterous.

By contrast, covenants are forever; they are impractical; they cost us everything. These three qualities might play out in a core homiletic idea for today.

An introduction might begin with some details about the call of Abraham as we see him in Genesis, moving from a nomadic existence to a relational one with God's call and covenant. Or another possibility would be to take either the book of Wisdom or the Letter to the Hebrews and touch on the persistence of memory and how such realities inform our faith experience.

   I. Covenants are forever.

      A. First Reading—sacred memory in the Passover; faith alive in the present through the past.

      B. Abraham leaves everything behind.

      C. Jesus' eternal covenant (Eucharistic Prayer IV).

  II. Covenants are impractical.

      A. Contemporary illustration: prenuptial agreements, safeguarding possessions, the risk-free society, the Internet and the "present tense."

      B. Faith as the most impractical virtue imaginable—but gave Abraham offspring (Second Reading).

      C. Memory of the past informs the faith of the present.

 III. Covenants cost everything.

      A. New covenant in Jesus' blood (Eucharistic Prayer IV).

      B. The church carries on memory of Jesus' covenant until the end when the Master returns to remember us, waiting on his servants.

      C. Example of service and self-giving comes from the Master, inspiring us to believe deeper (contemporary example).

Twentieth Sunday in Ordinary Time

Readings from the Ambo

Jer 38:4-6, 8-10; Ps 40:2, 3, 4, 18; Heb 12:1-4; Luke 12:49-53

The stories about the prophet Jeremiah's persecution, imprisonment, and eventual liberation play a crucial role in shaping the fate of Judea and Jerusalem in the three Babylonian invasions that occurred there from 597 to 582 BCE. The passage we have in the **First Reading** occurs after Jeremiah's imprisonment in 37:11ff., an event that was precipitated by the false accusation that the prophet was defecting to the Chaldeans. The passage for this Sunday heightens the drama still further, when Jeremiah is accused by the princes, this time of "demoralizing the soldiers who are left in this city, / and all the people, by speaking such things to them." Having washed his hands of Jeremiah, King Zedekiah allows the prophet to be thrown into a cistern to die, but is later freed through the intercession of the Ethiopian eunuch Ebed-melech, who is a slave and an outsider.

It is notable that the features of Jeremiah's imprisonment and release accentuate at least three components. The rulers of the powers object to Jeremiah's prophetic interference and truth telling to the people (i.e., that anyone who remains in Jerusalem will die). Secondly, King Zedekiah is easily persuaded by these courtly powers and hastens to be at equilibrium at their manipulative request, despite the demands of justice. Thirdly, an outsider, a slave and marginalized person, becomes the instrument of freedom. Because of his righteousness, Ebed-melech will eventually be spared destruction that awaits Jerusalem, according to Jeremiah.

It is easy to see from the **Gospel** how there emerged such a strong tradition linking Jeremiah with Jesus. Jesus was also oppressed by social powers; he was handed over to them by other rulers, and was freed from his own tomb-cistern by God's liberating force outside of the forces of earthly power. The psalmist echoes the experience of Jeremiah and Jesus when he says, "The LORD . . . drew me out of the pit of destruction, / out of the mud of the swamp; / he set my feet upon a crag; / he made firm my steps" (**Responsorial Psalm**).

When Jesus says that he has come to bring "division," he means the truth, the disclosure of which will always be the cause of a divided house. For this revelation of God's glory he knows that "[t]here is a baptism with which I must be baptized." He will die for God's truth, and, in the words of the Letter to the Hebrews, "he endured the cross, despising its shame, . . . endured such opposition from sinners, in order that you may not grow weary and lose heart" (**Second Reading**). So fixing our eyes on Jesus "the leader and perfecter of faith" becomes a source of both division and victory. The Christian community will face conflict, polarization, and division as it grapples with the truth; but our victory comes from Christ and from being "surrounded by so great a cloud of witnesses."

Connecting the Bible and the Liturgy

Prophetic oracles are not meant to be popular. We certainly sense the collapse of Jeremiah's world when he speaks the truth to the powers. Jesus recognizes that there is a baptism with which he must be baptized, enduring the cross, "despising its shame," as Hebrews tells us. The prophet shows the sword and fire that must come if God's truth is to be spoken.

Underneath the call to speak God's word of truth will almost always be faith in a kingdom that cannot be seen, a faith in a God who liberates from the cistern and the tomb. The **Collect** urges the assembly this day to be mindful of what lies beyond mere appearances and points, as the prophets and Jesus did, to something beyond Jerusalem, to a new order: "O God, who have prepared for those who love you / good things which no eye can see . . ." There is a truth here that the prophet knows, which recalls the promise of a heavenly city beyond the earthly Jerusalem that cannot last. The implication here, undoubtedly, is that we all face some kind of an earthly city that will be the source of division and conflict, especially in a post-Christian era. At the same time, there is no indication from the Collect that we will have any guidance on how to get to the heavenly home except from a very nebulous map, the consolation of God. That is the way of the prophet and Christ himself. As Hebrews says, we keep our eyes on Christ and, in the words of the Opening Prayer, we beg God to "fill our hearts, we pray, with the warmth of your love." This consolation will help us to "rid ourselves of every burden and sin that clings to us / and persevere in running the race that lies before us."

We are hastening to the heavenly home, thanks to God's gift of grace. Despite the division that will afflict all who embrace the truth in our age, the Christian community embraces the one thing necessary, Christ himself, "so that, loving you in all things and above all things, / we may attain your promises, / which surpass every human desire" (Collect). In a sense, no true Christian settles for a false peace or compromises with the truth, even if it means living with a harsh reality. Zedekiah allowed himself to be lured in by princes who would distort the truth and would, ironically, only come to the reality that Nebuchadnezzar would lay siege, destroy the city wall and the temple, kill his sons, blind him, and lead him off in chains. A parallel with Pontius Pilate may be made, as he hands himself over to those who would barter for the death of the Lord. Moreover, we might say that if the Christian community runs the race, some will be blind to the truth and others will try to throw obstacles in the path of the righteous. But asking God to fill our hearts with the warmth of his love allows us, like Jeremiah and Jesus, to run the race before us.

Strategy for Preaching

For those who proclaim the word of God, there are at least two questions that emerge this Sunday: Do you preach the truth to the powers? This is meant to be an interior confrontation for the preacher, which might be guided by Scripture, such as the present texts or 2 Timothy 1:8-14, for instance. Secondly, how does one do this in our era of postmodernity when truth seems to be more relativistic than ever? We get an encouraging model of Jeremiah or Jesus bringing "fire to the earth" and facing the inevitable consequences of the baptism that comes from such confrontation. Catholic social teaching has maintained a truthful witness, despite often intense opposition over the years, championing the dignity of the human person in the face of a contrary social and cultural construct. The matter before us in today's homily is not so much particular issues, such as "a just wage" or pro-life issues, as it is standing in the foundational truth from which these values are derived. So the core homiletic idea for today might be that Jesus came to bring a sword, but it is not a weapon of violence but the truth to which all of us are called to stand.

An introduction could recount details of prophetic mission (Jeremiah could be an example), either biblical or contemporary, and then narrow into an image of something like a sword or a fire. That could be followed by this:

The truth is liberating but also divisive. Jeremiah proclaimed truth to the status quo, the powers who resisted God's word and made alliances with destructive forces. In the end, he may have been imprisoned, but I wonder who was in the greater prison (First Reading)? Those who deny the truth or those who are made captive for preaching its values. In the end, Jeremiah was liberated by a slave, giving us an indication of how God will liberate those who speak the truth. Jesus himself was vigilant in proclaiming God's kingdom, for which he was persecuted and murdered. But those in political and religious power only sought their own kingdoms. He was handed over to Pontius Pilate, who, like King Zedekiah, made a compromise with earthly powers. But God liberated his Son from death in the final truth of the resurrection (Responsorial Psalm).

So we keep ourselves in the truth by looking to Jesus (Second Reading; Illustration: a practical, local story illustrating what this looks like). He is the model of prophetic witness, who helps us "run the race." Our house may be divided in this age, but that does not prevent us from standing in the truth. (Now an illustration of a more global figure, such as Nelson Mandela, John Paul II, Oscar Romero, Dorothy Day.)

The kingdom before us is our true homeland for which we speak the truth. That is where we are headed now and at the hour of our death (Collect). God does not abandon us but listens to our cries in the midst of our truth-telling (First Reading; Responsorial). We walk in the consolation of God's love (Collect) and that is all that matters when it comes to keeping us true to his Word.

Twenty-First Sunday in Ordinary Time

Readings from the Ambo

Isa 66:18-21; Ps 117:1, 2; Heb 12:5-7, 11-13; Luke 13:22-30

Scholars tell us that the section known as "Third Isaiah" (chaps. 56–66) is summarized in our present selection for the **First Reading** and focuses on a universal recapitulation of all nations into God's presence: "I come to gather nations of every language; / they shall come and see my glory." The nation of Tarshish was probably a port city in northern Africa, Put is Libya, Mosoch is possibly just west of Polatli and near the Sakarya River, Tubal a region in Asia Minor, and Javan is Ionia. This list is a spectrum of diverse nations that reach "to the distant coastlands." The oracle reveals that they will come together, a nation of outsiders. Where will they go? To the center of God's gathering place, Jerusalem. When will it happen? Now. At the same time, though, there is a commonality shared among these peoples. "They shall bring all your brothers and sisters from all the nations / as an offering to the LORD, / . . . to Jerusalem, my holy mountain, says the LORD."

The passage is somewhat reminiscent of Isaiah 60:6, where [c]aravans of camels shall fill you, / dromedaries from Midian and Ephah; / All from Sheba shall come / bearing gold and frankincense, / and proclaiming the praises of the LORD." This earlier passage in Isaiah, as we know, is the First Reading for all three years in the liturgical year for the solemnity of the Epiphany. Consequently, the very short **Responsorial Psalm** for today highlights the global event of God drawing all people together and, in an ecclesial context, the church's mission to foster that gathering: "Go out to all the world and tell the good news."

Yet it should come as some surprise to us that the **Gospel** refers not to the gathering of the multitudes but the narrow gate. And this image—the Greek word is actually *stenos thura*, or "narrow door"— seems directed against a kind of eclectic plurality of nations, a narrowing of the door to God's house. But it does not seem that Isaiah and Jesus are really at odds at all: the point is that those who think they are going to be gathered up will find themselves facing a narrow gate. Indeed, the doorway is going to be narrow even for those insiders who think they have a place with Abraham, Isaac, and Jacob. Rather, "people will come from the east and the west and from the north and the south and will recline at table in the kingdom of God." Yes, the kingdom of God is wholly owned by the Holy One; we cannot control who gets in and who does not, as much as we would like to do so. For those who insist on doing so, Jesus has a simple answer: "For behold, some are last who will be first, and some are first who will be last."

It would appear that there is a common feature that draws people into the narrow door, but not all will find that sacred commonality. I would like to speculate that it is understanding ourselves as children of God—no matter where we are from or how far—that grants us entry into the narrow door. Small bodies, so to speak, pass easily through such a portal. The Letter to the Hebrews suggests that the discipline we receive from God solidifies a filial relationship with the Almighty, training us to enter the narrow doorway.

Connecting the Bible and the Liturgy

There is a clubby side to religion that is inevitably social and has very little to do with Gospel values. Such groups of insiders seek to exclude others rather than invite them in, and would prefer to keep the doors to their church narrow, the entry to which can only be accessed by those who have the golden key. The horrible divisions of race, gender, ethnicity, and sexual orientation are incompatible with the God announced by Isaiah, who invites nations to come from afar; these aberrations of Gospel values are further still from the world of Jesus, who proclaims the last first and the first last at the table of the kingdom.

When the congregation gathers for Eucharist it is a chance to listen to the voice of the Father bringing his people together, but that reality comes through the discipline, self-knowledge, and recognition of our own sinfulness before God and one another. In the **Penitential Act**, the bidding is to our "brothers and sisters" to "acknowledge our sins." We do so in order that we might "recline at table" with "Abraham, Isaac, and Jacob and all the prophets in the kingdom of God." "[U]t apti simus ad sacra mysteria celebranda"—"and so prepare ourselves to celebrate the sacred mysteries." This is our preparation to enter into the narrow gate, which Jesus is opening for us. It is the call for the diverse people of God to come to the center of God's dwelling.

We might see this door opening still wider in using one of the optional tropes (**Appendix VI** in the *Roman Missal*) for the Penitential Act, which, in the case of today's readings, expand the other liturgical and biblical conversation partners.

Lord Jesus, you came to gather the nations into the peace of God's kingdom:
Lord, have mercy.

Lord Jesus, you come in word and sacrament to strengthen us in holiness:
Christ, have mercy.

Lord Jesus, you will come in glory with salvation for your people:
Lord, have mercy.

These marvelous addresses to Christ mirror the action of a church that stands knocking at the door, not as an arrogant group of insiders who think they should be first at table, but those who acknowledge their commonality with all people. The gate is narrow but only reducing ourselves through humility will enable us to gain access to what lies beyond those doors.

Strategy for Preaching

The homily for today will necessarily have to deal with what the hearers will make of the seeming disjuncture between the First Reading and the Gospel, or account for how God seems to be inviting many nations to come, but according to Jesus, the gate remains quite narrow. Can we explain it? This apparent anomaly can, of course, work to the preacher's advantage because the contradiction delivers a narrative tension created at the beginning of the homiletic text that wants to resolve into relaxation. The good preacher will set up the tension from the beginning (usually a very good tactic in narrative preaching) and wait to "spring the trap" as the clues finally yield to resolution. So the core homiletic idea for today might be this: although many are invited to recline at the table with the Lord in his kingdom, the true child of God enters the narrow gate opened to us by Christ's mercy.

The introduction should immediately point to the puzzle of the Lectionary readings being at odds: If Isaiah's vision is about all nations gathering to God's presence in Jerusalem, how could Jesus say we must enter the narrow gate? Keep the narrative tension going, which is the key to eventually applying the solution to the question. Doesn't the church say that Jesus "came to gather the nations into the peace of God's kingdom"? The introduction could then lead into the clue to the resolution:

I. But when we knock on the narrow gate we do so as sinners, with no expectations.

   A. Jesus gathering the nations is a sign that we have come together as one, but that means we have to let go of our prejudices.

   B. "The last shall be first."

   C. Penitential Act—acknowledge our sins.

II. So that we ask to recline at table with Christ and all the patriarchs and prophets, but through Christ's holding the door open for us.

   A. "[Y]ou come in word and sacrament to strengthen us in holiness."

   B. Discipline required: to become like a child of God. (Illustration: we come to a banquet with the manners of discipline so that we might be more welcomed at the table.)

III. And therefore we await the kingdom to unfold before us as a saving event.

   A. Isaiah's vision of restoration (First Reading).

   B. Children of God will come (Letter to the Hebrews).

   C. "[Y]ou will come in glory with salvation for your people."

Twenty-Second Sunday in Ordinary Time

Readings from the Ambo

Sir 3:17-18, 20, 28-29; Ps 68:4-5, 6-7, 10-11;
Heb 12:18-19, 22-24a; Luke 14:1, 7-14

With chapter 14 in Luke's **Gospel**, we have transitioned out of a rather heated moment in the life of Jesus in which the Lord laments for Jerusalem and its rejection and stoning of the prophets. Broadly speaking, chapters 14–16 showcase the importance of extending our confining boundaries, beginning with table fellowship and then moving to the marginalized in one family and society, especially the poor.

This instruction in the Gospel concerning desiring places of honor (occasioned by how one chooses to sit at a wedding banquet) seems to have a double purpose. There is a general admonition to all, having to do with presumption or choosing a lowly place rather than a higher one. Jesus is clearly putting our relationship with one another ahead of titles and rank. "Then you will enjoy the esteem of your companions at the table." Secondly, the instruction is also meant for the "leading Pharisees" and those who "were observing him carefully," hinting that for this group, titles and appearances are important values that ultimately come to nothing. Jesus, in fact, addresses this host-leader, telling him to "invite the poor, the crippled, the lame, the blind." The host should do so because he will be justified not by his position in society or by associating with the powerful, but "will be repaid at the resurrection of the righteous." The question seems to be whether or not the Pharisee will even consider the reward later rather than now.

The urgency to humble oneself is a virtue for the Jewish community, something that is not lost on Sirach, who wants to affirm this tradition to those who may be adrift. "Humble yourself the more, the greater you are, / and you will find favor with God" (**First Reading**). The table fellowship Jesus recommends allows those who participate to engage in a long-standing tradition, but they will have to let go of privilege, rank, and honor in order to see the table of the wedding banquet in the kingdom of God.

I would like to think that, in some sense, Jesus is speaking from a divine horizon that accentuates his own kenosis as incarnate Word. Even as God emptied himself for our salvation, when the Letter to the Hebrews says that we "have approached Mount Zion and the city of the living God . . . and Jesus, the mediator of a new covenant, and the sprinkled blood that speaks more eloquently than that of Abel," the author highlights the humility of God that made our salvation possible (**Second Reading**). This is the "sprinkled blood" of the Lamb who took the lowest place at the table so that we, the blind, the lame, the poor, the crippled—the sinner—may have a place at the eternal banquet.

Connecting the Bible and the Liturgy

When the **Gospel Acclamation** quotes Matthew's Gospel (11:29), it is summoning us to participate in the divine condescension made manifest at this table service: "Take my yoke upon you, says the Lord, / and learn from me, for I am meek and humble of heart." The Eucharist is an invitation to a banquet from a Host who has invited the lowly to dine with him. We come as his guests without title or privilege or political affiliation in order to share in the humility of the new covenant made perfect in the Blood of the Son of Man.

That covenant, so eloquently expressed in today's selection from the Letter to the Hebrews, in the Second Reading, finds a strong connection in **Eucharistic Prayer I** (Roman Canon) with the *anamnesis* (second part): "Be pleased to look upon these offerings / with a serene and kindly countenance, / and to accept them, / as once you were pleased to accept / the gifts of your servant Abel the just, / the sacrifice of Abraham, our father in faith, / and the offering of your high priest Melchizedek, / a holy sacrifice, a spotless victim." This remembering of the church at its sacred table recalls what the author of Hebrews also brings into holy memory as well: "a new covenant, and the sprinkled blood that speaks more eloquently than that of

Abel." Christ's humility has made room for the people of God at the banquet of the kingdom.

A salient connection in this regard is the moment the presider elevates the host over the chalice to show the people and exclaims, "Behold the Lamb of God, / behold him who takes away the sins of the world. / Blessed are those called to the supper of the Lamb." When we consider that Jesus has made room for me the sinner, me the cripple, me the blind one, these words have special meaning. *"Beati qui ad cenam Agni vocati sunt."* We are indeed blessed because we have been called by name, despite our condition. We have not been invited to this table because of our position in society, but out of a pure act of gratuitous love on the part of the Host himself, who has gone out into the streets in order to find those he loves, who are the lowly; these become *"Beati"* because they are blessed indeed to have come to this supper of the Lamb, the wedding banquet that requires no admissions tickets or special relationships in order to gain access. We come without money and status. Our response, then, is not to take a high position at this table, but to say, *"Domine, non sum dingus, ut intres sub tectum meum,"* "Lord, I am not worthy / that you should enter under my roof."

Despite our unworthiness, we are called to the banquet of the Lamb. Our response can only be what any guest would do at a wedding: "The just rejoice and exult before God; / they are glad and rejoice. / Sing to God, chant praise to his name; / whose name is the Lord" (**Responsorial Psalm**).

Strategy for Preaching

The Gospel must come as a cultural confrontation by anyone's standards, especially today. With the growing division in our own day between rich and poor, the haves and have-nots, the insiders and the outsiders widening by an exponential gap, Jesus' reversing the social order and status quo to which we have grown mighty accustomed may be just too much to bear. Yes, this is a social Gospel. When was the last time you went to a dinner party and sat next to a street person because the original guest could not make it? Or a family on welfare and out of work showed up for a little dessert at your friend's wedding reception? When was the last time you invited the marginalized to have a cheeseburger with you? When it comes to the bigger picture, this country still has a long way to go for establishing equality. Democracy is a nice idea, but rarely lived to the full extent of justice. But Jesus seems to be suggesting that our table service—or the way we behave locally—could begin to transform how we make sense of righteousness at every level. As far as Gospel values are concerned, live out of the lens of the first will be last and the last will be first.

An introduction could look at many things—civil rights, the growing number of enclaves in neighborhoods that have pushed out the poor. Honestly, does this resemble the kind of kingdom Jesus intends to bring? Start with Christ's own table service and let this form the core homiletic idea. Jesus came in humble service to invite us as sinners to his banquet, so we must also extend our hospitality to others—even those outside our comfort zone. (Who are these folks? Name some general possibilities.)

The remainder of the homily would move from a christological discussion (Hebrews) to a discussion on the value of humility and how that becomes manifest in the Eucharist. He was himself lowly and brought a new covenant with his blood (Second Reading). We are given a place at the table because of his sacrifice and so we are humbled by that offering (*Ecce Agnus Dei*). (A possible image here might be someone who gives up his place in the lifeboat on the *Titanic* so that a poor person might be saved, or a firefighter going into the house of a poor family to save them.)

The Eucharist is the table to which we are invited to share in Christ's humility (Gospel Acclamation). Jesus is the host who calls out to the lowly and the sinner to join him at this table. We see in God an example of humility that is not only taught, as Sirach does (First Reading), but enacted for us. (Love's actions always speak louder than words.)

So guess who's coming to dinner? We are. But you might remember that *Guess Who's Coming to Dinner* was the title of a feature film in the 1960s starring Sidney Poitier as a black doctor who was invited to dinner by a very proper white woman and her family. The woman was also his fiancée, or so her parents learned. It was a very tough night. We still have them. Even though we have come a long way. But not far enough. Who's coming to dinner at your table tonight?

Twenty-Third Sunday in Ordinary Time

Readings from the Ambo

Wis 9:13-18b; Ps 90:3-4, 5-6, 12-13, 14-17;
Phlm 9-10, 12-17; Luke 14:25-33

The author of the book of Wisdom, who is usually referenced in the scholarly community as "Pseudo-Solomon" because of the persona the writer adopted, offers the Jewish community (probably sometime after 100 BCE) two distinct parts in the overall shape of the book. Our selection for the **First Reading** comes at the end of the first of these parts. Chapter 9 is an extended prayer of "Solomon the Wise," which will be followed by a new section (chaps. 10–19) that is a historical survey of how Wisdom has worked its way through the ages in the lives of the great figures in Israel, beginning with Adam.

The contrast between the end of the first section and the beginning of the second is striking. The prayer that forms our selection today in the Lectionary is a passionate encounter with the unknown and mysterious God. The prayer frankly admits to the burden and inadequacy of human life, to say nothing of attempting to comprehend divine matters, to which there is an obvious surrender: "And scarce do we guess the things on earth, / and what is within our grasp we find with difficulty; / but when things are in heaven, who can search them out?" The question discloses the importance and necessity of petitioning God for wisdom and its gifts, even from a king. That is probably why the Judeo-Christian tradition sees these ponderings in the book of Wisdom as coming from Solomon the Wise, whose reputation for desiring wisdom above all things (cf. 1 Kgs 3:1ff.) is well known in the popular religious imagination.

The acquisition, then, of wisdom is difficult and, therefore, the one doing so should be prepared for hardship. In the **Gospel** it is as if Jesus senses that those following him do not really grasp the reality of what is at stake in seeking God and his wisdom. His abrupt turn on the way with a command to "hate" one's family (translated from the Greek verb *miseo*, which also could mean to "devalue" in the context) signals the zeal with which the disciple must follow the embodiment of wisdom, Christ himself. There is no room for casual discipleship. That attitude is pushed even further with a harsh recognition of what it means to follow the example of the teacher—not only in words, but in actions. "Whoever does not carry his own cross and come after me cannot be my disciple." In a word, if you intend to pursue a relationship with Jesus and his teaching and his example, be prepared for suffering. Jesus' admonition is a sober reminder that the journey toward and with God will involve passion, rejection, and death to this life. For the Christian faithful, the alliance with the Redeemer is constituted at baptism, when the neophyte renounces the world and all its attractions as contrary to the Gospel. That comes not only in words, but in action: we have been clothed in Christ, putting him on like a garment.

In the **Second Reading**, in his own way, Paul is gently and compassionately asking Philemon to let go of the issues concerning a runaway slave, Onesimus (now a Christian), and move further into discipleship. In the process, Paul illustrates for us the cost of following the risen Lord. There are several interpretations to this short letter, especially in regard to the horrendous issue of slavery that accompanies a text written out of a particular historical horizon. Indeed, the letter would be referenced by both sides in the slavery debate in the days of abolition in the mid-nineteenth century. In the end the letter, to a leader in the Colossian community from someone who is himself in the bondage of prison, is a petition for reconciliation. Indeed, Paul's epistle is a good example of the practical demands of wisdom and discipleship: discernment, reconciliation, and obedience.

Connecting the Bible and the Liturgy

How much security are we willing to let go of in order to be the Lord's disciple? Based on our baptismal promises, the answer should be "everything." Indeed the author of the book of Wisdom suggests that an encounter with the Holy is a petition into the unfathomable reaches of what a fourteenth-century Christian author would call "a cloud of unknowing." Do we know what we are getting into with a discipleship relationship with Jesus? Probably not. Discipleship will demand everything. Just like a general sending his troops into battle, we will need to know it will cost all we have.

Our sacramental encounter with Christ is like that: it faces us with the extreme demands of discipleship: the cross placed on our forehead at baptism and the partaking of the eucharistic mystery. Indeed the God we encounter in Christ asks us to leave our "possessions" as we are taken up into the life of the Beloved, the life of grace in Christ. The **Eucharistic Prayer for Various Needs III** asks the Father to "grant that we may be conformed to the image of your Son, / and confirm us in the bond of communion." We may not be able to ask as individuals for such a strong relationship with the Lord, but the church asks for us. Like Solomon, we can only ask for wisdom; in the Eucharist we will be conformed to the Body of Christ in his death and resurrection, the only path of discipleship.

As Eucharistic Prayer VN III continues, the prayer underlines the cost of discipleship as a dynamic event between the church and culture: "Grant that all the faithful of the Church, / looking into the signs of the times by the light of faith, / may constantly devote themselves / to the service of the Gospel." For this discipleship will invariably take us at our word, which are the words we profess and so believe. If we want to be the one Body in Christ, we become the tool of reconciliation as Paul did with Onesimus and Philemon, even in prison. For the good of the Body we continue to reach out for the good of all, even if we are struggling with imprisonment from our culture. As EP VN III continues, "Keep us attentive to the needs of all / that, sharing their grief and pain, / their joy and hope, / we may faithfully bring them the good news of salvation / and go forward with them / along the way of your Kingdom." We should expect nothing less than the cross, because where the Master has gone, we hope to follow.

Strategy for Preaching

Unlike so many things in our society, discovering the living God and, indeed, allowing the Lord to find us requires a full commitment of ourselves, meaning that we will need to let go of our egos or anything else that keeps us from the pursuit of wisdom. How many moments in our day, we may ask, are full of moments and opportunities of grace which go neglected or completely unnoticed? Still further, where have we fallen short to embrace those difficult life situations, the desolations, the crosses, and not, like good strategists, sought for terms of peace with God, ourselves, family, and friends? As we might intuit, the readings provide more questions than answers. So the core homiletic idea for today might be, how can we best embrace Christ the wisdom of God, even in the darkness of our cross?

I think Jesus means to sober us up about the demands of the Gospel. So an introduction that sketches out a society overtly dominated by entertainment and leisure pursuits works well as a point of strategic departure. And then to structure the homiletic text, the EPVN III provides a basic narrative outline to help the listening assembly unpack the proposed core idea. That might look something like this, albeit in a reduced format.

It is not easy to follow Christ, as the disciples learned in today's Gospel. The cross is a necessary part of discipleship and when we embrace its dark wood, we conform ourselves to Christ, the wisdom of God. We ask in the Eucharistic Prayer for Various Needs III "that we may be conformed to the image" of God's Son. Is that the laughing, happy, smiling Jesus we imagine walking with in a fragrant garden? Or is it kneeling with him at Gethsemane? Is it swapping parables with him on the road to dinner, or walking the way of the cross? Is it just conversation we want, or to hang next to him on the cross? That means being with him, day by day. In so doing, we become as our baptism implicates us, more like him. For a moment just imagine what Christ looks like and how you might become what he is. . . . We are the Body of Christ, the church, becoming more like Christ.

Yet we still face challenges as we become instruments of reconciliation for our culture, friends, and family. Paul was an instrument of peace in his Letter to Philemon, even while he was in jail (Second Reading). Solomon prayed for wisdom to govern a whole nation. So again, the Eucharistic Prayer helps us to understand: "Grant that all the faithful of the Church, / looking into the signs of the times by the light of faith, / may constantly devote themselves / to the service of the Gospel." The "light of faith" was given to us at baptism with a candle we keep shining brightly now. (Illustration: passing on a torch in the running of the Olympics.) With that light we can see the face of Christ, even in the midst of what an ancient author called, "the cloud of unknowing." The cost of discipleship is often the cross of reconciliation, handed on to us by Christ for the sake of the world. Like a wise ruler, we look at our armaments and ask for terms of peace.

Why? So that we might mission as a church to the world. This is, after all, the church that strategizes for peace and reconciliation like a good commander (Gospel). Jesus does not want us to be in a constant battle with our fellow citizens, but to search for ways of peace. We begin with family and friends. Where is the peace I can bring? I will have to let go of my dearest possession for me to arrange for such a peace: my own ego. (Illustration: garage sale). But we will be surprised at the wisdom of compassion that such desire for peace enkindles. So we pray that we can bring the Good News to all. (Image: perhaps a soldier on a battlefield informing the other side that the war is over and that both sides were gathering for prayer to the one God.) So we ask the Lord to "[k]eep us attentive to the needs of all / that, sharing their grief and pain, / their joy and hope," we come at last with them to the kingdom. That is what it means to encounter Christ, the wisdom of God.

Twenty-Fourth Sunday in Ordinary Time

Readings from the Ambo

Exod 32:7-11, 13-14; Ps 51:3-4, 12-13, 17, 19;
1 Tim 1:12-17; Luke 15:1-32

The readings for today showcase four (I am including the Responsorial Psalm) of the most powerful instances of sin and reconciliation in the Scriptures. Moses finds himself, once again, interceding for an ungrateful people in the book of Exodus. In a way, this **First Reading** becomes a paradigmatic instance of something we hear rather rarely, though I dare say it has far from vanished: corporate sin. One gets the sense of a kind of wild abandon as the Israelites made their shiny gold calf for an idol, yet this depravity shows precisely why the people need the law in the first place. The Decalogue serves as a structure, a moral armature, as it were, to guarantee the true *imago Dei* of our nature, so that we will not replace God with an idol of our own choosing.

It is important to point out that Moses, despite all his frustration, loves the people. In a brief moment of stunning irony, God tempts Moses with an invitation to power: "I will make of you a great nation," the Lord tells the Israelite leader, after God has promised to consume them all. The meekness of Moses shines through here as an example of humility and the ability to even turn down God's temptation to power. But as a true intercessor, Moses helps God remember, even as the people have forgotten. So the course of remembrance has saved the people from a bitter fate and God from executing a (admittedly just) sentence.

The father, whom Jesus portrays in the celebrated parable of the Man with Two Sons in the **Gospel**, needs neither an introduction to nor an explanation of his behavior. But like Moses, the wronged father was well within his cultural rights to disown the younger son because of the shame he brought upon himself, his father, and the family. The return of his wayward son is all he needs not to pass judgment but to throw a big party in the delinquent's honor. It is unclear how repentant the younger son really is—or maybe just so desperate he will do anything to come home. But at the same time, the younger son must have had some great love for his father in the first place simply to take the money and run—and then the colossal gall to come back. At the same time, there must be a trust already in a loving father who allows such rebellion to take place. So the big welcome, the celebration, and all the honors were probably not very surprising to this erring son. It may have happened before. The older son, by contrast, has calculated his risks all along. His image of his father is one who expects a *quid pro quo* kind of exchange and is shocked when the father displays such largess and lavish forgiveness. "Look, all these years I served you and not once did I disobey your orders . . ." This is the kind of relationship the elder son and the father seem to have, until the father sets him straight: "My son, you are here with me always; everything I have is yours." Somehow the elder son missed the unconditional love that the father possesses for both his children. Will the elder rejoice over his brother's return? We never find out even if he goes through the doors to the celebration for his portion of the fatted calf.

In the **Second Reading** Paul tells Timothy that God considered him trustworthy in appointing him to the ministry, even after he himself has been the "foremost" (*protos eimi ego*) of sinners. God's forbearance and welcome to those who have erred yields Paul gratitude ("I am grateful to him who has strengthened me, Christ Jesus our Lord, because he considered me trustworthy in appointing me to the ministry"), finally, demonstrating that "Christ Jesus might display all his patience as an example for those who would come to believe in him for everlasting life." So when Paul says that "Christ Jesus came into the world to save sinners," it can only be the God of mercy, who runs to all of us, embracing us and celebrating the return of the one he loves.

Connecting the Bible and the Liturgy

The Father's celebration for repentant sinners has begun with the Eucharist. The absolutely marvelous thing about proclaiming

Luke 15 to the Christian assembly during Mass is that, in a sense, all the faithful older brothers (and sisters) have gathered around the altar; we have gone into the party and completed the cliff-hanger in the parable. The coalescence of the particular Gospel with the Eucharist can only remind the assembly that in Christ, everything of the Father's is ours through the gift of reconciliation in Christ Jesus.

As I have suggested throughout these pages, alluding to the various liturgical texts for homily preparation and its preaching is fine in its own way; they do not necessarily have to be used in the same Eucharist in which the preaching occurs. That would be true in the present instance, since I will be recommending an alternative text for homily preparation, but not necessarily for the Sunday liturgy. **Eucharistic Prayer for Reconciliation II** makes what we do at the Eucharist through Christ's gift to us quite explicit during the epiclesis: "And now, celebrating the reconciliation / Christ has brought us, / we entreat you: / sanctify these gifts by the outpouring of your Spirit . . ." We beg the Spirit to come be with us in our celebration of the Spirit that has been sent forth from the Father. It is the same Father who tells the whole church, "now we must celebrate and rejoice, / because your brother was dead and has come to life again; / he was lost and has been found."

We were all lost in our idols, our golden calves, or whatever sparkling object floats our boat these days, and have been reconciled to God through the intercession of Christ, who, like Moses, pleads for us to God for our deliverance. "When we ourselves had turned away from you / on account of our sins, / you brought us back to be reconciled, O Lord . . ." (EP R II). In Christ, the new law has come into being, freeing us from our self-worship and leading us to love God and our neighbor. We become *imago Dei* in the truest sense. Paul reflects on the force of his own conversion in the Second Reading when he says, "I was once a blasphemer and a persecutor and arrogant, but I have been mercifully treated because I acted out of ignorance in my unbelief." Paul credits his turn toward the good entirely to the gift of Christ; it was his lack of faith that brought him to self-worship. "Indeed, the grace of our Lord has been abundant, along with the faith and love that are in Christ Jesus." With this conversion, Paul has been reconciled to God in Christ and with all his brothers and sisters as well. Similarly, we gather around the table of the risen Lord, "so that, converted at last to you, / we might love one another / through your Son, / whom for our sake you handed over to death." This is a celebration of the eucharistic banquet that unites the younger with the elder, a festive gathering where all have been brought to life.

Strategy for Preaching

The preacher would do well to remember that there will be a distinct mix of younger and elder sons and daughters in the listening assembly who will all have their own interpretive take on this particular parable of the Two Sons. The "younger" listeners will undoubtedly experience themselves as something like Paul does when writing to Timothy as "mercifully treated," following a flashpoint conversion. These folks have had an Augustinian conversion, a moment of profound insight and change that turned them from one way of living to another. But more important, this parable was meant for the elder sons of religion, since it was the Pharisees, scribes, and clerics—those loyal churchgoers, we might call them today—of the first century who provoked Jesus to speak of rescuing the lost sheep in the initial instance. To this observation, I would also add that the parable awaits a closure; will the elder son enter the celebration, which the Father has extended to his resentful older child as well as his younger rebel? In our own context, by accentuating the power of the Eucharist and Christ's role as the one who is "the Word that brings salvation, / the hand you extend to sinners," (EP R II), we see that the people of God have already been gathered into a celebration in Christ. Will the "elder children," figuratively speaking, embrace this reality, the eucharistic moment of reconciliation at hand, or will they resist the opportunity for grace, live out of an image of God who is calculating and judgmental, and become more and more resentful? The challenge is to preach a God who desires everyone at the table and affirms the loyal and the faithful that they are always with him. So the core homiletic idea for today could be that whether we converted yesterday or have been faithful all our lives, God wants everyone to be seated with Christ at the eucharistic celebration.

An introduction might account for the seemingly rational nature of the elder son's assessment of the situation in the parable: The younger brother was reckless, brought shame on his father, and is now rewarded. Why go into a house to celebrate wayward behavior? That just rewards irresponsibility.

I. But Christ has gathered every last one of us here, no matter where we have come from; we have always had an invitation to come through Christ's gift of reconciliation (EP R II).

   A. Contemporary story recounting a return to a family or church in a personal way.

   B. Paul's story of conversion (see Second Reading).

II. And we only celebrate in Christ who has opened the door to the Father's banquet.

   A. We have all turned away with our own idols (First Reading; name the idols that surface in contemporary society).

   B. We ourselves turned away, but then "you brought us back to be reconciled" (EP R II).

   C. Even the younger son senses that the Father will take him back; he must have had an intuitive grasp of the father's love.

III. Christ did that for us so that we might return not only to God, but to one another.

   A. We might love one another through your Son, says EP R II.

   B. The table has already been set. Will we allow Christ to open the door?

   C. Image: a mother hosting a party for her young daughter, inviting *all* the children from the neighborhood into the house (description of some who might not be well dressed or have very good manners).

Twenty-Fifth Sunday in Ordinary Time

Readings from the Ambo

Amos 8:4-7; Ps 113:1-2, 4-6, 7-8; 1 Tim 2:1-8; Luke 16:1-13

It is not an easy transition from Luke 15 to chapter 16 of today's **Gospel**. The invitation to the father's celebration in the parable to both his children allows the Christian community to lean into a liturgical feast in which all gather around the table of the Lord through the reconciliation of God's mercy and forgiveness. But chapter 16 is an infinitely more practical parable than the one that precedes it and really bears more resemblance to a previous parable (something like a king settling for peace when the war is lost; 14:31ff.) than a patriarch's largesse at the return of his prodigal.

Though the context of chapter 16 remains different from the previous passage, however, Jesus creates a reconciliatory alliance between the shrewd steward of this world and the one who is able to purchase real estate in the kingdom. "[M]ake friends for yourselves with dishonest wealth, so that when it fails, you will be welcomed into eternal dwellings." Though these words sound like they should be far from our Lord's lips, this advice is far from an invitation to be a lover of the world, but rather disassociated from its rewards. The parable seems to be the question, what do you have to do in order to partake in the kingdom? Answer: detachment from things and owning instead a good zeal for God. This little inquiry may help to explain the moral that Jesus attaches to the parable: "No servant can serve two masters. He will either hate one and love the other, or be devoted to one and despise the other. You cannot serve both God and mammon." A divided heart cannot enter the kingdom of God. In this regard, the father in the previous parable becomes a lovely example of detachment; he does not need to play the role of shamed patriarch, but, leaving this identity behind, discovers a merciful welcome for both his children.

The serving of mammon becomes a very pointed theme in the **First Reading** in which the prophet Amos calls the northern kingdom to honest reckoning. With the ministry that centers on social justice in the years before the Assyrian invitation, Amos denounces the power structures of his day, or those who serve two masters, "who trample upon the needy / and destroy the poor of the land." Like Jesus, Amos concentrates on the practical matters of defrauding and cheating the innocent. So it would seem that social justice does not come down to lofty ideals as much as acting locally with integrity. God will triumph because, as the **Responsorial Psalm** says, God "raises up the lowly from the dust; / from the dunghill he lifts up the poor / to seat them with princes, / with the princes of his own people." As Paul tells Timothy, God desires equanimity and not division among peoples: "This is good and pleasing to God our savior, who wills everyone to be saved" (**Second Reading**). As Christians we cannot help but be drawn into a paradox: the rejection of all that is unholy, but learning from the shrewdness that comes from the children of this world. When we are mindful of our heavenly home, our possessions and the need to collect debts from others, the compulsion to be in control and become powerful or to have others construct our false identity, begin to count for very little. Freedom awaits those who are able to settle for less, which counts for everything.

Connecting the Bible and the Liturgy

I think it is safe to say that we will act according to our personal horizon line. In other words, our stance in the world determines how to behave and orients the decisions we make. Luke has given us his own horizon, out of which he sees the Gospel of Jesus: chapter 4, verses 16ff. The prophetic Jesus, rearticulating, reinterpreting, and fulfilling Isaiah's words (61:1-2), giving sight to the blind and setting the captives free, is the framework out of which the Lukan community understands Jesus in the world and will become the challenge for discipleship in any relationship with the Lord.

Eucharistic Prayer IV recalls this foundation the Lukan Jesus unfolds for us when it says, "To the poor he proclaimed the good news of salvation, / to prisoners, freedom, / and to the sorrowful of heart, joy." Christ has come to liberate us from our possessions, especially our greed and deceit, our will to power, the sins that infuriated the prophet Amos because those human flaws crushed the poor. And from the beginning of the Eucharist today, the **Collect** has urged the baptized assembly to reorient itself with the liberating horizon that brings about social justice and equality: "O God, who founded all the commands of your sacred Law / upon love of you and of our neighbor, / grant that, by keeping your precepts, / we may merit to attain eternal life." The keeping of the two Great Commandments helps to free us from our most treasured possessions—our sins. By steadfastly keeping to the sacred law we deal shrewdly with ourselves and the debts that hold us fast. That does not mean compromising with sin, but learning how to deal wisely with our own illusions and self-deceptions.

Finally, God has left us as stewards of ourselves, our neighbor, and the earth itself. It is well for us to consider the implication of our global stewardship, or how we may have squandered the resources given to us, or, worse yet, exploited the poor in this country and throughout the world in order to become wealthy. Again, Eucharistic Prayer IV is an honest assessment of who we are, where we are going when we acknowledge our limitations, as well as the Giver of gifts: "[Y]ou have fashioned all your works / in wisdom and in love. / You formed man in your own image [*Hominem ad tuam imaginem condidisti*; note that the word translated as man is not *vir*, meaning that *hominem* could be translated as "humanity" because the word is not gender specific] / and entrusted the whole world to his care, / so that in serving you alone, the Creator, / he might have dominion over all creatures." I take it that *"creaturis omnibus imperaret"* is not the commission to rule and dominate, but to become honest stewards who do not exploit but serve and nurture what we have been given. For the earth is not our possession, but the Lord's; God owns the planet in all its fullness. The freedom Jesus brings liberates us from the need for narcissistic control of our ego, so that we might walk according to the love of God and our neighbor, the two Great Commandments.

Strategy for Preaching

The biblical reading for today, especially the Gospel, will cry out for some reasonable explanation on the part of the preacher. We can take our lead from the First and Second Readings, though, and ask ourselves what is our foundational stance or, if you prefer, religious and ethical horizon. Amos commits himself to preaching a God of justice for the poor; Paul understands his own calling as emerging from the risen Lord, of course, the "one mediator between God and men, the man Christ Jesus, who gave himself as ransom for all." This is the true servant who, though sinless, made friends with unrighteous mammon, and endured a shameful death to free us from our debts. So the core homiletic idea for today could be that Christ came to free us from our debt of sin so that we might live in freedom and as gracious stewards of one another and creation.

An introduction might make a very practical analogy between being in debt and sin. What is it like to owe something to another? Have we ever been in this position? This could move ahead by way of example through a story or brief self-revelation, followed by:

I. But Jesus has come to free us from our debt and lead us to the kingdom of God.

   A. Eucharistic Prayer IV.

   B. Second Reading—as we "come to knowledge of the truth."

   C. Image or illustration: someone being set free from prison, either in life or in literature (such as William Dorrit being freed from Marshalsea, the infamous British debtor's prison in Charles Dickens's *Little Dorrit*).

II. We are invited to embrace this freedom through the release of our possessions—our sins or whatever else binds us.

   A. Collect—live in the "sacred law" of love of God and neighbor.

   B. Resolve to cut our debts/sins (Gospel) using the example of the children of this world.

   C. Illustration: someone who wills to get somewhere, perhaps one who is running a race and must travel very light.

III. And so we are set free to be stewards of one another and creation.

   A. EP IV.

   B. Amos as a negative experience of exploitation.

   C. Environmental pillaging of resources here and in developing countries; social sin.

    D. Social justice demands we live out of the Christ who set all people free and made us stewards.

    E. Image or Illustration: city soup kitchen where the laborers must deal with difficult prices in the market in order to serve the poor.

I have included illustrations or images as recommendations for all three of these sections because there will need to be a reorientation in language for the hearer, likely more so than usual this Sunday. It is difficult to hear Jesus say, "make friends for yourselves with dishonest wealth," and the parable needs a practical, concrete reimaging of some sort.

Twenty-Sixth Sunday in Ordinary Time

Readings from the Ambo

Amos 6:1a, 4-7; Ps 146:7, 8-9, 9-10; 1 Tim 6:11-16; Luke 16:19-31

In today's **First Reading** in the Lectionary, we pick up again on the rage the prophet Amos reserves for those who are "complacent in Zion." This section in chapter 6 emerges from a lament prominent in the chapter previous to this one and follows through with a series of condemnations of which our selection is a part. Having given us cause for grief and mourning over Israel, the prophet rebukes the passive who fail to recognize the death of Israel to come. Here riches become equated with what we would call today "denial." "Lying upon beds of ivory, / stretched comfortably on their couches, / they eat lambs taken from the flock, / and calves from the stall." As Amos sees the problem in Israel, "they devise their own accompaniment," once again picking up the failure to sing a national song of lament for the coming day of doom that is at hand. Ultimately, the failure of the complacent is linked to a neglect of God and his people, not only the warning of future collapse, but of the past, ignoring the "collapse of Joseph." One senses here that the sin Amos condemns is the blindness of communal narcissism and neglect, all too common throughout our global history and to be repeated again and again. The inevitable stratification of communities leads not to stewardship but to marginalization, denial and, inevitably, collapse. How many revolutions have been caused by arrogant complacency and indifference to the suffering of those at the gates? Perhaps the most egregious moral disaster in the last century was ignoring the plight of European Jewry, which was indeed in anguish at our very gates. The systematic extermination in the genocide of our brothers and sisters counts to our everlasting shame, while many remained all too silent or, even worse, looked away. Saint John Paul II made it clear that the church itself bears a portion of this "denial," even though individual church members were attentive and even heroic while Lazarus was at our gate.

Amos has a poignant illustration in another outstanding parable of Jesus, rightly celebrated even in music by Ralph Vaughn Williams's *Five Variants of Dives and Lazarus*, composed for string orchestra and harp in 1939, at the height of the world's Great Depression and at the threshold of the Second World War. This parable will draw to a close Jesus' admonitions to those in power who neglect the poor. In some ways, the parable is a coda on what has come before, a preacher's dream illustration, gathered together with some previous teachings and sayings. That one person is rich and the other poor does not seem to be Jesus' main point as much as the blindness, denial, and neglect of one for the other. I see the parable closely connected to the First Reading, a kind of Amos *redux*—not as a national catastrophe, but as a moral and ethical collapse. Indeed, the rich man (who goes unnamed) will go to the fires of the netherworld, oblivious to Lazarus to the end, lying on his own "bed of ivory," as it were. There are a number of ironies, among them: the gulf between the rich man and Lazarus is repeated in death but now reversed; the rich man finally opens his eyes to see the potential problem facing his brothers (also in denial, presumably) but it remains a familial concern, stuck in an enclave of self-serving usefulness; even in death the rich seek their own self-interests. Overall, the postresurrection Lukan community has some pointed observations to make about its own failures, and whether or not they are moving toward conversion: "neither will they be persuaded if someone should rise from the dead" sounds like a warning to those who have heard the **Gospel** of life, but risk complacency in their hearing.

Taken together, Amos, Paul, and Luke all bear advice to "pursue righteousness, devotion, faith, love, patience, and gentleness" (**Second Reading**). These are the virtues that open oneself up to the world of others, so that these poor ones do not face neglect.

Connecting the Bible and the Liturgy

As is characteristic over the last several weeks, the Liturgy of the Eucharist has partnered well with the biblical readings to enrich the Christian community with insight and understanding, especially about mercy, forgiveness, and reconciliation. Of all the magnificent language that has been passed down to us this Sunday, one line should hit us directly and squarely between the eyes: "If they will not listen to Moses and the prophets, neither will they be persuaded if someone should rise from the dead." That resurrection is our trumpet call to boost us out of our humdrum passivity, ironically quite characteristic of those who are comfortable with the things of religion. After all, we have nothing in the Gospel indicating that the rich man was irreverent, or neglectful of religious observance.

What has the resurrection shown us? Or better put: What has the one who has returned from the dead preached to us about God's love and justice? God's mercy for those lying at the gates of death. Christ has crossed over that gulf and brought us back from the underworld. "For by his birth he brought renewal / to humanity's fallen state, / and by his suffering, canceled out our sins" (**Preface IV of the Sundays in Ordinary Time**). God's love in Christ is precisely the inverse of Amos's fat cats on ivory beds, or the rich man licking his sticky fingers. The **Responsorial Psalm** (146) blesses the Lord who "keeps faith forever" and "gives food to the hungry" and "sets captives free."

Preface IV goes on: "by his rising from the dead / he has opened the way to eternal life." We are mindful of the things of heaven and Christ's purchase of our redemption. If the way has been opened to us, we cannot be complacent as a Christian community. It is God's great love that has come to us with the balm of his compassion (unlike those who, according to Amos, anoint themselves) and healed the wounds of our sins. So the doors where we once sat in an unimaginable void between life and death have now been opened because "by ascending to you, O Father, / he has unlocked the gates of heaven."

The **Collect** further reminds us of the continuing outpouring of God's love, not just on me, but us: "bestow, we pray, your grace abundantly upon us." This Opening Prayer recalls for us the foundational experience of prayer, which is, at its heart, a work of charity. We do not pray only that our little enclave or nest of self-interest be free from torment, as the rich man does for his family, but that we all might "be coheirs in glory with Christ, / to whose suffering we are united / whenever we proclaim his Death" (**Prayer after Communion**). It is Christ who unites us as we cross the divide that separates us from one another and from God.

Strategy for Preaching

The death of any community will come from its inability to see beyond its own artificial, self-imposed boundaries. When St. Benedict of Nursia wrote his Rule for monasteries, he set in motion a system of checks and balances, as it were, so that the little community would not become self-aggrandizing, or some kind of ossified, self-congratulating enclave of the self- righteous. Indeed, the guest, the youngest members, the local townspeople, all serve as antidotes to break through the doors. As Benedict imagines these somewhat marginalized characters, they were the original gate crashers.

And so was Jesus, who broke the gates of death by God's great mercy, healing the wounds of sin and division. He is the great witness "who gave testimony under Pontius Pilate" and whose risen life witnesses to us continually that we are one Body, one Spirit in Christ. Therefore the core homiletic idea for today could be that Christ broke the gates of sin and death, and so we extend our own boundaries in love to one another.

As some may have gathered from my reading of these texts in the early section, I cannot resist the social and ethical claim the Lectionary has on us this day, particularly the Gospel, loaded as it is with potential references to the ironclad boundaries of race, gender, and all sorts of discrimination. The historical data seems to me altogether too overwhelming to see any other hermeneutic than one informed by social justice. Amos is clear that the justice God demands comes from an enlightened conscience about who lies outside our door. Those lying on their ivory couches do not get it so they don't get up from their place of rest; the rich man in Jesus' parable does not either. And neither do we, or we would not have an increasing gulf widening between the Lazaruses of our society and those who choose to separate themselves from their brothers and sisters: divisions between black and white, male and female, gay and straight, rich and poor. A very telling illustration in this regard is thinking of the United States as a kind of Dives with our neighbor Mexico to the south as Lazarus. Some would have the already strong gate of indifference be raised even further and lengthened to a seven-hundred-mile border wall. How long does it take for us to hear the cry of the poor who want to start a new life, free from the sores of horrible drug violence and war and poverty? Can we be content to lick our fingers while we fail to see the Hispanic community as what the American bishops have repeatedly called "a blessing"? We already watched one Holocaust, unimaginable and ghastly, transpire from our passivity and neglect. We watched the genocide of the Tutsis in Rwanda in 1994 from our La-Z-Boys in the living room. What will happen on the Day of Judgment when we are on the other side of the breach?

To break through the boundaries means recognizing Jesus' triumph over sin and death (Preface IV). He came because we were at the gates of death and gave testimony to the resurrection (Second Reading). Amos and the Gospel challenge us to heed the warning of complacent living and ignoring the invisible brother and sister in our midst. (Illustration: street people; how do we see them when we walk past? We may not be able to afford to give them anything at all, but we can attend to them by respecting them, not treating them as objects and praying for them; that opens up a boundary, which was formerly closed.) God has granted not just mercy to me, but to us. Those here present and beyond. What gate will we crash this week?

Twenty-Seventh Sunday in Ordinary Time

Readings from the Ambo

Hab 1:2-3; 2:2-4; Ps 95:1-2, 6-7, 8-9;
2 Tim 1:6-8, 13-14; Luke 17:5-10

The prophet Habakkuk makes a rare appearance on the scene in the Lectionary for the **First Reading** today, although we might remember that his role in shaping biblical theology is far from insignificant. The first half of the book is a protracted complaint to God, somewhat reminiscent of Job, insofar as the prophet is confronting God's silence and inaction in the face of evil and misery. The historical context was likely the deportation to Babylon in 597 BCE. We can see from just a few lines here that Habakkuk witnesses a great deal of suffering in Judah, betrayed as it was by the Chaldeans and punished for its alliance (due mostly to Jehoiakim) with Egypt. So saying, Habakkuk takes up the question of fidelity and righteousness in the midst of suffering, even national calamity. Paul will derive his theology of justification by faith evinced in his Letter to the Romans at least in part from Habakkuk: "The rash one has no integrity; / but the just one, because of his faith, shall live." Beyond its historical and political ramifications, the selection from Habakkuk is a model for prayer in the midst of silence and desolation. In a sense, Habakkuk becomes "Exhibit A" of the man of faith—and so shall live in God's light.

In the **Second Reading** Paul's address to Timothy clarifies the role of fidelity in a pastoral setting and, indeed, through the legacy of leadership that expresses such loyalty, "through the imposition of my hands." The hope is that Timothy will give courageous testimony "with the strength that comes from God." Scholars are fairly certain that the authorship of the letter is not from Paul himself, but the "witness" is authentic: it comes from a teacher urging his young apprentice to fight the good fight and to "bear your share of hardship for the gospel." We can assume that the letter was written in prison ("a prisoner for his sake"), which only underlines the testimony Paul himself achieves: even in the midst of hardship, the man of faith lives.

It is no small wonder why Jesus puts such an emphasis on faith, which, as he implies from the illustration of the mulberry tree, has a life animated by the person of faith: "If you have faith the size of a mustard seed, you would say to this mulberry tree, 'Be uprooted and planted in the sea,' and it would obey you" (**Gospel**). The life of faith should be the very part of our lives that animates us—and therefore the person of faith lives. And, like anything that lives, it can be increased. With Jesus' encouragement to his disciples, he is increasing their faith by his own witness and affirmation. Here he is in line with the prophet Habakkuk and the author of the Letter to Timothy, as they set forth their own testimony, even in the midst of suffering and chains.

Connecting the Bible and the Liturgy

When the disciples ask Jesus to increase their faith, they are requesting something every Christian desires, or at least should ask for, as a kind of echo of Mark 9:24: "I do believe, help my unbelief." The problem, of course, is silence—God's silence, sometimes even in the midst of great suffering, as Habakkuk learned. It is one thing to have Jesus encouraging the disciples in their faith, quite another to face the darkness of God's response. The Eucharist, though, is by its very nature a gathering of the faithful in praise and thanksgiving that seeks to keep memory, the *anamnesis* of the Lord in ritual action and faith; Christ increases our life of belief by our very lifting up of our hearts at the Eucharist.

The common feature for the Eucharistic Prefaces in the *Roman Missal* is an explanation for our thanksgiving after the **Preface Dialogue**: "It is truly right and just, our duty and our salvation, / always and everywhere to give you thanks, / Lord, holy Father, almighty and eternal God, / through Christ our Lord." In the context of the word of God we have just heard, we are confronted, like Habakkuk during the Israelites' deportation to Babylon, and like Paul in prison, with the words, "always and everywhere to give you thanks." The life of faith asks us to be present—sometimes in anger or disbelief, sometimes in joy, sometimes with a question—to the reality of the living God who may hide his face from us.

As a community of faith we increase our belief by speaking it aloud. Christ prays through the whole church as we articulate our belief that God is living and active. This tightly woven reality of faith is clear in the **Common Preface V** when it says, "His Death we celebrate in love, / his Resurrection we confess with living faith, / and his Coming in glory we await with unwavering hope." The death of Christ draws us into the mystery of human suffering and the difficulty of witnessing the inexplicable. In the offering of Jesus on the cross, however, we acknowledge that God in Christ remains with us in our own anguish and death. And therefore, "his Resurrection we confess with living faith." I would like to underline the expression "living faith" because this phrase seems to me to draw directly from Jesus' own example of the mulberry tree, animated by a faith with a new life. Such a faith, even if it is as small as a mustard seed, becomes a wellspring of the love we celebrate and the hope for Christ's return: "and his coming in glory we await with unwavering hope." The authorship of 2 Timothy may be uncertain, but there is a characteristic and steadfast hope in the letter that speaks of the author as a "prisoner for his sake." We are given the virtue of hope by the gift of grace and through the testimony of the clouds of witnesses who have gone before us. And so Paul says, "Guard this rich trust with the help of the Holy Spirit that dwells within us."

Strategy for Preaching

I think that the preacher ought to take to heart the request of the disciples: we need to make known to the Lord our need to "increase our faith." Every single eucharistic liturgy is an invitation to the preacher to orient and strengthen the faith, hope, and love of the baptized assembly. Habakkuk raises crucial theological questions that cannot be passed over lightly in the deepening of the faith experience; this is not a naïve celebration of those who wish to escape worldly distractions by ritual actions, but a confrontation with a living faith community in Christ Jesus, as we give thanks and praise, even in the midst of our sorrow and the difficulties of facing our brothers and sisters and the world around us. So the core homiletic idea for today could be that we come to the Eucharist, even in life's difficulties, to give thanks and live through faith, hope, and love.

An introduction might confront the occasional silence of God—or the kind Habakkuk faced at the deportation to Babylon in 597 BCE. The experience of exile has been an all-too-common event for the chosen people throughout their history, most glaringly obvious in the experience of the Holocaust. To some extent, the church itself faces an exile its own, as the members of all Christian confessions scramble to discover a faith in a post-Christian world. We might say that the global community of all men and women of goodwill, with a desire to discover and seek God in whatever faith tradition they come from, encounter the wall of secularism and the forgetting of God. Yet still they come to God, as the psalmist did: "If today you hear his voice, harden not your hearts." We should not close our brothers and sisters off and *impose* an exile; we are about building bridges to get to the other side.

The Spirit tethers us all in. No matter how we look for God, we will find the Spirit living and active (examples of interfaith experiences that reveal a trust and hope in God). Christians from all walks of life gather each week to hear the word of God proclaimed in the assembly. The Eucharist draws us into the experience of the living God, no matter where life finds us. As the Preface says to us each day, we "always and everywhere" give thanks to the Father. That is a tough one. Life beats people up. Sometimes God does not seem to hear (First Reading; a contemporary example).

Yet as a community of faith we witness to one another, even as Paul did for Timothy in prison for an increase in faith, hope, and love. We stand before the living God speaking again the words of his death, resurrection, and coming in glory. Listen, for instance, to what the church says is our christological focus in the weekday, Common Preface V concerning the three cardinal virtues of faith, hope, and love. These gifts all originate in Christ.

So when the disciples ask for an increase in faith, Christ is already giving it to them and to us; it is a living faith, a desire that has been enkindled by his presence. That desire itself is a gift from God, who is present with his community at the Eucharist. Look around. We are not alone. Some of us might be in a prison of suffering known to God alone (sketch out some parish scenarios of recent sicknesses and hardships). Yet still we come before the living God and one another always and everywhere giving thanks and praise. To these gifts of faith, hope, and love we can only say, "Amen."

Twenty-Eighth Sunday in Ordinary Time

Readings from the Ambo

2 Kgs 5:14-17; Ps 98:1, 2-3, 3-4; 2 Tim 2:8-13; Luke 17:11-19

The **First Reading** is something of a close-up shot of a longer story—all of chapter 5, as a matter of fact—and details the great Aramean general who has some kind of skin disease identified as leprosy (most likely not Hansen's disease, as we know it today). Through the intercession of a young Israelite girl, Naaman mistakes the king of Israel for the one who might cure him, even though the girl told her mistress that it is the prophet in Samaria who would cure him—Elisha. Having said this, Elisha tells Naaman to wash in the Jordan and after initially resisting, finally does so. The story picks up from this point, as we see Naaman was cured and is so grateful he converts to the religion of Israel. Although Elisha will take no offering of gift for this cure, his servant Gehazi tries to manipulate Naaman into giving him the gifts instead. As punishment for this greedy behavior, Elisha sends Naaman's leprosy on Gehazi and his future generations.

The story helps us to discover the important linkage forged between conversion and gratitude—and its mirror image, self-interest and greed. The avenue by which a powerful general comes to the God of Israel is a young female servant, and this aspect of the story is also important insofar as we see God healing the mighty and drawing the warrior into the one Holy God by means of the least in society. The eventual submission of the powerful man to the prophet contrasts with the wily and crafty Gehazi, who seems to be gesturing toward an early version of simony, which would be condemned in the book of Acts. Perhaps there is something else at work here, as well. The story is a triumph not of how the waters of the Jordan perform magical works, but of thoughtful and hopeful obedience to God's word, even when these signs emerge from the voices of outsiders. An Aramean general has submitted to an Israelite prophet and a young girl and has been cured. The prophet Elisha does not work alone, but God's power runs through an entire network of those who serve and mediate God's divine purposes.

The parallels with the First Reading and the **Gospel** are clear enough, with some important distinctions. Jesus acts alone at the request of the lepers and these men are outcasts (not powerful generals) who are marginalized; they are then not only cured but restored to the community. The common feature of the earlier reading and the Gospel is the emphasis on gratitude by a foreigner, which Jesus is quick to point out to anyone who will listen: "Ten were cleansed, were they not? Where are the other nine?" Luke is obviously interested in showcasing the gratitude shown to Jesus by a Samaritan—the marginalized of the marginalized—and how Jesus returns this outcast to society. Once again, the emphasis of the story of Naaman and the ten lepers is on inclusion based on faith. The other nine lepers may be cured, but they miss the opportunity to partake of the community of the grateful, an action that triggers the Aramean general's conversion to the God of Israel. The reality of the faith experience is the human trait that not only saves but brings the outcast into the circle of God's love. As Paul tells Timothy, "the word of God is not chained." The Word himself has been unleashed to call all humankind back into the community of love. The response may be gratitude or not; it is up to us.

Connecting the Bible and the Liturgy

Each of the biblical readings shows a dramatic transformation of one who was once at the edge of a faith community but now brought into God's full circle. Naaman and the Samaritan leper are brought into full healing and community by their gratitude to God. Even in chains, Paul recognizes that "if we have died with him / we shall also live with him" (**Second Reading**). The "we" here is all of us who are assembled for the eucharistic liturgy, participating in the death and resurrection of Christ, who now are made part of the circle of gratitude, a "living sacrifice of praise."

The word Luke uses to express the thanksgiving is *eucharisteo*. Quite literally, the Samaritan came back to *eucharist* God through Jesus. We are likely to forget that "eucharist" is a lively verb of thanksgiving and not only names "the source and summit" of the church's activity at prayer, but expresses the verbal reality of each and every worshiper in the assembly: we "eucharist" together; it is not enough to perform the ritual of "showing ourselves to the priest" like the nine lepers, but responding in faith and thanksgiving, which saves. As we give thanks, we are brought into Christ's everlasting gift of reconciliation. The text for **Eucharistic Prayer for Reconciliation I** serves as a nice reference point, even if this Preface is not deployed on this Sunday.

Let us explore this possibility and its connections a bit deeper. As Jesus travels through foreign territory, the Christian community will remember that he has also become incarnated in our flesh to bring us back to God from the marginalizing of our sins: "though we once were lost / and could not approach you, / you loved us with the greatest love / . . . and did not disdain to be nailed for our sake / to the wood of the Cross" (EP R I). Jesus allows the lepers to come near him with cries of, "Jesus, Master! Have pity on us!" Surely this is the cry of the church as well, as we beg Christ's intercession at the Eucharist to free us from the shame of sin and death, a work he has already accomplished once and for all.

And indeed, the dead, the most marginalized of all, are brought into the company of those who gather at the Eucharist and restored to community by God's saving act. "Be pleased to keep us always / in communion of mind and heart / . . . Help us to work together / for the coming of your Kingdom, / until the hour when we stand before you, / . . . with our deceased brothers and sisters, / whom we humbly commend to your mercy" (EP R I). Christ gathers all from the edge of life—from the edge of eternity—and returns them to the community of love in the Lord. In this way, the community, to whom the lost are returned, is the very kingdom of God.

Yet it would seem that only the grateful glimpse the true kingdom. The others (sadly, nine out of ten lepers failed to return to give thanks) settle for a socialized religion, an experience of reporting to the authorities that they are doing their bit. The one who returns in thanksgiving, like the man cured of leprosy, says *"eucharisteo"*—"I give thanks." Having seen the coming kingdom in our own healing, we return to the community with gratitude. "Then, freed at last from the wound of corruption / and made fully into a new creation, / we shall sing to you with gladness / the thanksgiving of Christ, / who lives for all eternity" (EP R I). The restoration Christ gives to lepers is not just a healing but a restoration to the human family, to newness of life, to a new creation.

Strategy for Preaching

When it comes to the miracles of our Lord, the preacher will need to help the listening assembly look beyond the naïve reading of the text and help the baptized understand the deeper faith issues at stake in these wonders. Healing is one thing; God's restoration to those in Christ into the kingdom is another. Moreover, if the Scriptures emphasize the gratitude of those who have been restored—Naaman, the single Samaritan leper, Paul—it is not the preacher's responsibility to tell the congregation that they, too, must be grateful. Gratitude cannot be forced or legislated, for obvious reasons, and Jesus does not hunt down the nine ungrateful lepers to give them a pious lecture on the virtue of thanksgiving. Ideally, gratitude arises from the human heart in thanksgiving after a provocation and an inspiration, not a moral correction. So the language the preacher chooses is to create an environment for gratitude to emerge rather than to insist on its betterment or, worse, harping on its guilty deficiency. The core homiletic idea for today could be that Christ has restored us from the world of meaninglessness into the center of reconciliation and love. Period. With the unfolding of that miracle of God's love, I would let thanksgiving well up on its own, even as Jesus allowed the ten lepers to respond in freedom. The preacher can only evoke an atmosphere of contemplative gratitude.

An introduction might focus on the experience of being an outsider; everyone has experienced this, some more so than others. The feeling of aloneness and alienation that often accompany such moments of marginalization are very painful indeed. (Illustrations: perhaps two or three brief examples.) Then transition to the following:

We are all outsiders, aren't we? I am speaking about the unfreedom of sin; it makes us trapped in our little caves like lepers, unable to come to the center of the human experience where God dwells so deeply. We can name our own rash of sins that keep putting us back as outsiders. (Name some contemporary "sin afflictions.")

But Jesus came to bring us back to God by reconciling us with the Father. Like the ten lepers, we stand afar off at the beginning of the Liturgy of the Eucharist and cry, "Lord, have mercy!" God wants to bring us to the center (EP R I), "though once we were lost."

Aren't we tired of being on the outs with God and one another? The coming together as God's family in community of mind and heart makes us united and knit together to the living and the dead at this Eucharist, more than we would be anywhere else on earth. (Contrasting situation: we talk a good game about the global village and connectivity, but how close are we? As far as I can tell, with all our good experiences on the Internet and social media allowing us to befriend one another, we encounter a dark side of this technology that is fundamentally alienating—identity theft, pornography, and bullying, just to name a few.) We have all come here because we seek the one who has invited us, even as Jesus healed the ten lepers, and Elisha told Naaman to wash in the Jordan. Like Paul, we are united with Christ, even if we are in chains.

Encountering the community of faith at the Eucharist of praise and thanksgiving is a wonderfully healing and comforting experience. We should thank God for all those moments of invitation into the kingdom and express apologies for those we have refused (Gospel). This Eucharist reminds us that the kingdom awaits us when, "made fully into a new creation, / we shall sing to you with gladness / the thanksgiving of Christ, / who lives for all eternity." As Christ's Body, we share his everlasting gratitude for the Father and have been taken up with him in fellowship with the living and the dead in our perfect hymn of praise.

Twenty-Ninth Sunday in Ordinary Time

Readings from the Ambo

Exod 17:8-13; Ps 121:1-2, 3-4, 5-6, 7-8;
2 Tim 3:14–4:2; Luke 18:1-8

The selection for the **First Reading** from the book of Exodus points us in a number of interesting directions, especially because of the context of the present selection in the Lectionary. Chapter 17 begins with the famous quarrel that Israel brings to both Moses and God. Give us water! Why did you bring us out of Egypt so that we would starve in the desert? Familiar complaints. So the Lord provides water. Manna comes to satisfy the hunger on their journey as well. But the more basic question remains: Is the Lord among us or not?

Verse 8 looks like a battle scene between Amalek and Israel but answers the question posed above. As long as Moses keeps his staff raised—the staff of God—"Israel had the better of the fight." Interestingly enough, Moses cannot keep the staff perpetually raised on his own, but requires the assistance of Aaron and Hur. With the help of his associates in his battle scene, we get a preview of chapter 18 and Jethro's advice to Moses to find collaborators to help him with his work to act as officers over the people (v. 18). In some sense, our selection today is a pivotal point for God's revelation not only in wonders (water and food in the desert), but in the gathering and listening of the faithful where the question, "Is the LORD in our midst or not?" is answered in a resounding affirmation (17:7).

The collaboration with others as a witness of faith is necessary for perseverance. I mean the witness of the past as well. When Paul tells Timothy to "[r]emain faithful to what you have learned and believed, / because you know from whom you learned it, and that from infancy you have known the sacred Scriptures," he is reminding the young man of the support the inspired word of God remains "for teaching, for refutation, for correction, and for training in righteousness" (**Second Reading**). Figuratively speaking, Scripture is the twin support of Aaron and Hur; it supports the staff of faith, hope, and love—our tools of good works throughout our discipleship. Collaborating with those who reveal and hold the word of God to us is not a luxury but a requisite, since these are members of the community of faith, disclosing the presence of God in our midst.

The Lukan community portrays Jesus as very well aware of the need for communal support, "about the necessity for them to pray always without becoming weary." At least on one level we might read this **Gospel** passage as a bolster for prayer and not becoming tired or discouraged. Christ demonstrates the force of the word of God, of parables to keep us supported. Again, figuratively speaking, Scripture is the widow who keeps after us, provoking us, in a dialogue with our reason so that we might stay continually alert in our prayer. Scripture is the gift of consolation in the midst of battle, supporting and provoking, a widow who will not give up so that the Son of Man will find faith on the earth when at last he comes.

Connecting the Bible and the Liturgy

As always, the word of God returns us to basics: the need for perseverance in prayer, despite all our struggles in faith; the witness of the tradition in biblical history "for training in righteousness"; and perhaps most fundamental of all, the more than frequent provocative question on our desert journey: Is the Lord among us or not? The people of Israel found an answer to that inquiry not only in water from the rock but also in the collaborative witness of Moses, Aaron, and Hur during a battle. The Christian community gathers to celebrate so that we might hear once again: the word of instruction as well as inspiration. We participate in the greatest act of witness, Christ's intercession for us to the Father.

Eucharistic Prayer for Various Needs II immediately recalls that God is not only with us but among us, the church at prayer. We are gathered precisely to give thanks and praise to the God who never fails to accompany his people on their pilgrimage of life. "You are indeed Holy and to be glorified, O God, / who love the human race

/ and who always walk with us on the journey of life." Again, we might say, with the chosen people in the desert, when we look for his presence among us and find it through our victory, "Our help is from the Lord, who made heaven and earth." The **Responsorial Psalm** recognizes God's help by acknowledging God's presence as Creator of all things.

The Lord's presence is disclosed by those who have responded to the Lord's word—most of all and supremely Christ himself—who has gathered us as Word, even as the Scriptures have instructed us and edified us by their witness. The very proclamation of the Scriptures is capable of giving us "wisdom for salvation / through faith in Christ Jesus." "Blessed indeed is your Son, / present in our midst / when we are gathered by his love." (EP VN II). The prayer brings to the collective consciousness of the assembly the God who is with us in Christ, the one who has gathered his people to hear the word proclaimed and the bread broken: "and when, as once for the disciples, so now for us, / he opens the Scriptures and breaks the bread." Christ's presence in the breaking of the bread empowers the faith community as tireless believers, as persistent widows in the Gospel, knocking on the judge's door. Through Christ, the baptized assembly relentlessly offers its prayer persistently, proclaiming the passion, death, and resurrection of the Lord, "whether it is convenient or inconvenient." In so doing we will be found faithful when the Son of Man comes.

Strategy for Preaching

The dynamic present in the readings in our Lectionary today reminds us of the end of Matthew's gospel: "They worshiped, but they doubted." These seemingly paradoxical and puzzling words are meant to acknowledge that the law of worship, although meant to fortify the law of belief, sometimes falters. *Lex orandi, lex credendi* imagines a seamless transition from faith to worship, but the Christian community, like the chosen people, asks for reminders of God's presence among them. Noticing the God who is in our midst and naming the wonders he has done—past and present—will witness to the presence of God and orient our faith for the future; it will make us persistent widows, storming the judge's bench with our prayers. So the core homiletic idea for today might look something like this:

even if we wonder if God is in our midst, the Scriptures and the sacramental presence of Christ among us affirm and embolden our prayer.

A good place to start could be to use a battle metaphor, a simple recognition that sometimes life will be more uphill than downhill, fraught with difficulties, burdens, and hardships. Numerous examples come to mind, but it would be useful to draw on an allegorical reading of the battle between Israel and Amalek to talk about the way in which God supports us in the midst of our difficulties with Scripture and the witness of faith around us.

Jesus' remedy is simple enough: keep going and be persistent. He preaches a parable about a tireless widow, which serves as an image for prayer. The old widow is, in fact, a prayer partner for us; she supports us with our staff of faith, even as Aaron and Hur kept Moses going during the battle and, indeed, even as Paul kept Timothy strengthened by his encouragement. God "love[s] the human race" and "always walk[s] with us on the journey of life" (EP VN II). There is nothing the Amaleks of this world like better than convincing us that we are alone. The widow did not fall for that one, but kept going.

We are not alone either. Christ is present in the midst of the faith community (name the graces of the parish, for example) and especially when we gather at the Eucharist by his love (EP VN II). We keep each other going because we see the persistent widow in one another, a prayer that will not give up. (Illustration: the so-called "Greatest Generation" could be named as those who are now in their 80s and 90s who have been persistent in listening to God's word over the years, despite the Great Depression and World War II.)

We witness that faithful gathering in love with the celebration of the Eucharist. The disciples were terrible examples of faith before the resurrection and Pentecost. They fled. They denied. They bowed down in worship, but some doubted. The disciples at Emmaus were in despair until they witnessed Christ in the Scriptures, which he would interpret for them and break the bread that revealed his divine presence. Then, and only then, their hearts were burning within them. And so "as once for the disciples, so now for us, / he opens the Scriptures and breaks the bread" (EPVN II). We can see with our own eyes and hear with our own ears that God is present among us.

Thirtieth Sunday in Ordinary Time

Readings from the Ambo

Sir 35:12-14, 16-18; Ps 34:2-3, 17-18, 19, 23;
2 Tim 4:6-8, 16-18; Luke 18:9-14

If last week's readings were an encouragement to be persistent in prayer while witnessing God in our midst, today's Scripture asks us to be attentive to the quality of the prayer as well as the one who makes those petitions. Israel has typically concerned itself with the orphan, the widow, and the stranger throughout its long history, marking these lowly *anawim* as deserving special care from others and God. "Though not unduly partial toward the weak," the **First Reading** from the book of Sirach says, "yet he hears the cry of the oppressed." God's attention to the needs of the poor is substantially linked to the call they make from the poverty, the depths of their heart, "the wail of the orphan," the widow who "pours out her complaint." This is the prayer not of many words, but of the heart. Therefore, "The prayer of the lowly pierces the clouds."

It would seem that even in antiquity, the powerful multiplied words in a flurry of verbiage to get a good hearing. So Jesus' parable in the **Gospel** telling of a tax collector's righteous prayer in contrast to the self-righteousness of the Pharisee becomes an apt illustration of the tenants held by Sirach in the First Reading and, indeed, the **Responsorial Psalm**: "The LORD is close to the brokenhearted; / and those who are crushed in spirit he saves. / The LORD redeems the lives of his servants; / no one incurs guilt who takes refuge in him." There is a wonderful irony in the prayer Jesus recounts in his example of the Pharisee and the tax collector, intuiting the sense of a false self that accompanies those who may be professionals in religion, but lack the self-insight and understanding of their own humanity. The expression Luke uses to describe the "prayer" of the Pharisee is *pros eauton*—or "within himself" he prayed. That is far from "pierc[ing] the clouds," or the powerful "prayer of the lowly." On the other hand, the tax collector humbles himself, even though we could not describe him as an *anawim*; it is his disposition at prayer, not his economic condition, that makes his prayer authentic. He does not raise his eyes to heaven, but penetrates the skies with a simple utterance, "O God, be merciful to me a sinner." This prayer is less a word game of rhetorical tricks than it is a disposition of the heart. The prayer does not compare itself with others, but exists solely as an intimate encounter with God through contrition and petition.

In the **Second Reading** Paul poignantly captures "the cry of the poor" in his Letter to Timothy when he says, "I am already being poured out like a libation . . ." A contrast between Paul and the Pharisee suggests that they both seem to see their place before God as a competition. The Pharisee hopes that God will see his works in contradistinction to the rest of humanity—"greedy, dishonest, adulterous." But Paul's race is against no one except himself; that is his "competition." "I have competed well; I have finished the race; I have kept the faith." But Paul was able to accomplish the attainment of the "crown of righteousness," not by virtue of his behavior, but because "the Lord stood by me and gave me strength, so that through me the proclamation might be completed and all the Gentiles might hear it." Recognizing that the Lord alone can accomplish what we cannot makes Paul's race a prayer journey that God alone is able to perfect through grace.

Connecting the Bible and the Liturgy

The *Catechism of the Catholic Church* references the tax collector in today's Gospel as a model for righteous and pure prayer (2631). When the community of faith gathers to celebrate the Eucharist, there is a reason that the **Penitential Act** follows so closely on the heels of the Greeting; it is a reminder of our essential disposition before God as a humble people in need of forgiveness. Moreover, the wisdom of the eucharistic liturgy recognizes that this is human language on the lips of ordinary sinners, not the prayer of the perfect. Christ perfects our prayer insofar as we are humble enough to stand afar off and say, "O God, be merciful to me a sinner." In so doing, we allow Christ to be the single word that brings salvation in gratitude to the Father, a prayer devoid of the artifice and titles and honors that so often accompany daily human language, so that we might go home justified.

As we know, there are a number of options available for the Penitential Act, but one impresses me as being directly related to our Lectionary readings this day. Having invited the faithful into the Penitential Act itself by acknowledging our sins so that we might be prepared to celebrate the sacred mysteries, the prayer goes right to the heart—or, even more, pierces the clouds. Priest or deacon: "Have mercy on us, O Lord." People: "For we have sinned against you." Where else in the secular public forum is there any acknowledgment of corporate and personal guilt? Answer: Nowhere. But in the sublime act of the eucharistic liturgy, the church admits it has sinned and that almighty God remains the Giver of all blessings and forgiveness. The Pharisee used his public worship in the house of God as an occasion to blame someone else, compare his virtues, and "pray" within himself. He sounds like a politician. But the church prays as a sinner, a tax collector for mercy. Recent popes have demonstrated the reality of this confession by admitting to the church's guilt in some very serious and egregious areas, notably anti-Semitism and the priest abuse scandal.

But there is more. We need to see that act of divine compassion unfolding for the sinner when we ask for that mercy. Priest: "Show us, O Lord, your mercy." People: "And grant us your salvation." In a sense, the prayer of the church helps to complete the tax collector's prayer; we ask to see and benefit from salvation. We do so because Christ completes the church's prayer, now poured out as a libation in blood and water. This Penitential Act is an acknowledgment of our weakness and God's strength. We come to the Lord, knowing that the cry of the poor will be heard by the God of justice. We also know that the One who hears our prayer gives heed to our groaning because of the humble Christ who embraced our humanity and his own death on the cross so that we might speak to God a word of love, faith, and gratitude. With Christ, we pierce the heavens with our prayers, no matter how base our condition.

Strategy for Preaching

When I look on the faces of those assembled for worship, I sense a deep eagerness for the presence of the Holy from the people of God.

How that experience of God in prayer might be deepened is the work of grace, but facilitated in Word and sacrament. The cry of the poor is all of us, because "we do not know how to pray as we ought," as Paul says in Romans (8:26), and the Spirit prays within us in our weakness, our poverty. Acknowledging our poverty before God, like the tax collector, begins the initial foray into the great prayer of thanksgiving, the Eucharist. So the core homiletic idea for today might be that we are all poor before the altar of God and acknowledge the need for mercy, which he hears in love.

I suggest that a good starting point is the *Catechism*'s teaching on prayer, particularly since it references the tax collector in Luke's Gospel as an iconic portrait of prayer. It may be a source of wonder to some why humility is the point of departure for the prayer of the righteous and that petition remains linked to our interior disposition.

The homily might then begin with an allusion to the Penitential Act as the church's disposition before the heavens, which we will pierce through the Eucharist we celebrate. "Have mercy on us, O Lord" articulates the church's voice humbling itself before God, not with words but through the admission of faults: "For we have sinned against you." (Illustration: the tax collector admitting who he is before God.)

So God hears the cry of the poor. (Contra example: the Pharisee prays "to himself.") Sirach draws from a long history of God's love for the weak and the poor and the oppressed. The church's stance for the poor and justice for the afflicted is everywhere in the social teaching of the Catholic Church and especially in the celebrated phrase, "the preferential option for the poor."

So the signs of God's action for all of us in need are everywhere. We see it in Scriptures as Paul pours himself out as a "libation." We see it before us in the Eucharist, where in our poverty we are given to eat and drink from the one bread and one cup. We ask, then, to see that salvation now (Penitential Act) through God's mercy. This Eucharist is the saving sign for God's love for the poor. We are fed and come to the waters without cost, as the prophet Isaiah says (55:1ff.). Humility before the Lord makes our prayer perfect through the God who became one of us.

Thirty-First Sunday in Ordinary Time

Readings from the Ambo

Wis 11:22–12:2; Ps 145:1-2, 8-9, 10-11, 13, 14;
2 Thess 1:11–2:2; Luke 19:1-10

The charming episode portraying Jesus and Zacchaeus is a quirky little story with a funny little man at the center. Although the **Gospel** describes him as "a chief tax collector and also a wealthy man," Zacchaeus is clearly on the edge of society because of his function as a tax collector and, therefore, a sinner. Underlying Zacchaeus's marginal characteristic is his current vantage point, which, as it happens, is a sycamore tree. The thought of a powerful man seeing Jesus by climbing a tree because he was short of stature has its comic side. I wonder about this man and the humor he brings to the Gospel, not to mention the potential for conversion to those who hear his story. That *metanoia* comes because Jesus has invited himself over to Zacchaeus's house as a guest for the evening. According to the way the narrative progresses in Luke, this stopover is a change of plan, since Jesus originally "came to Jericho and intended to pass through the town." Also, this self-invitation on the part of Christ to enter the house of a sinner is something of a reversal of the Roman centurion in Luke 7:1-10, where the Gentile expresses his unworthiness for the Lord to come under his roof. By contrast, Zacchaeus "came down quickly and received him with joy."

But what seems to provide the moment of further conversion is being named a sinner by the grumbling crowds, a remark really directed mostly at Jesus for his audacity to board with a tax collector. Zacchaeus takes their remarks to heart: "Behold, half of my possessions, Lord, I shall give to the poor, and if I have extorted anything from anyone I shall repay it four times over." The translation here is notoriously ambiguous. As we have it here, the tense is rendered into English in the future ("I shall give"), but the tense in Greek is really just the simple first-person singular *didomi*. The point is, though, that the verb only makes sense as a reference to the future, if we reckon Zacchaeus coming to a moment of conversion. If not, this little man is just defending what he usually does—"I give to the poor." Indeed, Jesus' response only makes sense in the context of a *metanoia* on the part of the one he is about to sanctify by his presence: "Today salvation has come to this house." It is a transformation or change of heart that repositions Zacchaeus into the chosen people, since "this man too is a descendant of Abraham." Jesus has brought back a lost sheep, somewhat different from the Prodigal Son in Luke 15, but marginalized by wealth rather than poverty and youthful arrogance.

The divine urgency that caused Jesus to change his plans provides a conversion in Jericho and lies behind every change of heart. Grace will meet us where we are—even if we are, so to speak, too short to see and climb up a sycamore tree. Paul's prayer for Timothy in the **Second Reading** carries this same determination for conversion. Perhaps Timothy is to move further toward God's consolation when Paul says to him, "We always pray for you, that our God may make you worthy of his calling and powerfully bring to fulfillment every good purpose and every effort of faith, that the name of our Lord Jesus may be glorified in you, and you in him." This prayer begs the intercession of God for the conversion of every person, even those already on the way, to make us all "worthy of his calling."

Paul senses, I think, that the God of the living wants only our good and can will only our good. As the book of Wisdom says, "you spare all things, because they are yours, / O LORD and lover of souls / . . . you rebuke offenders little by little . . ." (**First Reading**). Perhaps this observation in the text explains why Luke 19:1-10 has always struck me as having such a humorous side; it is because Jesus just seems to be inching up little by little on the little man, Zacchaeus, until the moment when salvation has come to his house—quite literally staying at his door and inside his very home.

Connecting the Bible and the Liturgy

Zacchaeus's conversion already occurred when he was halfway up the sycamore tree. Indeed, the desire to see Jesus is the fire that burns for the peace Christ offers, the salvation that ultimately visits our house. Immediately prior to our reception of the Body and Blood of the Lord, our moment of conversion to be one with him as members of his Body, the celebrant gives us a vision of Christ the Bridegroom, the Lamb, who awaits the church, his Bride: "Behold the Lamb of God, / behold him who takes away the sins of the world. / Blessed are those called to the supper of the Lamb." The new translation in the *Roman Missal* for "Behold" (*Ecce*), which was changed from "This is," emphasizes that we have come to see him, to behold him out from our own vantage point, even as little Zacchaeus has done when Jesus comes to visit him.

Our response to the Lord on the occasion of his visit to our house in this communion, like the centurion in Luke 7:1-10 and indeed the small man in the sycamore tree, is humble conversion: "*Domine, non sum dingus, ut intres sub tectum meum, sed tantum dic verbo, et sanabitur anima mea.*" A change from the previous translation as well, this new version puts an emphasis on the "*tectum meum*"—my roof—as well as the sanctification of the soul. The change clearly duplicates the centurion's response to the Lord. But further, if Zacchaeus received the Lord under his roof with joy, we take the news that Christ has also come to our daily dwelling with elation.

The affirmation of our communion with the Lord is the "salvation [that] has come to this house" not tomorrow but today—now. He will say the word and, like the astonished centurion, we will find that the Word has come in an instant to sanctify our house. In this regard, the Gospel is often used as one of the options for the rite **For the Dedication of a Church and an Altar**, and the **Collect** for such a celebration is a fitting rejoinder to the affirmation of the salvation that has come to sanctify our house. "Almighty ever-living God, / pour out your grace upon this place / and extend the gift of your help / to all who call upon you, / that the power of your word and of the Sacraments / may strengthen here the hearts of all the faithful." Christ's sanctification of our house can only cause us to love more— to give away what we have and receive the only possession that matters as the door of our hearts are open to receive him. With Paul, we ask that God make us "worthy of his calling and powerfully bring to fulfillment every good purpose and every effort of faith, that the name of our Lord Jesus may be glorified" in us. The word that has been spoken to us is "Jesus," which brings salvation to our house;

that is the word that has been uttered so that our souls may be healed.

Strategy for Preaching

Luke's account of the story of Zacchaeus is one of those disarming Gospel narratives that grabs us before we realize we have been touched by its power. Like Jesus himself, the passage sneaks up on us in our quiet little town, our small house, and moves us to conversion. The passage is vivid, humorous, and profound. The congregation will probably find itself inevitably taken by this erstwhile wealthy tax collector who is curious about the rabbi from Nazareth passing by and who winds up as a houseguest at his table. That Jesus is no ordinary houseguest may be hidden for now, but the Lord's forward behavior would suggest that there is more at stake than just an interest in table fellowship; it is a matter of Christ seeking out the marginalized and bringing them to the center. So the core homiletic idea for today could be that we have come to zealously seek the Lord, but he wants to find us even more so that he may bring us sanctification and love.

The preacher might consider an introduction that handles one of life's more quirky episodes: getting to a new place by following an older one. I am thinking here, for instance, of a couple who eventually married and who met on a double date, but each was with a different partner originally. Or getting a new job—a life career—because one assigned work with an agency from a former employer. Zacchaeus starts out to gawk as a tourist, a curiosity seeker in part, but winds up as a host. Such began his journey and that is our path as well. So much of true conversion is really related to hospitality, how we welcome God and one another into our hearts. That guest comes slowly, as if we were welcoming this stranger from room to room. Faith development, together with its partner, conversion, is like that: we are drawn into its world slowly by God's healing forgiveness (First Reading). We come to see Jesus in the Eucharist from our own vantage point. Maybe we have been estranged from the community of God, but "Behold the Lamb of God" is an invitation to come down from the tree of isolation and eat.

God seeks us out, even though we are ill-suited to be the host of such a Guest. Just before communion we reach a point of conversion as did Zacchaeus, when we can receive Christ with joy, but know we are unworthy to have him "enter under [our] roof." We receive strength knowing that salvation and sanctification have come to our house (Gospel; Second Reading; Collect for Church Dedication). Our union with the Lord brings us the joy of coming down from our individualism and surrendering our property to the one who loves us and cannot do otherwise (First Reading). We become consecrated to the Lord by his very act of abiding with us. (Consider using a hymn text for an allusion, such as "Lord Jesus, Abide with Us.")

Thirty-Second Sunday in Ordinary Time

Readings from the Ambo

2 Macc 7:1-2, 9-14; Ps 17:1, 5-6, 8, 15;
2 Thess 2:16–3:5; Luke 20:27-38

The First and Second books of Maccabees are positively loaded with very interesting and very complex Jewish history. Our selection from Second Maccabees for the **First Reading** represents something of a climax in an ongoing story of oppression and revolt transpiring during the second temple period. With some exceptions, the Jews during this period believed in the resurrection of the dead, which finds an echo in the speech of the fourth brother about to be slain during the reign of Antiochus IV when that faithful son of Israel says, "It is my choice to die at the hands of men with the hope God gives of being raised up by him; but for you, there will be no resurrection to life."

Despite the historical density involved in decoding Second Maccabees, Catholic Christians will find the heroic martyrdom of the seven brothers rather familiar, since their refusal to comply with Antiochus's order to disobey the law resembles the hagiographies of many Christian martyrs, especially in the first centuries of the early church. Yet to modern ears, however, this dietary transgression on the part of the Maccabean brothers sounds fatally scrupulous, but what was sacred to the brothers was keeping the law of Moses. So they say, "We are ready to die rather than transgress the laws of our ancestors. . . . you are depriving us of this present life, but the King of the world will raise us up to live again forever. It is for his laws that we are dying." These are witnesses from the past recorded to strengthen the lives of those who remain. Indeed, after the grotesque details in chapter 7, Judas Maccabeus leads a revolt of faithful Jews, who defeat General Nicanor in the Battle of Adasa. Antiochus dies and Judas and his followers restore and purify the temple.

It may appear ostensibly that the linkage between the First Reading and the **Gospel** concerns the parallel between the seven brothers. But the deeper issue is, of course, the resurrection, which the Sadducees, the elite keepers of the temple, categorically deny. And so, these Sadducees attempt to trap Jesus into a conflicted answer about the law, ordering a brother to marry his deceased brother's wife (Deut 25:5). But instead of falling into their snare, Jesus interprets salvation history to them as precisely that—salvation, a point they have missed entirely in their dusting off the scrolls of the law. "[T]hose who are deemed worthy to attain to the coming age and to the resurrection of the dead neither marry nor are given in marriage." Jesus' understanding is that life and death are interpreted by a comprehension of God, who alone made himself known to Moses, "and he is not God of the dead, but of the living, for to him all are alive." Ironically, the Sadducees themselves would be all but dead as a group after the temple is destroyed in 70 CE.

Jesus and the Maccabees place their hope in the God of the living. As Paul tells the Thessalonians, "the Lord is faithful; he will strengthen you and guard you from the evil one" (**Second Reading**). In a sense, a belief in the resurrection remains a pledge to God's fidelity and strength, already present in this age and destined to be revealed in full in the age to come. We have the testimony of faithful witnesses, the martyrs, to keep us mindful of God's own witness as the Creator who loves those he has fashioned in his image.

Connecting the Bible and the Liturgy

If we believe that when we gather to eat this bread and drink this cup, we proclaim the death of the Lord until he comes again, we are testifying to the resurrection of Christ and witnessing to the hope of our own eternal life with him. The Eucharist reveals to us a God of the living, working in and through his people. Even in the midst of life's difficulties, we recount our belief in the God of salvation and life, as Jesus did to the Sadducees. We proclaim the truth heroically, with the models of the Maccabean brothers handed down to us as faithful witnesses to the resurrection of the dead.

Certain selections from **Preface I for the Dead** are a fitting analogue for today, establishing appropriate coordinates for the belief we profess. When the faithful typically hear this Preface, they are obviously in a state of grief. But while not deploying this Preface today as a performance text—for obvious reasons—but rather as a reflective touchstone for shaping the biblical witness, the language of hope in the resurrection will prove altogether fruitful.

Every Eucharist announces, "In him the hope of blessed resurrection has dawned." We count ourselves among those who testify to the reality of Christ's resurrection and indeed the God of the living. The use of the word "dawned" picks up on the image we have from the resurrection accounts of our Lord, but I think there is something even more at stake. The resurrection has dawned after the night of salvation history has reached its climax in the witness of witnesses, Christ himself. Denied and betrayed, Christ was put to death by earthly powers, but the temple of his earthly body was raised up and glorified by the God who is faithful. As we know, the second temple would be destroyed, together with the Sadducees and their legacy, but Christ lives on in his faithful church.

"Indeed for your faithful, Lord, / life is changed not ended." This was the mantra of Jewish and Christian martyrs who believed that "the King of the world will raise us up to live again forever." The faithful are those who die in Christ and so, like him, they will be restored to a lasting temple because "when this earthly dwelling turns to dust, / an eternal dwelling is made ready for them in heaven." In his response to those who would deny the resurrection, Jesus looks through his life and the lives of those around him from the vantage point of the age that is to come, an eternal city for the undying and the faithful witness. "They can no longer die, for they are like angels; and they are the children of God because they are the ones who will rise." In the end, these readings—biblical and liturgical—are meant to convey the presence of a faith community witnessing to a God who keeps faith forever and keeps us safe, even in death.

Strategy for Preaching

As I have suggested before, we do not preach nearly enough about the joy of the resurrection and the age to come. But proclamation of the kingdom and the God who keeps faith forever are deeply associated with the Creed we profess, as well as with the biblical and liturgical readings for today. Moreover, the witness of the truth shows itself as a legacy, as Jesus points out to his hearers and scoffers, from God's manifestation to Moses in the burning bush. When the Maccabees say, "It is for his laws that we are dying," they are affirming the God of history who continues to animate and give prosperity to all things; that is the reality of the resurrection: the good news of Jesus Christ brings us life through his faithful witness as Son of the God who loves us all. So the core homiletic idea for today could be that we worship a God of the living, who continues to bring us new life in the risen Christ in the witness of the Eucharist and beyond.

An interesting starting point might be one of the options from the **Mysterium Fidei**: "When we eat this Bread and drink this Cup, / we proclaim your Death, O Lord, / until you come again." Bringing this affirmation of Christ's paschal mystery to consciousness in the listening assembly suggests the testimony of the resurrection in the Eucharist we celebrate, the life that has been given to us through Christ's death and resurrection.

We celebrate the God of the living whose Son rose from the dead. "In him the hope of blessed resurrection has dawned" (Preface I for the Dead). We know that God is living here among us now in the risen Lord, just as God showed himself to Moses in the burning bush (Gospel; Exodus 3). Think of the men and women you have known who are graced with the joy of new life each day. (Name some folks from the local community who fit this description.) They are witnesses to the resurrection. Consider those who have died who have gone not to their graves but the hope of the resurrection; their lives were testimonies to Christ's own bursting from a dark tomb (First Reading; contemporary examples).

But we are often surrounded by dead thinkers, like the Sadducees who are content just to unfurl the scrolls and the temple that will be fated to crumble in a heap of dust. We are surrounded by what we know to be "a culture of death," which simply cannot see life beyond the grave and forces others to abide in its shadow. The martyrdom of the Maccabees shows us that our society is nothing new in regard to its allegiance to dead thinkers (First Reading; some historical allusion, but brief). The Sadducees at the time of Jesus were more wedded to their own positions and way of thinking than thinking out of the box—or rather, thinking outside the tomb! They were more interested in trapping Jesus than allowing the Lord to set them free. I am sure we can think of contemporary examples of things that do not give life (name some briefly: abortion, euthanasia, capital punishment); it is a whole mentality, not just one demon, that plagues the community of life. We are witnesses to the seamless garment of life against those who wish to tear and divide Christ's robe to shreds.

But we know that God keeps faith (Preface I for the Dead). Paul tells the Thessalonians that God "has loved us and given us everlasting encouragement and good hope through his grace." So we will find the strength, then, to enliven one another even as countless martyrs throughout the ages have done, men and women of all different persuasions and confessions who have died for the truth. Together with our family, friends, and those here present, we testify in the Eucharist that God keeps his promises forever.

Thirty-Third Sunday in Ordinary Time

Readings from the Ambo

Mal 3:19-20a; Ps 98:5-6, 7-8, 9; 2 Thess 3:7-12; Luke 21:5-19

As we approach the last days of the church year, the transitory nature of life and the coming of the Son of Man are consistent themes in our readings, with a massive crescendo on the solemnity of Christ the King. For the **Second Reading**, Paul's seemingly benign reflection to the Thessalonians about not being lazy seems a bit out of place today, more like a manual on ethics for good living than a text that would suggest the last days. But scholars tell us that this Second Letter to the Thessalonians was a kind of "updating" for a community that once expected the immanent return of the Lord, but now longed for and wondered about Christ's coming at all. The theme of eschatological hope is obvious in chapter 2, in which Paul notes that the Day of the Lord has yet to come and not to despair. The prophet Malachi is even more dramatic than Paul about the Lord's coming in a book fraught with fiery zeal about God's coming righteousness. The selection for the **First Reading** is quite short and occurs at the end of the book, but the prophet's point is clear enough: the Day of the Lord will separate the proud evildoers from those who fear God's name, and then, "there will arise / the sun of justice with its healing rays."

Returning to Paul, we can see that his immediate concern is what to do while we wait for the Day of the Lord. The issue at stake is fairness and justice in the order of charity before that Day dawns upon us. In this regard, Paul uses the expression *ataktos*, which can have a whole range of associations, ranging from lazy to immoral and chaotic lifestyles. Part of his rhetorical reason for raising such an issue is to contrast this ruffian behavior with his own, "so that you might imitate [*mimeisthai*] us." Paul wants to stabilize those who are "not keeping busy but minding the business of others." Attending to the work of the self and one's own affairs and the interior life associated with that practice prepares for the Day of the Lord. Those busying themselves with trivialities or living like freeloaders on others are not part of the justice and righteousness that is the kingdom of God.

Jesus has the same advice as Paul, but puts the recommendation in terms of the apocalyptic fragility of the temple that will be destroyed in the days to come, "when there will not be left a stone upon another stone that will not be thrown down." In the context of Jesus' position in the **Gospel** of Luke, the keepers of the temple are angrily resisting him, as we noted last week with the conflict with the Sadducees concerning the resurrection of the dead (20:27-40). The temple's destruction signifies the coming of the end time, together with false signs indicted by false prophets. Steadfastness of mind and heart is the rule of order; there is no place for *ataktos*, when the Body is in jeopardy with persecutions. How, then, to live while waiting for the coming of the Lord? In justice and constancy because "[b]y your perseverance you will secure your lives."

Connecting the Bible and the Liturgy

As I have stressed throughout these volumes, the integration of Scripture and liturgy through preaching comes from prayer, interpretative reading, and artful organization of ideas, stories, and images in order to theologize for the baptized, listening assembly. The *Roman Missal* provides an inventive conversation partner for the Scriptures, which can inform the dynamic of preaching from the first days of the church year to its last moments. When *The General Instruction of the Roman Missal* suggests sample tropes for the **Penitential Act**, I take it that the presider may construct similar rhetorical structures. These may be touchstones for integration, where the presider/preacher prayerfully absorbs the biblical witness in the Lectionary and then prepares to use them in the liturgy accordingly. The next step would be to deploy these in the homily itself, something I will take up in the subsequent section. I have invented some tropes below for this Sunday as an example of what might be done to shape Word and sacrament together.

Lord Jesus, you give your disciples wisdom to speak the Gospel. *Lord, have mercy.*

Christ Jesus, your grace makes us zealous in your ministry. *Christ, have mercy.*

Lord Jesus, you will come with justice to rule the earth. *Lord, have mercy.*

We can detect the patterns in the readings in these three features above, which take their lead

1. from Paul;
2. from the Gospel;
3. from Malachi.

In a sense, these three tropes prepare the congregation in a subtle way for what is to come, as many have discovered in preparing the liturgy for a particular day. But I am also keeping an eye open for how these petitions to Christ for intercession will inform the preaching for today.

Strategy for Preaching

Some may guess without too much difficulty where I am headed. If the three-part trope used at the Penitential Act implicates the congregation early in the liturgy with God's word, the preaching that follows the proclamation will bring these words to fulfillment. The Penitential Act is an utterance of eschatological hope for the coming of the Just One and asks that we might be made righteous before the coming of the Son of Man; preaching discloses God's promise still further in faith, hope, and love. So the core homiletic idea for today might be this: Jesus gave us the grace to persevere so that we might be diligent in seeking God's justice until he comes again in all righteousness.

An introduction might raise the frustrations of the kind that the Lukan and Pauline community could have been experiencing—or, better put, the absence of God's righteousness here on earth. There are too many confused—so where is God's wisdom? There are those who have given up on the Gospel and lead mediocre lives of faith—where is our zeal for Christ? There remains injustice after injustice—so where is God's righteousness? (Note that these are echoes of the Penitential Act.)

We live in the *meanwhile* of God's return. What we do "meanwhile" matters. Paul's community was very frustrated and became disordered, lazy, and even chaotic. They lived not in a state of righteousness but a bit of a free-for-all, getting very complacent. Perhaps there are some in this church who have given up. They are here in body, but not in soul. They are not alone. (Name some potential discouragements in contemporary society.)

But Christ gave his disciples wisdom to speak the Gospel in the face of persecution (Gospel references). And we face similar obstacles today, blocks to Christ's wisdom. They tell us that Christ will never come, or that he never came, or that he never said who he really was and on and on and on. How do we find zeal for doing the work of Christ?

That desire places us right at the core of hope, which the prophet Malachi says will come, together with the Lord himself (First Reading). Until then, we keep our lamps burning by stoking the fires of justice in our families, among our friends, and at the workplace. What does that look like? It means we walk away from gossip at the watercooler in the office. It means we start cultivating an individual relationship with Christ alone at different times during the day. It means we are zealous for the good. We stand up for civil and religious rights when we know that Christ's little ones are persecuted. This is what we do "meanwhile," that small island where we have been asked to wait until the coming of the Lord and all his saints.

We ask the question of "meanwhile" as we end the church year next week and wait for the season of Advent to begin. But each day requires us to see how God is breaking into our lives with mercy and justice. The One who is to come will arise "with its healing rays."

SOLEMNITIES
OF THE LORD
DURING ORDINARY TIME

The Most Holy Trinity

First Sunday after Pentecost

Readings from the Ambo

Prov 8:22-31; Ps 8:4-5, 6-7, 8-9; Rom 5:1-5; John 16:12-15

The book of Proverbs comprises one of the three classically de-fined Wisdom texts of the Hebrew Scriptures (the other two are Job and Ecclesiastes). The character of Proverbs is readily apparent to most, since the book is meant to provide instructional musings and guidance, often using very concrete situations (with a paternalistic tone and point of view) to accomplish these educational ends.

The selection for the **First Reading** on this solemnity comes by way of contrast to the previous chapter (7) concerning the avoidance of loose women and their seductive snares. Consequently, chapter 8 personifies Wisdom as the perfect consort and scholars have noted the first-person narration present in this chapter (i.e., verse 12) is most often associated with the divinity. Verses 22-31 follow this pattern as a kind of recollection of prehistory or preconsciousness in order to grasp the mystery of God. The Hebrew verb translated here as "possessed" is often rendered elsewhere as "created." But from a Christian perspective, we might understand Wisdom as the Logos, cocreating the world and present with the Almighty in the beginning, evidenced in the first-person plural deployed in Genesis 1:26: "Let us make humankind in our image, according to our like-ness" (NRSV). The christological overtones and associations for this passage on Trinity Sunday are obvious enough. This beautiful pas-sage, then, becomes a meditation on the Father's only-begotten Son, present with the Creator from the beginning of time: "then I was beside him as his craftsman, / and I was his delight day by day, /

playing before him all the while, / playing on the surface of his earth; / and I found delight in the human race."

Wisdom personified acts as an agent of God, through God the Creator. And Jesus identifies himself in today's **Gospel** as a relational subject in harmony with the "Spirit of truth" who "will guide you to all truth." This same Spirit "will glorify me, because he will take from what is mine and declare it to you. Everything that the Father has is mine . . ." These are the words of the Son mystically contemplating the whole of divine agency, something of an echo of Wisdom's delight in the Creator before time began. Paul himself will develop his own famous theology of justification based on the "peace with God through our Lord Jesus Christ, through whom we have gained access by faith to this grace in which we stand, and we boast in hope of the glory of God" (**Second Reading**). Yes, it is precisely this place in which we stand—our humanity created in *imago Dei*, which is the life of the Trinity who has come to dwell in the baptized. So Paul is not merely contemplating a speculative theology of God's essence, but a reality that has already been accomplished by Christ's work of redemption and lived out in the church through the gift of the Spirit.

Connecting the Bible and the Liturgy

Taken together, the splendid ensemble of readings today focus our attention on divine agency—gratuitous action in love by God. The **Collect** gathers the congregation together in order to remind the assembled church of the triune God who is living and active in history and in his creation. "God our Father, who, by sending into the world / the Word of truth and the Spirit of sanctification, / made known to the human race your wondrous mystery . . ." The "sending into the world" (*mittens in mundum*) is a point to observe here in this first part of the Opening Prayer because *mittens* is a predicate use of the present participle—indicating that it is contemporaneous with the verb. This suggests that God's work is ongoing: Christ is still revealing his truth and the Spirit still sanctifies. So the Collect calls our attention to the historical moment of God's revelation in Christ and the outpouring of the Spirit on the church, but we also celebrate at the liturgy our continued participation in these manifestations of divine gifts. As the **Prayer over the Offerings** reminds us, "Sanctify by the invocation of your name, / we pray, O Lord our

God, / this oblation of our service, / and by it make of us an eternal offering to you."

How do we participate in the life of the Trinity? For Paul, "we have gained access by faith to this grace in which we stand." Therefore, the Collect continues: "grant us, we pray, that in professing the true faith, / we may acknowledge the Trinity of eternal glory / and adore your Unity, powerful in majesty." We ask for the grace to be able to, "*in confessione verae fidei*," come to a fuller relationship with the triune God. When we profess this faith, it is not done in some kind of arrogant or superior way; but if we are asking for the grace to profess God's truth, we are petitioning to live in the life of the Trinity, our baptismal reality, to abide with all truth and neither deceive nor be deceived. Christ has already given us access to God and so in faith "we have peace with God through our Lord Jesus Christ / . . . because the love of God has been poured out into our hearts / through the Holy Spirit that has been given to us." Although the Trinity has something of a reputation of being the most difficult and speculative doctrine to understand, its foundational, mysterious reality is far from abstract. Quite the contrary, the faith we profess is a dynamic relationship with God as three Persons in majestic unity. The confession of God's beauty, truth, and unity leads us to the mystery where the Spirit will speak to us and guide us "to all truth."

Strategy for Preaching

I mean this statement to sound as direct as possible: we need to stop boring the Christian assembly with our preposterously abstract preaching on Trinity Sunday. Is life at God's center and the communication of the Blessed Trinity so tedious and ponderous that the homily must resort to instructional sound bites or shallow bon mots? When Moses encountered the mystery of the one true and living God in all radiance and beauty at Mount Horeb, the vision drove an outlaw and an exile into servant leadership for a nation. Preachers would do well to tear up former homilies on the Trinity, take off their sandals, and behold the burning bush before them. So the core homiletic idea for today might be that the Father burns with desire to love us and continues that relationship in Christ by the work of the Spirit.

Again, this could go very abstract on us. But another way to get started might be to lay all the cards on the table: if the hearers are expecting a lofty series of conceptual observations, they have come to the wrong place. The Trinity is about the Father's love and the sacrificial gift of Christ into which we are drawn by the labor of the Spirit. Today we have to look no further than Jesus' promise in John's Gospel.

The introduction should be very concrete. Begin with asking the assembly a rhetorical question: When was the last time we made a promise to someone? (Cite possibilities in real life by name and example, from the simple to the more solemn: Mary made a promise to her daughter Linda that she would take her to shop for her wedding dress after lunch, etc.)

The promise God has given us was from the beginning, before history even started. Can you imagine what that looked like? The book of Proverbs gives us a glimpse of Wisdom playing on the earth before time began. (Theological explanation: the Word of God shaping creation, the only-begotten Son, destined to reshape us.) God keeps his word and the Word keeps us; God has already shown us his love in Christ as truth and in the Spirit sanctified us.

There are at least three ways the Word of God in Christ continues to shape us if we acknowledge its presence among us as a faith community. We have it in a complete sentence: (1) The Word of God has come in Christ (Second Reading), (2) which was with us from the foundation of the world (First Reading), and (3) continues to sanctify us in the Spirit (Collect).

The remainder of the homily can be a concrete expansion of this premise in its various parts:

I. If the Word has come among us in Christ, that is something like getting to know a friend or a future spouse. (Illustrate a small sketch of what that might look like.)

II. The Creed allows us to penetrate the mystery of God's gift (name grace for the assembly here), which is ongoing and began before the foundation of the world.

III. Paul says that this is how we have access to grace: faith in our relationship with Christ and sanctification comes precisely in that faith experience. (Tell a contemporary story of faith.)

The Most Holy Body and Blood of Christ
Sunday after the Most Holy Trinity

Readings from the Ambo

Gen 14:18-20; Ps 110:1, 2, 3, 4; 1 Cor 11:23-26;
Seq., Lauda Sion; Luke 9:11b-17

The identity of the mysterious figure of Melchizedek, king of Salem, who appears seemingly out of nowhere in the **First Reading** from the book of Genesis, represents something of a conundrum to scholars. His name can mean either "king of righteousness" or the "one who is legitimate king of Salem" (i.e., Jerusalem) or his name may be associated with a Canaanite god, *Sidqu*. Be that as it may, the verses that precede and follow our selection in the Lectionary are equally informative about this puzzling personage and his place in these readings. Abram had just returned from bringing back his nephew Lot and all his people in a battle that established a coalition of kings, among whom was the king of Sodom. Bera, the king, offers goods to the patriarch, who refuses them (vv. 21-24). But Melchizedek's offering is more like a gift that is gratuitous and refreshing for both Abram and his company. Significantly, Melchizedek's blessing identifies him as some kind of priest, as well as a king. Therefore Melchizedek becomes an important link to Christian sacramental life and theology; as a symbol, Melchizedek foreshadows Christ's own identity as High Priest, as it does for the author of the Letter to the Hebrews (6:19-20; 7:9-25).

So Melchizedek's offering of bread and wine was both gratuitous and refreshing, an instance echoed in Luke's **Gospel** account of the feeding of the five thousand. The disciples are of the mind that bartering with the surrounding towns and villages will satisfy the needs of the multitude, much like the quid pro quo rationale of the king of Sodom, from whom Abram refuses payment. But Jesus thinks differently; he introduces a divine economy of nourishment in line with Melchizedek: it is a gift for sustenance for the kingdom of peace, the new Jerusalem. There is instruction here for the disciples, as well, even as there is food for the multitude. "Give them some food yourselves" requires the self-giving service of all who follow Jesus, not just those called to ordained ministry. The priesthood of all believers offers its gifts through the great High Priest for the feeding of the world with the food that will provide true nourishment.

That service is repeated, as Paul tells the Corinthians (**Second Reading**), in remembrance of the one who offered himself and was handed over. Christ is handed over as the true Bread, offering himself to the Father for the sake of the "many." This section of Paul's address to the Corinthians deals with the institution of the Lord's Supper, with its parallels in the Synoptics (Matt 26:26-29; Mark 14:22-25; Luke 22:14-20). There is possibly a little pun deployed for theological purposes with the use of the Greek verb *paradidomi*, the root in the same sentence to describe that Paul is "handing over" a tradition even as Jesus was "handed over." As we hand over the remembrance of the Lord, we are handing him over in proclamation of his death.

Connecting the Bible and the Liturgy

It should strike no one as odd that there is a sublime connection between the Scriptures and the liturgical texts today. Indeed, the Scriptures themselves become something of a mandate for the very celebration in our midst. As Paul says, "For as often as you eat this bread and drink the cup, you proclaim the death of the Lord until he comes." The "you" here are those gathered for worship either in first-century Corinth or now at this Eucharist. As the **Collect** for today prays, "O God, who in this wonderful Sacrament / have left us a memorial of your Passion," we see the link between memory and proclamation of Christ's saving work.

The famous **Sequence** for today, *Lauda Sion*, takes up this memoriam when it says, "*Quod in cena Christus gessit, faciendum hoc expressit in sui memoriam.*" "What he did at supper seated, / Christ ordained to be repeated, / His memorial ne'er to cease." For what purpose? The Collect tells us, "so to revere the sacred mysteries of your Body and Blood / that we may always experience in ourselves / the fruits of your redemption." In a way, this memorial of Christ's death and resurrection helps us to respond to Jesus' provocation to his disciples to feed the five thousand. "Give them some food yourselves" can be answered by the church's memory of what the Lord has done, since what we can do is incomplete and can only act in *anamnesis* through the agency of the Holy Spirit: the memory of Christ's handing over his sacred meal on the night he was handed over is the proclamation of his saving work. "When we eat this Bread and drink this Cup, / we proclaim your Death, O Lord, / until you come again."

In a very real sense, Christ becomes the one who speaks this word of salvation for his people back to the Father—and the only one who can do so, "[f]or he is the true and eternal Priest, / who instituted the pattern of an everlasting sacrifice / and was the first to offer himself as the saving Victim, / commanding us to make this offering as his memorial" (**Preface I of the Most Holy Eucharist**).

That Christ offers gifts—his own life—as a gratuitous offering for us, not in bartering with God but as an offering for sustenance and salvation, put Jesus the High Priest in line with Melchizedek, who supplied nourishment for Abram and his household unbidden. As **Eucharistic Prayer I** (Roman Canon) reminds us, our offerings are taken up into Christ's pleasing sacrifice as High Priest, "as once you were pleased to accept / the gifts of your servant Abel the just, / the sacrifice of Abraham, our father in faith, / and the offering of your high priest Melchizedek, / a holy sacrifice, a spotless victim."

Strategy for Preaching

The solemnity of Corpus Christi celebrates the Lord present among his people in the Eucharist. The distinct advantage the preacher holds on this occasion is that, by and large, most Catholics who are regular churchgoers have some level of eucharistic piety. These faithful come to have that spirituality deepened in a special way this day and the present biblical and liturgical readings provide an abundance of theological meanings for heightening the assembly's awareness at the presence of the eucharistic Lord. So the core homiletic idea for today is meant for those who gather in memory each week and know what it is to keep remembering and to be remembered by God. I think that when the preacher performs an exegesis on the assembly of those gathered for this particular solemnity, a discovery, perhaps unique to this solemnity, will follow. For "they all ate and were satisfied." So here is the core: Christ feeds us continually with his Body and Blood as we keep the memorial of his passion, death, and resurrection.

One advantage that those who preside regularly at the Eucharist share with those who are eucharistic ministers is witnessing the devotion of the congregation as they come to receive the Body and Blood of Christ at the distribution of Holy Communion. It is a point of view that could be highlighted at the introduction to the homily, affirming the faith of the assembly in the celebration of the source and summit of the church's life.

This eucharistic devotion of receiving the Body and Blood of the Lord reveals love but also lets us know that we are a hungry people who keep coming back here because we were satisfied. World hunger continues to plague this planet. Every day millions of children go hungry (illustration, though brief). And we may sense what this need is all about when we place ourselves before the eucharistic Lord and he asks us to give something to the crowds ourselves. We are all poor. We have nothing but our open hands to offer, even as Abram received gifts from Melchizedek.

That is why we, the church, the Body to whom this memorial was handed on by the one who was handed over, say over and over, "This is my Body"; "This is my Blood." It is the only language that answers human hunger (Collect). The Eucharist is rightly referred to as the Bread of Life, even as that sacrament proclaims the death of the Lord until he comes again (Second Reading; *Mysterium Fidei*; Preface I of the Holy Eucharist).

These gifts of bread and wine are free from God's High Priest, his Son. He is Melchizedek, giving nourishment to famished troops, and we do not have to return even a fraction of what has been given to us—nor could we (First Reading). Each time we approach the altar to be fed with this life-giving sacrament, we are one step closer to a discipleship that humbly recognizes that only Christ can feed us with what we need.

The Most Sacred Heart of Jesus

Readings from the Ambo

Ezek 34:11-16; Ps 23:1-3a, 3b-4, 5, 6; Rom 5:5b-11; Luke 15:3-7

Chapter 34 in the book of Ezekiel addresses the role of shepherding with a metaphor used by the prophet to preach to the exiles, according to which God is about to reestablish divine authority in Israel. The first part of the chapter denounces the wicked leadership of the institution that has fed themselves rather than the sheep. But the second half of the chapter deals with the reconstruction of justice by rescuing the sheep from the mouths of corrupt shepherds. Instead of falling into the hands of bad leadership amid the dispersion of exile, God says, "I will rescue them from every place where they were scattered when it was cloudy and dark. . . . I myself will pasture my sheep" (**First Reading**).

This promise to "seek out" and bring back is the testimony of a very proactive God asserting his steadfast love. Jesus pushes Ezekiel's image of God as the one who seeks out the lost and proposes a shepherd who is crazy-mad for love of his lost sheep: he would leave the ninety-nine and go look for the one who has strayed. That search is crazy as it is reckless and makes not a bit of sense, except if one are in love; the French call it *l'amour fou*. We know that the parable of the Prodigal Son follows shortly upon these verses. And so we find a gloss on the shepherd who loves to excess, as illustrated in Luke 15, by a father who forgives unconditionally. It is clear that this is the pastoral (literally) role of the Shepherd, as Psalm 23 makes clear: "He guides me in right paths / for his name's sake" (**Responsorial Psalm**). This is for the sake of the name of the Lord, who only wants our good.

The biblical readings for the solemnity of the Sacred Heart in Year C point very particularly to a God who seeks out the lost. Ezekiel frames divine love as the power to rescue a scattered people—broken even by their own leadership—back into a single reign from exile. One wonders if Jesus has the Pharisees and scribes in mind when he asks them, "What man among you having a hundred sheep and losing one of them would not leave the ninety-nine in the desert and go after the lost one until he finds it?" (**Gospel**). Clearly, Jesus intends this as something of an ironic rhetorical question because the scribes and Pharisees are not in the business of rescuing the lost but of making themselves "sleek and strong," as the prophet Ezekiel would say.

Finally, Paul sums up the lavish love of God when he tells the Romans, "The love of God has been poured out into our hearts through the Holy Spirit that has been given to us" (**Second Reading**). This gift of the Spirit was made possible not only for the lost sheep of the house of Israel at the time of the exile, and sinners and tax collectors at the time of Jesus, but for all of us now: "For Christ, while we were still helpless, died at the appointed time for the ungodly." Paul uses the Greek expression *"ekkechutai en tais kardiais hemon"*—"poured out into our hearts"—in order to express the love of one who gives to his flock without reservation so that none need be lost. There is something of a poetic twist going on here in this solemnity, that as God's own heart longs to rescue the sinner, it is our hearts that become the beneficiaries of that divine love. God will never be outdone.

Connecting the Bible and the Liturgy

The **Entrance Antiphon** (Ps 33) for today suggests a wonderful interface for the biblical readings, filled as they are with references to the God who actively seeks out the lost. "The designs of his Heart are from age to age, / to rescue their souls from death, / and to keep them alive in famine." There are a few things of importance to note here. *"Cogitationes cordis eius"* recalls the God who knows, wills, and plans *"in generatione et generationem,"* from one age to the next. In the readings for today, we see the unfolding of God's designs from Israel's exile through Christ's mission to seek out the lost sheep to Paul's theological understanding of the God who *"ekkechutai en tais kardiais hemon"* his great love in Christ through the work of the

Spirit. In other words, this is the plan of God's desire—the Sacred Heart intending our salvation—that is, "to rescue their souls from death / and to keep them alive in famine."

The **Collect** absorbs the overall spirit of the Entrance Antiphon when it acknowledges that those who have gathered for worship, "who glory in the Heart of your beloved Son / and recall the wonders of his love for us, / may be made worthy to receive / an overflowing measure of grace / from that fount of heavenly gifts." This Opening Prayer puts liturgical language on the spine of Paul's Letter to the Romans, excerpted for the Second Reading. For we acknowledge God's wonders as we count among them the love of God, which "has been poured out into our hearts." The Collect, then, asks that we may be made worthy to receive "an overflowing measure of grace / from that fount of heavenly gifts." Arguably, Paul might say that we have already received this outpouring "while we were still helpless" and "ungodly," and yes, unworthy. But it is God who justifies. There is the overflowing, immeasurable grace that cannot be counted. We might ask for the grace, but we have already received this gift in abundance because "God proves his love for us in that while we were still sinners Christ died for us." That love is the design of his heart from age to age. We come to the Eucharist not to earn God's love but to celebrate its wild, unfathomable reach beyond our human reckoning.

Strategy for Preaching

The popular devotion to the Sacred Heart has wavered in recent years, even though there was a time when many Catholic homes enshrined a painting of the Sacred Heart of Jesus on a wall in the dining room or on the mantelpiece. Today, the devotion is particularly important to the Hispanic community. The occasion of the solemnity arose historically to counter an excessive European rationalism, which tended to eclipse the understanding of a personal God whose heart yearns to bring his people to salvation. At the same time, though, we know that this God has a design for his heart from age to age; he is no great Watchmaker, as the Deists often picture the Lord. And in a very interesting way, God's heart beats not only with passion but with intention and a will: there is a knowledge and providence that deserves to bring forth salvation from the beginning of history to its conclusion. Such design was definitively expressed in Christ, whose Sacred Heart celebrates the Father's outpouring of the Spirit to sinners and invites them to the table. The solemnity of the Sacred Heart takes the picture of Christ off the mantel and lets that heart beat with fiery love for those celebrating the Eucharist.

The core homiletic idea for this solemnity might be that God's designs are never separate from his heart. This is a crucial theological point to convey to the Christian faithful because it expresses that God's will is completely entwined with God's love. God only wants our good; that is his will. An introduction might trace God's biblical wonders as the preacher reads those marvels, from generation to generation. Then move to the body of the homily with a strong sentence: God knows what will bring us to salvation (Entrance Antiphon; Second Reading). There is plenty of theology to explore here regarding the will of God to bring justification to sinners in Christ.

And that divine will beats with the heart of love for each one of us as if each of us is the only one God loves (First Reading; Gospel). The preacher might briefly speak of the exile in which Ezekiel finds himself preaching about God as shepherd. I would also include contemporary examples of those who are in "self-exile" and long to be brought back. Christ's invitation to the lost sheep is more than an engraved invitation to a fancy dinner party. He himself has purchased us with his blood and carries us to the altar—even though we are unworthy (Collect). We can only respond in gratitude that love has found us and rejoice with the Shepherd who has brought us to the green pastures of this Eucharist.

Our Lord Jesus Christ, King of the Universe

Last Sunday in Ordinary Time

Readings from the Ambo

2 Sam 5:1-3; Ps 122:1-2, 3-4, 4-5; Col 1:12-20; Luke 23:35-43

A good way to set up the preaching for this solemnity is to set the appropriate context by looking back at how we got to this point in the liturgical year. Fittingly enough, the journey we have taken, which has faced Jesus and his disciples in a web of conflicts with those in power in Jerusalem, has reached its endpoint: the cross. The opposition against Jesus still continues with the rulers and soldiers (both signifying worldly and religious powers) mocking him. Another person, one of those condemned with Jesus, joins in the mockery as well. "Are you not the Christ? Save yourself and us." At the same time, however, an affirmation of Jesus' kingship comes from two unlikely sources: the sign that reads "This is the King of the Jews," which ironically names a reality rather than providing additional mockery; and secondly, the criminal on the other side of Jesus (literally, the other's foil) who says, "Jesus, remember me when you come into your kingdom." In a way, the repentant criminal becomes the everyman in this scene, a stand-in for all those who repent. That said, it may be a little hard to identify with the man, good as he is, since the translation here is somewhat stilted and appears like forced language rather than a sincere moment of repentance (for a contrast, see NRSV, Luke 23:40-43).

Speaking of linguistic features, several have pointed to the ubiquitous use of the verb *sozo*—"I save"—in this very short passage, which reaches its dramatic climax when Jesus saves the repentant criminal who acknowledges Jesus' kingship. Jesus tells the man, "today you will be with me in Paradise," meaning he has been saved and will be with the Savior at the end time. In the **Second Reading** Paul puts theological wings on this saving moment when the criminal (read: the rest of us) inherits the kingdom, as it were. "He delivered us from the power of darkness and transferred us to the kingdom of his beloved Son, in whom we have redemption, the forgiveness of sins." The cross of Christ has given us all a share in the kingdom, "[f]or in him all the fullness was pleased to dwell, / and through him to reconcile all things for him, / making peace by the blood of his cross." We can see that the powers who mock Jesus bring their sin up to the foot of the cross, but it is precisely here that they are reconciled as Christ takes on their sins for the sake of redemption.

That is the role, after all, of the Servant King: to bear the hardships of his people. The model for this kingship is David, to whom the Lord said, "You shall shepherd my people Israel." The kingship of the Lord is celebrated because we have been brought into the kingdom by the Servant King. So we exult with the psalmist, who says, "Let us go rejoicing to the house of the Lord."

Connecting the Bible and the Liturgy

If we are able to "go rejoicing to the house of the Lord," then we do so because of Christ, who is "head of the body, the church." So this day celebrates the victory Christ has gained over death and rightfully affirms his place as King—a Servant King. It is also a liturgy that acknowledges in grateful praise and thanksgiving the Father of all blessings who has given us this inheritance and "transferred us to the kingdom of his beloved Son."

The various **Presidential Prayers** and the **Preface** for this solemnity remind us of how we, like the repentant criminal on the cross next to Jesus, have been *metestesen*—literally removed from one place where we were standing or stationed to another—to be with Christ when he has come into his kingly power, the *paradeisos* of the resurrection. That is what has happened to the reformed criminal when he was conveyed from the cross next to Jesus to paradise with the Lord; and it is what has happened to us. The **Collect** sets at work at once to remind the assembly of God's plan to transform all things in Christ, transferring us to the kingdom when it says, "Almighty ever-living God, / whose will is to restore all things / in your beloved Son, the King of the universe, / grant, we pray, / that the whole creation, set free from slavery, / may render your majesty service / and ceaselessly proclaim your praise." Clearly, the repentance the criminal models for us recognizes the kingship of the Lord, even as he admits his own creaturely status, literally in need of transformation or, more particularly, transference.

Christ restores not only me, justly condemned for my sins, but all humanity as well. So the Eucharist we celebrate is "the sacrifice / by which the human race is reconciled to you, / we humbly pray / that your Son himself may bestow on all nations / the gifts of unity and peace" (**Prayer over the Offerings**). I believe we should sense in a very tangible way that, as we go to God's house rejoicing this day, the Eucharist is a taste of the kingdom, the eschatological end-time banquet of the King, the resurrection into which we have been transferred. As David was anointed a shepherd king to bring his flock together under the rule of God, the **Preface: Christ, King of the Universe** reminds us that "you anointed your Only Begotten Son, / our Lord Jesus Christ, with the oil of gladness / as eternal Priest and King of all creation." It is the cross from which the Servant King finds his majestic throne, because he brought peace and reconciliation to those who asked—and even to those powers who mocked him, "so that, by offering himself on the altar of the Cross / as a spotless sacrifice to bring us peace, / he might accomplish the mysteries of human redemption." This solemnity is a celebration of the God who has brought the kingdom into being, the anticipation of which is evoked in the Preface, bringing to the ears of the baptized God's rule, which is at our doorstep. The Eucharist unfolding before us is the site of the altar of the cross where the king gave himself for his people "as a spotless sacrifice to bring us peace." He did so in order that "he might accomplish the mysteries of human redemption / and, making all created things subject to his rule, / he might present to the immensity of your majesty / an eternal and universal kingdom." What is that kingdom? "Truth and life," "holiness and grace," "justice, love and peace" (Preface: Christ, King of the Universe). Having tasted that kingdom through the gift of the King himself, we pray that "we may live with him eternally in his heavenly Kingdom" (**Prayer after Communion**).

Strategy for Preaching

The solemnity of Christ the King in Year C is going to share certain characteristics with Years A and B, but today has a unique Lukan flavor that the preacher might access from both the biblical and liturgical readings. Luke has taken the assembly gathered for worship each week on a journey with Jesus to Jerusalem from 9:51 to 19:48. We have seen the confrontation in the temple in Jerusalem and now the culmination of human sin as well as its redemption stands before us on the cross. Together with the repentant criminal, Christ has transferred us to the long-expected kingdom, the coming of which was promised in the Lord's teaching on prayer. So preaching today might form a summary of what has been and what is going to be with a core homiletic idea that stands at the crux of the end of the church year: we have made our pilgrim journey with Christ to Jerusalem; and now at the cross the King brings us into his reign. Not surprisingly, the tactics for accomplishing this core idea will involve solving questions such as, How will our transference to the kingdom take place? What does this look like? And so what?

An introduction might focus on the church as a pilgrim people of God, the well-known metaphor and theological description from *Lumen Gentium* from the Second Vatican Council. As a pilgrim people, we walk with Christ on his journey to Jerusalem. It would be important to name significant episodes from 9:51–19:48, which gather together the "plot" of Luke's journey motif during those chapters. In the process, the hearers are stitching together their own recollections of the various healings, encouragements, and confrontations of the Lord with the various cast of characters. What these episodes reveal does not matter so much as that they are included. And now we find ourselves with them to that place under the cross. Then transition to the following:

I. We have journeyed with Christ to the moment of reconciliation for all people, those who weep for him and those who despise him.

   A. Gospel.

   B. Second Reading, especially the reference, "transferred us to the kingdom."

   C. Prayer over the Offerings.

    II. Eucharist is a foretaste of that kingdom where we are set free.

       A. Collect.

       B. Preface, "a spotless sacrifice to bring us peace."

       C. Servant-King-Shepherd (First Reading).

   III. So we give thanks for God's anointed here as we await the kingdom.

       A. Preface: "kingdom of truth and life," etc.

       B. Preface: oil of gladness as King (First Reading).

       C. Second Reading: God's reign will be of reconciliation, all creation making peace by the blood of the cross.

       D. As we participate in the rule here and now with the Eucharist, let us share the kingdom with the Christ and his Body, who draws all things to himself, and be one with him and one another.